*Drawing
the
Line*

WEAPONS

THAT

DO

NOT

WEIGH

ONE

DOWN

**FREE LIFE
EDITIONS**
41 UNION
SQ. WEST
NEW YORK
N.Y. 10003

DRAWING THE LINE

THE POLITICAL ESSAYS OF
Paul Goodman

EDITED BY TAYLOR STOEHR

DRAWING THE LINE: The Political Essays of Paul Goodman

First Edition

Published 1977 by
FREE LIFE EDITIONS, INC.
41 Union Square West
New York, New York 10003

Library of Congress Number 77-71943
ISBN 0-914156-17-9

Book Design by Sidney Solomon
Jacket Design by Elliot Kreloff

Acknowledgments

The editor and publisher wish to thank the following for permission to reprint material included in this book:

Dissent—for "Berkeley in February." Reprinted from *Dissent*, Spring 1965.

Encyclopaedia Britannica—for "Anarchism and Revolution." Reprinted from *The Great Ideas Today*, 1970, with permission of The Great Ideas Today, and Encyclopaedia Britannica, Inc.

Hart Publishing—for "The Present Moment in Education." Paul Goodman, "The Present Moment in Education," from *Summerhill: For and Against,* copyright© 1970 Hart Publishing Company, Inc.

Horizon Press—for "Power Struggles." from *The Society I Live In Is Mine*, copyright© 1962 by Paul Goodman, by permission of the publishers, Horizon Press, New York.

Liberation—for "Declaring Peace Against the Government," *Liberation*, March 1962;—for "Our Standard of Living," from *Liberation*, April 1964;—for "The Duty of Professionals," from *Liberation*, November 1967.

The New Republic—for "Television: The Continuing Disaster." Reprinted by permission of *The New Republic*. © 1963, The New Republic, Inc.

New York Times Magazine—for "The Black Flag of Anarchism." © 1968 by the New York Times Company. Reprinted by permission.

Partisan Review—for "Vocation and Public Conscience." Copyright© July 1942 by *Partisan Review*.

Politics—for "Notes on Neo-Functionalism." Reprinted from *Politics*, December, 1944.

Random House—for "Jails and blows, being a coward." Copyright© 1972, 1973 by the Estate of Paul Goodman;—for "When our demonstration was a dozen." Copyright© 1972, 1973 by the Estate of Paul Goodman;—for "Flags, 1967." Copyright© 1967 by Paul Goodman;—for "Blessed is the landscape that around." Copyright© 1972, 1973 by the Estate of Paul Goodman. Reprinted from *Collected Poems* by Paul Goodman, edited by Taylor Stoehr, by permission of Random House, Inc.

Acknowledgments

Random House—for "Horatio's Mourning Song." Copyright© 1942, 1946; copyright© 1959 by Paul Goodman. Reprinted from *The Empire City* by Paul Goodman, by permission of Random House, Inc.

Random House—for "Pornography and the Sexual Revolution." Copyright© 1961 by Paul Goodman. Reprinted from *Utopian Essays and Practical Proposals* by Paul Goodman. Reprinted by permission of Random House, Inc.

Resistance—for "Dear Graduate..." Reprinted from *Why?*, April 1946;—for "To Young Resisters." Reprinted from *Resistance*, March 1949.

School of Living Press—for Last Public Speech. Reprinted from *Humanizing Our Future*, edited by R. Bruce Allison, School of Living Press, Hinsdale, Illinois, 1972.

Smithsonian Institute—for "Two Points of Philosophy and An Example." Reprinted from *Smithsonian Annual II, The Fitness of Man's Environment,* © 1968 Smithsonian Institute.

Burton Weiss—for parts of "A Young Pacifist."

Contents

PREFACE   **VII**

INTRODUCTION   **IX**

I.

THE MAY PAMPHLET

Reflections on Drawing the Line   2

On Treason Against Natural Societies   11

A Touchstone for the Libertarian Program   17

Natural Violence   21

Revolution, Sociolatry, and War   25

Unanimity   36

II.

SOME PRACTICAL PROPOSALS

Notes on Neo-Functionalism   48

Two Points of Philosophy and an Example   55

The Present Moment in Education   67

Pornography and the Sexual Revolution   82

Television: The Continuing Disaster   99

III.
ACTIVISM

Vocation and "Public Conscience"   106
"Dear Graduate..."   111
To Young Resisters   116
Declaring Peace Against the Governments   120
Berkeley in February   127
A Young Pacifist   145
A Causerie at the Military-Industrial   156
The Duty of Professionals   166

IV.
THE BLACK FLAG OF ANARCHISM

Reflections on the Anarchist Principle   176
The Forms and Content of Democracy   178
Notes on Decentralization   185
The Black Flag of Anarchism   203
Anarchism and Revolution   215
Confusion and Disorder   233

V.
TALKING SENSE: THREE IMPROMPTU OCCASIONS

"Our Standard of Living"   248
"Power Struggles"   255
Last Public Speech   264

Preface

*T*his selection attempts to bring together Paul Goodman's best and most characteristic thought, from among the hundreds of things he wrote over a long and prolific career. Before the decade of his fame much of his writing was published in out of the way places and went unnoticed; even some of the more celebrated essays have been out of print since their first appearance. Although he rescued two or three volumes of miscellaneous pieces during his lifetime, they represented what he had on hand more than any retrospective view. This is the first attempt to collect his work systematically.

Goodman's favorite genre was the occasional poem. In prose too he always kept his eye on the present moment ("the kind of books these are, you're talking about the cases which are in *The New York Times*, no?''), so it is remarkable how well his work has held up. I have made no effort to prune the texts of dated material, but aside from a few references to other contributors in a symposium, other speakers from a platform, the reader will find little to remind him that these thoughts were not written yesterday. The issues he addressed are still with us, and his radical solutions are all the more appropriate as the problems persist and multiply. This applies to his literary as well as his social criticism; they were not so different.

Since this edition is meant for use, not for the record, its priorities vary from those of the usual "standard edition." Instead of the last text corrected by the author, for example, I have picked the fullest, strongest, and most characteristic version whenever more than one exists. To preserve rather than muffle their occasions, I have chosen to handle the texts as lightly as possible, letting idiosyncrasies of time, place and manner of publication stand. The inconsistencies (some magazines changed *tho* to *though, thru* to *through,* others didn't) reflect the tastes of editors, easy enough to live with. For similar reasons I have not worried about the few cases where Goodman borrowed whole paragraphs from one essay to use in another; it is interesting to see what he thought bore repeating. In short the individual essays have not been trimmed, nor the speeches tidied up, except for punctuating a few tape-recorded sessions.

For the most part I have avoided reproducing much from Goodman's famous books—*Growing Up Absurd, Communitas, Gestalt Therapy, The Structure of Literature*—because they are still in print and likely to be widely available for a long time to come. Moreover, although readily excerpted, these books have a certain integrity and are best *read through*. Rather than a sampling of classics, I have striven after some sense of the range and development of his thought over several decades, with emphasis on the way he lived the intellectual life—his commitment to ideas. Whenever it has been possible, I have chosen writings that give a personal turn to the issues; and some selections have been included because you can hear Goodman's voice there, still sounding with his lively idiom.

For their suggestions and counsel I thank my fellow literary executors Sally Goodman, George Dennison, and Jason Epstein. Others too have been invaluable sounding boards for me as I wrote the introduction, especially Susan Goodman, David and Diva Wieck, and Ruth Perry. Maurice and Charlotte Sagoff made reading proof a pleasure, and Chuck Hamilton has proved what an advantage it can be to have a publisher who is an enthusiast.

T.S.

Introduction

*I*t is hard to be political in the modern world. When Aristotle said man was a political animal, he meant that it was the essence of human nature to deliberate courses of action and to choose the good. We do deliberate and choose much in our daily lives, and so far we are political, but in those areas that have to do with civil government and public policy our voices are not heard. What we call "politics" is electioneering and office-holding. We are so used to the nation-state and its bureaucratic lumberings that most of us have lost the taste for direct action on public issues. Nonetheless few fail to notice the distance between a private citizen's desires and the machinations of government. This recognition is usually flavored with resignation. Most people no longer even want a voice in public policy; probably they are right, for in these circumstances one cannot really deliberate and choose the good anyway: all choices are bad when they must apply to cases so complex and on such a scale that no policy could allow for any but the crudest fit. Most people think that the nation-state is necessary or valuable in spite of all this, but increasing numbers do not. The few who are committed to its dismantling are called decentralists these days; they used to be called anarchists.

The problem in being an anarchist is this: how to abolish the state without also destroying society? Although some anarchists speak of revolution, in the conditions of modern super-states it is not realistic to think that any political revolution would do more than alter the terms and personnel of power. How then can we act in our world without complicity in its corruption? Is it possible to bring our lives into closer touch with our ideals? Can our daily living help make a better world for us all?

Our exemplary figures are those who try to live this life of principle, Thoreau, Tolstoy, Gandhi. Of modern American decentralists or anarchists, by far the most important was Paul Goodman. All through the 1960's he campaigned for a new attitude toward politics and government, and poured out ideas for practical changes that would return autonomy to individuals and especially to small neighborhood groups. He also wanted to live a life of principle. It is easy to be cynical about his motives, or sophisticated about his methods, but we do not have so many heroes of this spirit that we can afford to condescend to any of them. And although it is too soon to know his precise effect on our political history, it is nevertheless clear that Goodman's ideas have begun to seep down among people who never even heard of him.

It is strange to think that people who never heard of him have absorbed his ideas, for like most anarchist thinkers, much of Goodman's appeal comes from the integrity of his life and thought. It makes little sense to have anarchist ideas if one doesn't act on them. Long before he began to call himself an anarchist Goodman adopted the maxim of D.H. Lawrence, Consult Your Deepest Impulse, and made a touchstone of his own nature. His anarchism was based on an antinomian optimism, that was religious before it was political. I do not think he ever really abandoned this principle, though in later years he had already worked through so many questions (he rarely changed his mind) there was less need to consult the oracle of impulse: he knew what he thought about most things, his life had been the test.

People are always glad to find someone who is sure of himself. Even more appealing, Goodman made it clear that his self-assurance was not prudential or limited to matters of opinion. This is what first fascinated me when I met him over twenty-five years ago: he seemed to live entirely without regard to the hedging conventionalities that dominated (so I thought) the lives of almost everyone else, myself included. What daring! to live, as he said, "in present society as if it were a natural society." As one got to know him, this freedom and autonomy lay more and more in the shadow of the spiritual price he paid for it—but let me not say anything to diminish his example or my admiration for it at a time when I needed such a hero.

Part of the reason that he appealed to young people so much was that their propensities were encouraged and flattered by his own. He dared to lead an unconventional bohemian life, refused to be cowed by authority, called a spade a spade, flaunted his sexuality. His detractors said he was childish and rude. There was a boyish impudence in him, to be sure: it was a pleasure to see some of those high hats knocked off. But for the most part he maintained his dignity better than they, for it was no mere posture with him but founded on complete openness in his life. For a long time I thought he had no secrets whatever, no private thoughts, nothing reserved or intimate. That in itself was awe-inspiring, and gave him a sort of authority few others could claim. It was one source of his clear-sightedness too, for if there is nothing to hide, the attention may be directed at the obvious facts. Common sense is the political virtue *par excellence,* but it has largely vanished from political life because everyone is busy manipulating images and putting his best face forward. Goodman's directness cut through all this like a knife. It was unsettling to some, intoxicating to others.

Goodman struggled with the anarchist dilemmas personally, for like Thoreau he was not fundamentally political: "I do not have the character for politics," he said in his last political tract *The New Reformation.* "I cannot lead or easily be led, and I am dubious about the ability of parties and governments to accomplish any positive good." Nonetheless, like Thoreau with the Fugitive Slave Law, Goodman found himself confronted with encroachments by the state that could not be ignored: World War II, the Cold War, and finally—especially through his son—the Vietnam War. How he tried to maintain his principled anarchism in the face of these monstrous complicities is a story as full of hard lessons for our time as Thoreau's support of John Brown and the Civil War was for his.

Goodman was a poor Jewish kid, fatherless, bisexual, growing up more or less unsupervised on the streets of New York City. Like many such boys not handy with their fists, he learned eloquence early. He was what used to be called a "golden mouth"—though his Hebrew name, which translates "brazen mouth," was perhaps more accurate. At the beginning of the Great Depression, when most twenty-year-olds were scrambling for jobs, and many were "radicalized" in the process, Goodman appointed himself an artist. This was an auspicious beginning for an anarchist—articulate, insubordinate, and dedicated to a calling that promised to keep him poor if not disgruntled.

Although his friends of the Thirties remember him as apolitical, this is not quite true. It is fairer to say that he took pleasure in mocking the political pretensions of others, especially doctrinaires of the left. He claimed that at City College he used to bait his Communist classmates by reading Trotsky out loud. At the University of Chicago he made fun of the Stalinists who came to indoctrinate the Poetry Club, and at the beginning of the Second World War he shocked a young Trotskyite who had joined the Navy by praising the Black Market as a model of small business initiative with the added virtue of undermining the war effort.

The war soon forced him to sift his politics deeper than these easy jibes. What was the correct response to Hitler? Fascism, like slavery, was not something one could simply wash one's hands of. Thoreau might have picked up a gun, just as he defended the guerrilla exploits of John Brown. Goodman was closer to the "non-resistant" wing of abolitionism, activists like William Lloyd Garrison and Henry Clarke Wright, who argued in classic anarchopacifist fashion, War is the State. Like them Goodman considered himself already engaged in his own guerrilla action, and the problem was not how to join the larger campaign against the Third Reich and Imperial Japan, but how to keep from joining the United States Army.

The state offered only two choices, army or jail. Some men refused to register and went to jail; or refused induction and went to jail or concentration camps, depending on their religious beliefs. One out of every six inmates of federal prisons during the war was a C.O.—over 6000 men—and many times that number were locked up in the "Civilian Public Service" camps. Others joined the Merchant Marines, got jobs in defense plants, or went on the lam. Almost 350,000 draft evasion cases were officially reported. Still others were drafted and decided to "bore from within."

Goodman himself was lucky, classified III-A

> ...because of a marriage (not quite regular)
> and a dependent child (I can't support).

But he was typically unable to follow the advice he gave to himself and others—to lie low in his "little hole of lies and honorable pretensions," as he put it in his "War Diary." While his friends were going into prison or hiding or the army, he chose to make a nuisance of himself, thereby risking his position of relative safety. His brazen mouth cost him dear, though as it turned out, not at the hands of the authorities.

At this point in his career (Spring 1942) he had seemed on the verge of the great literary success he was continually expecting. He had two books newly published, one of them his masterpiece *The Grand Piano.* New Directions was including his stories and poems in its annuals, and *Partisan Review* had accepted a batch of stories and was running his film criticism as a regular feature. Klaus Mann (the novelist's son), editing a prestigious new international journal, said Goodman's voice reminded him of "the accents of Goethe's mellow wisdom and fatherly confidence"!

With our entry into the war this pattern of luck and reward fell to pieces. If he had been willing to play the apolitical artist everyone considered him in the Thirties, Goodman might have nursed along this ripening career as an avant-garde novelist. But that was not consulting one's deepest impulse. Already in the Spring of 1941 Goodman had written a public letter in the *Partisan Review* complaining that James Laughlin had dedicated the New Directions annual to the R.A.F. without consulting his contributors. This bit of "scrupulousness" did not keep Goodman out of later annuals, because Laughlin was looking for talent not orthodoxy, but others who had Goodman's career in their hands were more easily offended.

The editors of *Partisan Review* were themselves deeply divided on the question of "critical support" of the war, and Goodman poured oil on the flames by submitting an extraordinary pronouncement "with regard to the war, draft, and sedition," for publication in the late Spring of 1942, when the Allies were rapidly losing the war. Goodman was asking for trouble when he sent them this piece. First of all, he refused to consider the war as a struggle between fascism and democracy: "By the war I do not mean something subsequent to the attack on Pearl Harbor, but the activity of decades which has adapted itself with such astonishing smoothness to the present world-wide national unities." And just as he explained the war in these terms of "continuity between the past and present," so he accounted for, and justified, his own response to it in terms of "the next step following from each man's past." If all along one had refused to acquiesce in the social drift that led to the war, he might in good conscience now refuse to take part in it.

He then distinguished the possible responses of three kinds of citizens: (1) those "who concurred in the social ideals" all along "are unlikely to dissent now, unless by a strange ignorance, a want of feeling for the horrors long present, they did not realize where they were headed and now undergo a late revulsion"; and (2) those who dissented all along, but "thought the people were persuasible to a more or less imminent political change," are in the present circumstances "committed to sedition," but might lie low "if they think the odds are at present too great." This was an accusation or a dare; readers and editors could take their choice between responsibility for the global insanity and going underground.

The third group consisted of those "who so strongly dissented from the authoritative institutions and mores that they despaired even of political persuasion," and had been working instead as "educators, artists, and religious persons" toward a future society more in touch with basic humanity. This group, among whom Goodman counted himself, was further divided into those "whose lives are given...to the purity of their principles and moral agitation," and those "who sacrifice themselves to free works, living privately for the good of all." Of these, the religious persons—like Dave Dellinger and the Union Theological seminarians who refused to register for the draft in 1940—would choose civil disobedience and jail rather than the army; the free artists, on the other hand, would employ "cunning, fraud, or flight" just to go their own way. Again it was the latter group that Goodman found himself among, and he went on to explain "that persons of this kind have always lived in the society more or less as in a state of nature, accepting the social conventions only pro tem and conditionally. Now when the social events have so far deteriorated that life and liberty themselves are in jeopardy, it is their duty to criminally do their best for themselves and their work. So Hobbes taught."

When the editors at *Partisan Review* saw these opinions, they immediately consulted their lawyers—"to purify it for the mails." Goodman savored the nuances of this censorship: "Everywhere I wrote 'we ought' or 'we must,' it came out that 'such people in the past often have.' Do you catch it?" "Cunning, fraud, or flight" became "seizing various private opportunities." "To criminally do their best for themselves and their work" emerged as "even in violation of social sanctions."

At this point the *Partisan Review* was still publishing a fairly wide range of political opinion, including in the next issue a controversy over "Pacifism and the War" by D.S. Savage, George Woodcock, Alex Comfort, and George Orwell. For at least a year the editors had been arguing among themselves over the proper line to take toward the war, Rahv and Phillips pro, Macdonald and Greenberg con. According to Goodman, Rahv wanted to squelch any discussion of the draft or sedition, since those issues brought the war itself into question; "what people are *really* interested in, he said, is 'The Cultural Dilemma of the Intellectual in Society.'" As it turned out, this was the position that finally won control of the magazine in the Summer of 1943, and from that point on Goodman's name was not to be found in its table of contents but at the top of its black list. Goodman regarded the loss of the *Partisan*'s backing as fatal to his literary career, which never recovered, even in the days of his fame as a social critic. He later believed—and there is some evidence of it—that the *Partisan* editors were responsible for the general freeze he felt thereafter in the circles of literary power and prestige. Of course Goodman's opinions and life-style gave enough offense to most people, without the need for a campaign against him, nor was Rahv quite that much the literary czar.

When Rahv and Phillips gained control of *Partisan Review*, Dwight Macdonald left to start his own alternative magazine, *Politics*, which became the most distinguished political journal in America's history. Although it had nothing like the literary and intellectual following of the *Partisan Review*, it was the major conduit of radical thought during the middle and late Forties. Goodman immediately began to publish there, and his influence on its developing anarchist position was clear to many readers. With the loss of his literary audience, Goodman was more or less constrained to take advantage of his new reputation as an extremist, and he wrote a great deal of lively social and political commentary during the next few years, hammering out a career between the war and his art.

About this time Goodman also began to write for the anarchist magazine *Why?*, published by a group of young radicals who met every Saturday in the Spanish Anarchists' Hall on Lower Broadway (*Solidaridad Internacional Anti-Fascista*). *Why?* could trace its lineage back to the old *Vanguard* of the Thirties, and during the first years of the war some of the older syndicalists and wobblies continued to come every Saturday afternoon to argue with the younger generation who had "gone off on a tangent," tempted into bohemianism and personalism. The *Vanguard* group had been a melting pot of European revolutionary movements. Not everyone carried proper papers, or the name he was born with; their interests were pre-war: trade unions, deportation, internationalism, Spain, the Moscow Trials, Kronstadt. The younger anarchists were still mostly working class, but native born, from Brownsville and the Bronx. The state that was their enemy was the U.S. Their vocabulary was different: they rarely talked about who had the better "analysis," who was a "wrecker," how to organize this or that group. The war made certain topics obsolete, brought others to the fore. Even more than conscription and pacifism, they wanted to talk about mutual aid, communal living, and decentralization—the topics of the Sixties.

These concerns were right up Goodman's alley, for he and his architect brother Percival Goodman had just finished writing

Communitas, a radical history and compendium of community planning that was twenty years ahead of its time. In 1944 Goodman was already thinking about ecology, a guaranteed annual wage, and banning the cars from Manhattan, as well as how to evade the draft. He quickly became the Dutch Uncle of the anarchists, older and more learned than these twenty-year-olds, and not quite one of the family (he rarely went on the Sunday picnics), but looked to for intellectual energy. He brought his friends around to give talks, and he met new people with ideas and talents that interested him. The range of occasional voices went from Tuli Kupferberg to Ernest van den Haag, from Robert Duncan to James Baldwin, from Paul Mattick to Julian Beck and Judith Malina. For the most part these were one-shot speakers rather than regulars, and not all of them were anarchists by any means. It was the great civic contribution of SIA Hall that it provided a forum for all sorts of radicalism during a period when almost no public opportunities existed. If *Politics* magazine gave Goodman an audience for his political and social thought, the *Why?* group gave him an intellectual community.

This sense of community was especially important for people as thoroughly at odds with the surrounding society as Goodman and his anarchist friends. In the Forties it was considered despicable to hold the views they held. Even after the war the victors were not willing to let anyone off lightly. Truman's amnesty, for instance, left thousands in jail, and six months after the armistice the *Why?* group joined in the picketing of Danbury Prison, where their friends were still doing time. Local patriots, the *Danbury Times* reported, "hurled insults at the demonstrators.... The crowd of onlookers at times appeared to be in an ugly mood, especially the war veterans and the parents of youths who served their nation and some of whose sons were killed and others wounded in defense of their country." That ominous cliché "ugly mood" conveys a sense of the sullen aftermath of the war hysteria. On the picket line Goodman is remembered as calming down the Brownsville anarchists, who were ready enough for a fight if it came to that; later, inside the prison as part of a delegation to the Warden, he called for the release of *all* the convicts, not just the C.O.s—a typical anarchist demand that infuriated most people.

Goodman was not predictable in his anarchism. Often you saw how it all hung together only after you had heard him out completely, and sometimes not even then. Basically he was a pacifist, but not opposed to all forms of violence, and not among "those whose lives are given...to the purity of their principles and moral agitation." Rather than public civil disobedience, his announced *modus vivendi* was "cunning, fraud, or flight." The duty of artists was to "sacrifice themselves in free works," not jail. He advised others to avoid both the army and jail if they could: "I have the strongest objection to enlisting in jail!" exclaimed the hero of *The Empire City.* "Institution for institution it is worse than the army." But he also tried to impress upon his friends the importance of acting out of long-standing conviction, in order that one might not later have to deal with guilt and self-accusation. "Do not let either your enemies or your friends prematurely assign 'your' principles to you. Stubbornly work for the personal goods that you know and desire, and your underlying principles will emerge."

When he was finally ordered to report for his own physical in the Spring of 1945, Goodman was again very much in need of comrades: they were the jury of peers to whom he addressed his defense. Yet so far as I have been able to discover, Goodman did not discuss his own draft case with any of his anarchist friends. He had been considering his alternatives ever since he first registered in 1940 (he regretted *that*!) but I do not think he had yet come to terms with his fears or his principles, as he advised others to do. He now needed a sympathetic hearing as he tried to write out his political credo, in half a dozen essays on the difficulties and consequences of "drawing the line." One story has it that he went to his confrontation with the U.S. Army carrying these essays under his arm. Certainly they would have been enough to stamp him "not military material," even if he had passed the physical.

He published most of these essays in *Why?, Politics,* and *Retort,* and then collected them as *The May Pamphlet*, which remains the major philosophic statement of his anarchist position. In all his social criticism of the Sixties, the closest thing to it is *People or Personnel,* but there is a big difference between that recipe-book of decentralization and his earlier attempt to write a formal political treatise. In some ways the later book is more appealing, for Goodman faced no questions in it that he had not settled in his own mind long before. His marvelous common sense shines in every page. By contrast *The May Pamphlet* was a painful struggle of self-definition. He was not content to call himself a pacifist, since in fact there were many forms of violence that he accepted as "natural" or inevitable—to which he devoted an entire essay—nor did he simply fall back on the traditional political arguments of revolutionaries who refuse to serve the state in its wars. He set himself the task of creating his own anarchist ethics from scratch. This was his weakness and his strength.

The argument of *The May Pamphlet* is that present society is not free, but trapped in coercion and compromise. Each man must "draw a line" beyond which he will not go along with society's demands, or be party to its acts. What then? The libertarian program of free action was "to live in present society as though it were a natural society." This required more than the drawing of a line, for unnatural conventions have become habitual and their renunciation will necessarily be accompanied by conflict and suffering. Nor will present society permit men to live in it as if free. Here we glimpse Goodman's sense of his own embattled situation, his defense of his Hobbesian withdrawal from the social catastrophe, and his way of dealing with the opprobrium his behavior occasioned.

To discover just which conventions were "unnatural" and deserved defiance, he invented his "touchstone for a libertarian program," that is, "to advocate a large number of precisely those acts and words for which persons are in fact thrown into jail." As an anarchist touchstone, this makes a certain amount of sense—the point was not to get thrown into jail, of course, but to find the heart's-blood of the coercive society—yet one wonders why he did not go on to discuss the issue that was surely uppermost in his mind: what if the "acts and words" amounted to draft refusal and sedition, and what if one were "in fact thrown into jail"? I don't mean to suggest a failure of candor here, but only that the whole negative side of his anarchist philosophy—all the ways of avoiding complicity and abstaining from evil—seems to have been as difficult for him as for most other enemies of the state. One feels the misgivings in the very syntax, full of parentheses and connectives like "contrariwise" or "nonetheless."

It was a happy fact of his character that the positive aspects of his libertarian program came easier to him, and one can see in them an early formulation of the social thought he lavished on the Sixties. First of all, the program must attempt to bypass conventional institutions by going back to "primary nature" (the animal instincts) for sources of energy, and to the community of friends for a more thoroughgoing participatory democracy, based on the unanimity of fraternal love rather than the rule of the majority. The planks in the program were six: (1) a demand for work "that realizes our human powers"—"cooperative jobs themselves worth doing, with the workers' full understanding of the machines and processes, releasing the industrial inventiveness that is in each man"; (2) a reassessment of the standard of living; (3) encouragement of childhood and adolescent sexuality; (4) "direct political initiative" in housing, community planning, education, etc.; (5) a more humane naturalistic ethics; and (6) abstention "from whatever is connected with the war." It was essential that all of these be practical, and not merely utopian proposals. They were directed at areas within the control of small groups, where by mutual aid and free initiative something might be done immediately. One can find little in his books of the Sixties that cannot be traced back to these aims and principles.

Nowhere in the six essays does Goodman discuss the draft or his position on the war so pointedly and personally as he did in his *Partisan Review* statement, or in the advice he later gave to draftees in the pages of *Why?* and its successor during the Korean War, *Resistance.* Yet there is no doubt that *The May Pamphlet* grew directly out of his need to justify his own draft-dodging (to whom? not the government, for it was all strictly legal, but rather to his friends and fellow-anarchists). For my part, I find the political ethics thoroughly convincing, but the justification of his own case must be read in his tone of voice, which seems to me strained and even a little desperate. This was not the first or the last time in Goodman's life that he wrote some brilliant analysis in order to justify his own acts, and in the end was left with his anxiety unallayed. I admire the way his politics grew out of his own predicament, and his deepest impulses about how to cope. His faith in this principle was one of his most attractive qualities. On the other hand, he did not always know what his deepest impulse was, or he would not have been looking for other touchstones. Also, the problems that Goodman faced in his life were not the sort to be solved by intellectual genius or insight. He put his finger on it in his very first essay on drawing the line: "No particular drawn line will ever be defensible logically...the inner conflicts now begin to appear, in the details of drawing the line, and all the fear, guilt, and rage. Let us draw our lines and have this out!"

In later years, after his psychotherapy, he learned to court confusion in such cases, a Taoist faith that sometimes helped, though it was very difficult for so articulate a man. Too often he pretended to know his truth all the more certainly when he was most at a loss, and *The May Pamphlet* is not free from this forcing. It is the source of its uneven tone—sometimes full of conviction, sometimes merely knowing. The combination is eerily reminiscent of "Civil Disobedience," probably the last serious attempt to "draw the line" in America, written almost exactly 100 years earlier. *The May Pamphlet* has the same power to inspirit and dismay as Thoreau's more famous *apologia*.

Beyond the circle of anarchists at the SIA Hall, and the readers of *Politics* magazine, Goodman had little audience for these reflections. Significantly, *Partisan Review* was one of the handful of magazines to review *Art and Social Nature* when it came out featuring *The May Pamphlet*. That review was a mere hatchet job, treating the book as Goodman's self-serving theory that "If we systematically introduce children to sexual experience,...we shall get the revolution." A few more such reviews might at least have made it notorious, but it sank into oblivion instead. Before long copies of *Art and Social Nature* were being remaindered at 45 cents. Although he was still publishing books at a terrific clip, nobody was reading them. *Communitas* acquired a modest following in departments of architecture, but *The Facts of Life, The State of Nature, Kafka's Prayer,* and *The Break-Up of Our Camp* fared no better than *Art and Social Nature*. In 1949 he had to publish the best single book of his career, *The Dead of Spring,* by subscription ($5 each from 200 friends). And for the next ten years his audience remained at this depressing size. It got so bad in 1956 that Goodman gave up starting new works and began to keep a journal instead, gloomy little thoughts he jotted down like a tramp staring greedily in the restaurant window at the customers eating.

Then came the decade of his fame and influence, so sudden and overwhelming. *Growing Up Absurd* began as a book on juvenile delinquency, commissioned by a publisher who realized, on seeing the completed manuscript, that it was not the quick cash-in on a vogueish subject that he had bargained for. Goodman kept the advance and once again began to hunt for a publisher. If his count can be trusted, sixteen others also failed to recognize a best-seller. Then Norman Podhoretz at *Commentary* and Jason Epstein at Random House "discovered" him. Overnight it was no longer juvenile delinquency that was faddish, but Goodman himself.

Goodman had said in the early Forties, "*this* time the duration will last longer than the war!" By 1959 it was no joke. The reason *Growing Up Absurd* was so popular—and remains in print almost twenty years later—is not because it focused on the plight of young men trying to find their manhood, but because it was the first book to show how modern American society systematically thwarts and betrays its youth by not providing a viable community to grow up in. Goodman did not claim that the Cold War was responsible for this disaster; the war mentality was simply the continuing inter-national manifestation of the lives we all led, and the institutions we all served. At this level, his view was precisely that which he had held at the beginning of World War II. Since the emergency was now more obviously chronic rather than cataclysmic, public hysteria was not so widespread, which made for an audience ready to listen. As for Goodman himself, he had "the nerve of failure." Almost fifty years old, he complained that he had already missed out on everything he ever wanted. His tone was not so cocky, but he was surer than ever of his ideas. Whatever the causes, his voice had become steadier, with less anxiety and more of his character in it, at the same time that the public had finally caught up with the ideas he had been propounding so long.

This opportunity to speak to a very large audience was totally unexpected, just as the whole phenomenon of the Sixties was a surprise. Goodman was quick to respond, for he had been brooding on his subjects for many years of "exile," but it is unlikely that he would have addressed himself so unwaveringly to social criticism during the next ten years had not the chance of an audience come upon him so suddenly, and been so emphatically a "second chance"—not so much to salvage his own career as to redeem its principles. Something of the sort must explain his writing so many essays and books of social commentary in spite of the fact that he did not "have the character for politics" and always thought of himself as an artist, who should be devoting himself to the creation of "free works." He wrote no plays or fiction after the early Sixties, only the little poems he could jot down on the backs of envelopes as he waited in airport lobbies and empty hotel rooms for his ride to the campus.

It might seem obvious that a writer who finally finds his audience after many years of poverty and neglect would then busy himself to address it. But there is room for disagreement about whether his genius was for politics at all, or whether he betrayed his true calling to become a publicist. He himself felt the conflict, as I have been suggesting, and in the end he regretted his choice, though he continued to think it had been his duty to make it. What else could he have done? Among the handful of essentials to any artist are subject matter and audience. There was no way of avoiding the subject that forced itself on his generation, even if he could have turned away from the vast audience every writer dreams of.

At first he liked to think of himself as a gadfly who was also the philosopher of the movement. This unlikely combination suited his former reputation as the *bête noir* of the intelligentsia. Out of this self-image from the Forties, which had plenty of truth in it, grew his activism of the Sixties—a sort of hit-and-run guerrilla tactic. "Cunning, fraud, or flight" had been the defensive posture; now, on the offense, it was one-night stands on the college campuses, picketing his publishers during the General Strike for Peace, tongue-lashing the Military-Industrial Complex in Washington. Moment by moment there was excitement and justification, and even some results and glory, but for Goodman personally it was a desiccation of the spirit.

Ocean, Sexuality, and the Sun,
and Death, and Flora are the gods for real
that sway my soul, so I freeze or smile
or am awestruck. Secretly I often
salute them when I meet them. But this ruin
of my lifetime for the commonweal,
I do it as my duty and I feel
nothing but weariness and indignation.

The Holy Ghost is also my acquaintance
whom I when I encounter sing and dance
with the musicians. But there is one god
for whom I have the others all betrayed,
Adam—wasting me for fifty-six
winters in waiting and peace politics.

In truth Goodman had no character or taste for politics, even "peace politics." Paradoxically, that was at the heart of his radicalism. His fertility in thinking up practical alternatives, for example, was a direct result of his disbelief in "the ability of parties and governments to accomplish any positive good." If one did not look to the state for solutions, one might discover them for oneself. He was marvelous at this sort of thing: putting together orphans and the elderly, subsidizing farmers by establishing rural hostels for slum kids, setting up neighborhood mini-schools and using the city as a classroom, and dozens of other ways of coping with the world as we find it.

The old libertarian program of *The May Pamphlet* had foreshadowed these ideas, but it was phrased like a manifesto, purportedly addressed to his fellow-anarchists and whatever readers of *Politics* might be won over, but really for himself. In those circumstances there was no point in trying to explain how such sensible miracles were to be accomplished; how else but in one's own life, where autonomy begins? To end the alienation of labor, quit your job; to ban the cars from Manhattan, ride a bike; to fight the draft, dodge. But in the Sixties Goodman found himself rubbing elbows with people who ran things—planners, educators, jurists, senators. He did not get many ideas for educational reform by sitting on the local school board, but his new tone of voice, patiently spelling out the details, was the result of that face-to-face familiarity with his audience. He began to speak as if his program might actually be put into practice.

This was good for his style, perhaps not so good for his politics. In Washington he amused his colleagues at the Institute for Policy Studies by taking it for granted that politicians meant all the fine phrases and patriotic sentiments they spouted—and he puzzled the Congressmen and public officials he met by proposing ways they might act on them! This too was a guerrilla tactic. However, beyond the momentary jolt his provocative naiveté gave a few pious liberals, Goodman's influence in the nation's capitol was minimal. To make any dent there, it was necessary to believe in myths like the desirability of the standard of living and the efficacy of power—the ends and means of American democracy.

What business had Goodman being in Washington anyway? This was no place for an anarchist. It was not power that interested him, and of course he already had his audience. But Goodman did take pleasure in solving problems and accomplishing tasks—one result, I suppose, of his having lived so long in voluntary poverty. "Coping" was one of his favorite words. He was full of expedients, whether he was making a salad or running a group session or inventing the free university. His favorite scientists knew how to ask the right questions, think up the relevant experiment, and fashion the necessary equipment out of makeshift parts and junk—what he called, lovingly, "dumb-bunny apparatus." When suddenly he found himself invited to think up alternatives for a whole country, his first impulse was to look around for useful scrap.

Even at this level his inclination was to suggest something that required no massive funding or retooling, more likely a simple reallocation or even retrenchment. His idea of educational reform, for instance, when he testified before a Congressional committee, was "don't give them a penny!" Another time, he was asked whether man's institutional needs and spiritual development might not be deeply incompatible, so that there could be no hope for civilization without a change in our whole system of values; Goodman replied that what "we need at present for our social ills seem to be to be prudence, temperance, courage, justice—they seem to me to be perfectly excellent...and these are all very old-fashioned virtues, which I think are quite sufficient."

It was precisely these old-fashioned virtues that Goodman shared with the readers of his books and essays. Young people especially were outraged at how the Established Order—government, the military, industry, education, the media—connived in the abuse and disregard of every traditional value. Our resources were wasted, our lovely countryside polluted, our cities a shambles; the entire network of public communications was in the service of a venal standard of living and soporific entertainment; the young were taught to behave themselves in educational salt-mines; public monies were poured into wars which destroyed other countries, or into the roads and cars which destroyed our own; young men were conscripted and sent to die in foreign lands or, if they refused, to rot in jail at home; citizens were systematically lied to about all of this, knew it, and had lost their faith in human nature, including themselves.

Goodman changed the lives of many of us simply by naming these outrages. He knew them well, could quote you the shocking facts and figures. His critique of the educational system, for example, was based on years of experience as a teacher (ages six to sixty, he used to boast), and close familiarity with school board and PTA as well as juveniles of every class and race. But he never criticized anything without proposing a better way of doing it—or more often, a good reason for not doing it at all. When he proposed mini-schools in store-fronts, he had in mind Mabel Chrystie's First Street School where his daughter Susan Goodman taught. When he recommended doing away with the high schools, it was no spur of the moment notion tossed off for shock effect, but an estimate of the human situation of adolescents, informed by his clinical experience as a psychotherapist as well as a teacher. Jobs, travel, and other experiments in independence made more sense than the increasingly prison-like conditions of urban high schools, or even the milder drudgery of middle-class prep schools in the suburbs. Again, as a learned man Goodman considered himself an "academic" and urged that universities return to their duty to conserve and transmit the Western tradition, instead of staffing a mass holding-pattern for unemployable youth. Most students were not bookish, and did not belong in college. He called for more trade schools, folk-schools on the Danish model, apprenticeship programs, and public service projects, to supply the real needs of teenagers for vocational training. He demanded the reform of the licensing requirements for many jobs that did not really depend on formal lessons in college.

The fact that any authentic attempt to deal with such questions immediately raises other questions—about the viability of American habits of work and leisure, about consumerism, the products and services rendered, about family life, child-rearing, sexual mores—shows how far we have already gone astray in establishing unnatural institutions to preserve our precarious social balance. Prudence, temperance, courage, and justice have been in abeyance for a long time, or we would have a looser, more flexible world, with room for risk-taking, innovations that would not threaten the whole interlocking structure. It was Goodman's special gift, unlike any other social critic of the Sixties, to see this complete picture, and to understand that it was not some single institution, or even a group of institutions, that needed reform, but the overall drift of society. Once you saw that you could not make corrections here or adjustments there without altering the entire machine, it became clear that such changes were not the point; the key was not knowing which institutions to attack or what modifications to propose, but how to bring people to their senses. How to revive the old-fashioned virtues, and give people choices to exercise them on.

In this Goodman's own example was crucial. Consider his influence in a few particularly problematic areas. One might admire his essays on academic freedom, censorship, and the media, but his most important contribution to free speech was his own insistence on printing what he believed, no matter how offensive to his potential audience or the authorities. This fundamental candor is at the heart of his political and literary power. Or take a different sort of example: his psychological and educational writings are full of passages that analyze and defend sexual practices at extreme variance with conventional mores, and his stories and poems celebrate his boys in the most explicit language, but the most telling argument for sexual freedom was simply his public enjoyment of his love-life. More than any other single person, he helped make present-day sexual honesty and the gay liberation movement possible, because of his courage in the sexually repressive Forties, Fifties, *and* Sixties. In these and other areas, his effect on society must be measured not merely by the books he wrote, or the ideas he circulated, but also by the life he led.

The radical complaint about Goodman's work in the Sixties was that it was merely reformist, patchwork on a crumbling wall.

What else was he doing in Washington? how else did he happen to be asked to testify before Congressional committees or to write for the *New York Times*? From this angle his practical proposals can be viewed as playing footsie with the status quo. On the other hand, the liberals criticized him as utopian; even if some of his suggestions might be feasible, they were worth nothing if he couldn't convince anyone to adopt them.

Both these estimates miss the point of his contribution. Much as he loved "making do," he did not think of himself as a facilitator of progress. If he had been nothing but an expert in one field or another, deeply invested in his own expertise, he might very well have conceived his role in this way, a technician laboring on his special part of the social machine. But he was no such thing: what professional educator would have recommended to Congress *no* budget for the schools? Anyone else would have come up with a million-dollar idea to make everything better.

Goodman was not trapped in this problem-solving syndrome because his ideas had never taken the impress of any one particular set of categories. By the time of *Growing Up Absurd* he had made his mark in several fields, having written *Communitas, The Structure of Literature, The May Pamphlet,* and *Gestalt Therapy.* He was able to combine politics and psychoanalysis, or community planning and philosophy, etc., so as to command a perspective that entirely escapes the parochialism of the technocrat. Since he was never wedded to the particular problems of a single field, he developed a remarkably unproprietary attitude toward his ideas. The point was not to institute these ideas, but to develop the habit of mind that could see alternatives. This is the crucial distinction that both the liberals and the radicals failed to see. He had already thought up most of his schemes ten or twenty years earlier, in his more theoretical books, or in his conversations at the SIA Hall. It was all there, and only needed rephrasing in the new political vernacular. But what he was now trying to convey was neither those ideas nor the philosophies that lay behind them; rather he was trying to impart the anarchist attitude.

The anarchist attitude is not something that can be taught systematically, like Marxism. It is impossible, a contradiction in terms, to be a doctrinaire anarchist. This was why it was necessary to work empirically, concentrating on cases. As he explained, "when you're writing the kind of books these are, you're talking about the cases which are in the *New York Times,* no? which are on the front page, front-page stories. And what you're trying to give is a tendentious series of statements which would give an attitude of what to do with these front-page stories. That is, there's no point of writing systematic work of this kind, it has no political function."

Of course his wisdom was philosophical and systematic at some level—he could always explain to you how his view of human nature, his understanding of English Common Law, and his anarchist principles, all went together—but when he talked about these things he was always dealing with instances and circumstances that actually confronted us, like a slap in the face. He, above all the leaders and personalities of the movement, seriously deserved the title *guru,* for he turned to these actualities like the Zen master, and gave answers that taught "the way." People kidded him about being a sage, and he thought it was funny too—"Come off it, Paul!"—but that is probably the best term we have for what he became in the Sixties. To be his sort of anarchist, you could try to learn his system by reading *Communitas* or *The May Pamphlet,* but that was scholarship, not understanding. It was better to read *People or Personnel,* not so thoughtful a book perhaps, but in it you could get the feel of his way of coping, the attitude of anarchism. It did not contain a political ethics or a libertarian program, because it was not the theory of anarchism but its practice:

There is a pervasive attitude, which is an anarchist tendency—there's not an anarchist philosophy, that would be a mistake, and there's certainly not an anarchist system, that would precisely be non-anarchist—there is a general attitude which is founded on what I think is an empirical proposition, which is probably true, namely, that by and large, animals, and human animals preeminently, function best if you let them cope concretely with what they're doing and make their own decisions about it.

As the decade wore on, Goodman devoted more and more of his energies to the antiwar movement. This was a different sort of activism, for it depended less on ingenuity or insight than moral sensibility and the willingness to risk something ("justice" and "courage" among his old-fashioned virtues). Early in the Sixties, when he helped Julian Beck and Judith Malina form the Worldwide General Strike for Peace, he was reluctant to do anything that went against the grain of his character as a literary man—he wrote leaflets and he picketed Random House ("No Business as Usual") on the day of the strike—but he steered clear of the nitty-gritty organizing, which felt boring and manipulative to him. On the other hand, he did serve on the editorial board of *Liberation,* where A.J. Muste, Dave Dellinger, and others tried to coordinate, anarchist fashion, increasingly large-scale efforts to stop the war. That involvement crept up on him, for when he came on the magazine it was still just a forum for libertarian views. As both the bloodshed and the protests intensified, so did Goodman's sense of an obligation to make some serious personal sacrifice. In 1967 he joined Karl Bissinger and Grace Paley in organizing Support In Action (the New York wing of Resist), which provided financial and legal assistance for draft resisters, and recruited non-draftable citizens to risk their own necks by "counseling, aiding, and abetting" the handing-in or burning of draft cards. Goodman fully expected to be indicted for this activity, and was surprised not to be among the Spock defendants.

Support In Action was especially important to Goodman, not only because of his own "seditious" history in the Forties, but also because his son Mathew was a non-registrant and one of the Cornell activists who organized the first mass draft card burning in Central Park on April 15, 1967. After Mathew was killed in a mountain-climbing accident that summer, Goodman continued for a few years in the same harness—doing it for Matty, one could see—but an iciness had come into his heart that distanced him from everything but grief for his son. At the same time the "Movement" was now being spelled with a capital "M" and drifting further and further from the libertarian ideals that characterized its early stages. Even in the heady days of Berkeley and the FSM Goodman had been wary of the anti-intellectualism of some student rebels, just as they mistrusted his harping on professionalism and the Western Tradition. He liked the new emphasis on confrontation politics even less. To his way of thinking, it was a far cry from anarchist "direct action." A.J. Muste had died the same year as Mathew, and since then Goodman's fellow editors at *Liberation* seemed to him to have abandoned their libertarian-pacifist position for a more intransigeantly revolutionary stance; one day he walked into the office and took his name off the masthead. When radicals began to give themselves titles like "collectives" and "cadres," Goodman began to call himself a "conservative"—as he certainly was, and always had been, though in a sense few understood: "It is only the anarchists who are really conservative," he had argued in a revised version of *The May Pamphlet* put out in the early Sixties, "for they want to conserve sun and space, animal nature, primary community, experimenting inquiry."

Goodman had his first heart attack in 1971. He died August 2, 1972, just short of his sixty-first birthday. His last works were his most moving poems, of loss and mourning for his son, and the fear of death. I think he felt that both his son's life and his own were somehow part of the price he paid for his political career, though of course accidents and heart attacks happen in peace and war, to all men. He took it as defeat. In 1970 someone asked him what the overall effect of his work had been; he answered, "Nothing. My feeling is, nothing."

When he said that, there were people in his audience to deny it on the spot, and I suppose the ultimate answer *is* up to us. If we could simply say that he was again twenty years ahead of his time, and take his suggestions as a blueprint for the Eighties, that would be some comfort, for the warnings and the solutions seem as apt and practical today as they did when he first announced them. We have not yet banned the cars from Manhattan, or decentralized our schools. But will we? It is depressing to think of how he was twenty, thirty, a hundred years ahead of his time. His time will never come if it is not already here. That was the lesson of *The May Pamphlet*. It is the attitude of anarchism we must learn. He knew from the beginning, when his audience was perhaps a couple of hundred, that the secret was to propose only that which one was willing—and able—immediately to put into effect, in concert with one's friends. "The libertarian is rather a millenarian than a utopian. He does not look forward to a future state of things which he tries to bring about by suspect means; but he draws now, so far as he can, on the natural force in him that is no different in kind from what it will be in a free society, except that there it will have more scope and be immeasurably reinforced by mutual aid and fraternal conflict. *Merely by continuing to exist and act in nature and freedom, the libertarian wins the victory, establishes the society....*"

Taylor Stoehr

Stateless, yet we have a flag
of the raw stuff the neutral color,
a march without a rhythm or key
our drum and trumpet muted play.

Unarmed, yet we have the power
of when the bottom drops out.
Lonely, loyal, murky-minded,
doubt-free we go our way.

Chuangtze is dead as I shall die
unnoticed by the wayside,
his spirit does not haunt the world
and his death-grip is relaxed.

I

The
May
Pamphlet

Reflections
on
Drawing
the
Line

I.

A free society cannot be the substitution of a "new order" for the old order; it is the extension of spheres of free action until they make up most of the social life. (That such liberation is step by step does not mean, of course, that it can occur without revolutionary disruption, for in many spheres—e.g. war, economics, sexual education—any genuine liberation whatsoever involves a total change.)

In any present society, though much and even an increasing amount is coercive, nevertheless much is also free. If it were not so, it would be impossible for a conscientious libertarian to cooperate or live there at all; but in fact we are constantly "drawing the line" beyond which we refuse to cooperate. Especially in creative work, in episodes of passion and sentiment, and in spontaneous recreation, there are healthy spheres of nature and freedom: it is the spirit of these that we most often extrapolate to all acts of a utopian free society. But indeed, even the most corrupt and coercive functions of the present society draw on good natural power—the pity of it—otherwise the society could not survive for one moment; for free natural power is the only source of existence. Thus, people are fed, though the means, the cost, and the productive relations are coercive; and the total war would be the end of us all were it not for the bravery and endurance of mankind.

Free action is to live in present society as though it were a natural society. This maxim has three consequences, three moments:

(1) In many spheres which in fact seem uncoerced, we exercise personal excellence and give mutual aid.

(2) In many spheres which in fact seem uncoerced, we have nevertheless been trapped into unnatural ways by the coercion that has formed us, for example we have become habituated to the American time-table and the standard of living, though these are unnatural and coercive through and through. Here the maxim demands that we first correct ourselves.

(3) Finally, there are those natural acts or abstentions which clash openly with the coercive laws: these are the "crimes" which it is beholden on a free man to commit, as his reasonable desire demands and as the occasion arises. (See below, "A Touchstone, etc.")

The libertarian is rather a millenarian than an utopian. He does not look forward to a future state of things which he tries to bring about by suspect means; but he draws now, so far as he can, on the natural force in him that is no different in kind from what it will be in a free society, except that there it will have more scope and be immeasurably reinforced by mutual aid and fraternal conflict. *Merely by continuing to exist and act in nature and freedom, the libertarian wins the victory, establishes the society;* it is not necessary for him to be the victor *over* any one. When he creates, he wins; when he corrects his prejudices and habits he wins; when he resists and suffers, he wins. I say it this way in order to teach honest persons not to despond when it seems that their earnest and honest work is without "influence." The libertarian does not seek to influence groups but to act in the natural groups essential to him—for most human action is the action of groups. Consider if several million persons, quite apart from any "political" intention, did only natural work that gave them full joy! the system of exploitation would disperse like fog in a hot wind. But of what use is the action, really born of resentment, that is bent on correcting abuses yet never does a stroke of nature?

The action drawing on the most natural force will in fact establish itself. Might is right: but do not let the violent and the cowed imagine for a moment that their weakness is might. What great things have *they* accomplished, in practice, art, or theory?

II.

Now I have been freely, even liberally, using the terms "nature," "natural," and their contraries to attribute value and disvalue, as: "natural and unnatural institutions." Do not these terms in this use lead to self-contradiction? for obviously the bad institutions as well as the good have come to be by natural process. A bad convention exists by natural causes; how are we to call it unnatural?

Let us consider the example of a language like English, and I want to distinguish three notions: physical and social nature, natural convention, and unnatural convention. It is physically and socially natural for people to speak: they have speech organs; they communicate with these; children express their feelings with determinate cries and imitate their parents' speech behavior. But any speech is some language or other. Speech organs, need to communicate, the expression of feelings, the desire to identify by imitation: these give the potentiality of speaking some language or other; historical circumstances make the language in fact English. It is usual to call the historical language conventional, but surely it is a "natural convention," in that the convention of English is a means of making the power of speech into a living act. Here at once we have the clue of how we can speak of an "unnatural convention": *an unnatural convention is one that prevents a human power from becoming a living act.* Thus, English is becoming unnatural because of its use in advertising. The technique of advertising is to establish an automatic reflex response, and immediate connection between certain words and the behavior of paying out money: thus it debauches the words so that they no longer express felt need, nor communicate a likeness of affection between persons, continuous with the original imitation of parents, nor correspond to the desire for objects really experienced—all these functions of honest speech are shunted over by a successful advertisement. But these functions are the strongest and the creative power in speech. Therefore we can say that such a use of English prevents the power of speech from becoming a living act; it is unnatural.

On the other hand, it is objected, automatic response is also natural: it is physically and socially necessary for life, as consider the words "Look out!" or "Fire!" To this objection the libertarian responds: Let us patiently consider the order and ratio of such alarm-words to the rest of speech. If they are too numerous, their emergency is blunted, just as indiscriminate profanity has no expletive force. What is the natural order of emergency and non-emergency situations, so that the strongest powers of health, safety, and pleasure may not be prevented from becoming living acts? The sense of emergency, natural in itself, inhibits vegetation, memory, reflection. (It likewise inhibits, by the way, the religious, eschatological, sense of emergency.) Taken at face value, the techniques of advertising and automatic political slogans express a state of continuous alarm!

Yet to be sure, as we consider it deeper, this is the true historical situation; there is nothing conventional about such techniques; and our poor English, like a faithful servant, is sacrificed to urgent need. The society that needs to buy up the products of its industry *is* in a state of continuous alarm: what time has *it* for vegetation, memory, reflection? And the "high" standard of living thus purchased exists in emergency conditions that are preventive of any natural standard of living whatever, for there is no vegetative pleasure and reflection; it is unnatural. But further: this habit of alarm, in the hearing of words and the consumption of commodities, lays people open to still further coercion in whatever direction, for a man is swept along.

One does not need to go thus roundabout through the analysis of linguistic usage to show that the modern industrial system, with its time-table and minute division of labor is against reason, freedom and nature! But in general: *the analysis of the forces constraining any strong natural power will show that they themselves are under constraint.* (Thus libertarian argument, like any other free expression, gathers force by its exercise.) Conversely—tho I shall not attempt to prove it here—the analysis of any great synthetic achievement, in art, theory, or practice, although it will show the cooperation of many powers in one effort, will also finally show the direct expression of each of these powers in the result.

III.

Concerning coercion itself, to take an extreme example, the libertarian must ask: *what is natural and what is unnatural coercion?* I doubt that I can answer this question to my own satisfaction, but perhaps we can find a clue in the following considerations.

Natural coercion would seem to be the correlative of natural voluntary dependency. An infant is dependent; a child is voluntarily dependent: it is on a basis of security of felt love and care that it grows in independence, partly by imitation of and withdrawal from precisely those in whom it is secure. A certain amount of coercion and even apparent violence strengthens this necessary security. (Obviously the violence is only apparent, that is, it is action that would be violent among adults; for absolute violence is destructive.) So much is matter of common observation. Again, a pupil voluntarily depends on a teacher who exercises authority and intellectual coercion; and again, the progress of the pupil and the aim of a good teacher, as Fromm has said, is the independence of the pupil from the teacher. If the previous childish dependency has been unfortunately insecure or cowed, a young person both will not trust his teachers and cannot grow to become their brother: he is prevented from drawing on new knowledge and power. (Thus we can say that the parental coercion was violent and unnatural.) Again, it is certain that discouragement of childish sexuality, or even *lack of encouragement*—as good parents encourage other developing powers such as walking, talking, drawing—leads to later general anxiety and timidity and may therefore be called unnatural coercion. (So Wilhelm Reich.)

Given these few, but important facts, let us psychologize as follows: The Ego gradually forms in between the inner desires and the stream of outer impressions, both sources of natural power. And the Ego must be said to have a power of its own; Freud calls it the "organized part of the Id," but I should say boldly that it is the organizing part of the Id: when the specific work of organizing has constructed enough patterns of concrete experience, the gradually cohering Ego comes to its great roles of interpreter, defender, purveyor. Now the danger to the child, it seems to me, is not generally that the Ego will not fail to crystallize, a case of extreme psychosis, but that it will crystallize too rapidly and inflexibly, in too tight a system, *against* the inner and outer worlds from which, in the end, we must draw the forces of life. This has been especially noted with regard to the inner sexual drive, against which the Ego sets itself (becoming erotized in turn); but not enough stress has been laid on the uncanny ignorance, stupidity, incuriosity, and lack of observation and perception which characterizes us all and which are also to be attributed to inhibition by the too narrow, shut-in, and erotized Ego. Now natural dependency, the need for security, is twofold: first, of course, the satisfaction of the vegetative and erotic instincts of the child; but secondly—and this is the point I am driving at for our purposes—*the furnishing by the adults of large imitable patterns of interpretation and attitude by using which the Ego can take its time and not feel called on too quickly to stand alone as sole authority.* The adult decides, where the Ego ought not yet to decide: this is coercion, always partly corporal, putting the child in the way or out of the way of some experience. Natural coercion is the adult decision that in fact gives the Ego the greatest inner and outer power to work up into experience and art. Since such decisions are imposed, cultural, and not spontaneous, I should call such adult coercion a natural convention. (For the purpose of this analysis, "adult" may mean single, dual, or multiple parents, or natural or foster parents.)

A pupil, even very small, is not dependent in the same way, for it is only of the parents that there are actual pre-ego memories. The relation with the parents remains always somewhat intra-personal. (Intra-personal *and* social; it has been the shrewd disservice of Sullivan and others to equate the social with the interpersonal.) The relation with the teacher is interpersonal, ego to ego; but the intra-personal dependency persists in symbols and attitudes, and the teacher is symbolically *in loco parentis* (this is sufficient, for the arts and sciences are also at first only the teacher's voice; a person who cannot surrender to such archaic attitudes is probably not truly docile.)

We come finally to our present goal: Of the simple goods, food, shelter, safety, over which great constituted bodies like governments and industrial systems claim authority, there is not a single one that the average adult person is not competent to decide about. If his ego has not developed to this point, it is that it has been maimed by previous unnatural coercion. I mean simply that every one knows he is hungry and it is food he wants, or knows enough to come in out of the rain. I am saying the same thing as the Tao, that it is "the affair of government to keep the people's bellies full and their minds empty," not that empty minds will not generate ideas but that this is not the affair of government. Therefore, all dealings on such simple matters should be ego to ego without dependency whether physical or symbolical; these are matters of discussion and reason, not persuasion and force. A man must make his own commitments. Any coercion in this sphere is unnatural in that, first, it prevents the ego from realizing its living power of interpreting and defending the most original instinctual demands; second, perhaps more important, it awakens archaic attitudes that then shunt off the power of the ego altogether and reduce the man to a child. What is the use of a man who cannot decide that he is cold or hurt, or who allows himself to be talked out of this primary experience by words and symbols?

At present of course, a man is not competent to cope with the arrangements for the simplest goods. The state does decide for him. And it exercises coercion. The ego is isolated from the primary facts by organizing which it first formed itself at all. It is in a continuous state of alarm. Under these circumstances, orators easily pose as fathers and leaders. Are we to call all this progressive and excellent?

IV.

A man is dependent on his mother Earth.

It is false that social relationships are primarily interpersonal. The strongest bonds in natural groups are continuous with passions and impulses previous to the organization of the egos of the members. These are love and fraternity. How different is the juridical equality of the social psychologists of "interpersonal relationships" from the creative unanimity and rivalry of revolutionary fraternity! the brothers vie to excel individually, but catching fire from each other they achieve what none of them had it in him to do alone.

The libertarian manifests the nature in him much more vehemently than we who have been trained to uniformity. His voice, gestures, and countenance express the great range of experience from child to sage. When he hears the hypocrite orator use words that arouse disgust, the libertarian vomits in the crowd.

We can conceive of a man whose ego takes far longer to crystallize than ours; whose ego still is forming out of vast systems of inner and outer experience, and works with forces beyond those that we have settled for. Such a vast ego belongs to a Christ or Buddha; we may confidently predict that it will perform miracles.

In the mixed society of coercion and nature, the characteristic act of libertarians is Drawing the Line, beyond which they cannot cooperate. All the heart-searching and purgatorial anxiety concerns this question, *Where to draw the line?* I'll say it bluntly: the anxiety goes far beyond reason. Since the extreme positions are clear black and white, and they exist plain to suffer and enjoy, and since it can be shown that one step leads to another in either direction: in the in-between murk *any* apparently arbitrary line is good enough. And one's potential friends among the people, to whom one wants to set an example, are moved by the big facts not the little details.

No particular drawn line will ever be defensible logically. But the right way from any line will prove itself more clearly step by step and blow by blow.

Yet to each person it seems to make all the difference where he draws the line! This is because just these details are the symbolic key to his repressed powers—and with each repression guilt for the acceptance of it. Thus one man will speak in their court but will not pay a tax; another will write a letter but will not move his feet; another is nauseated by innocent bread and fasts. Why are the drawn lines so odd and logically inconsistent? why are they maintained with such irrational stubbornness—precisely by libertarian people who are usually so amiable and easy-smiling? The actions of nature are by no means inconsistent; they are sequences of even rather simple causes; following the probabilities does not lead one astray but to see one's way more clearly. But the fact is that each of us has been unconsciously coerced by our training and acceptance; the inner conflicts now begin to appear, in the details of drawing the line, and all the fear, guilt, and rage. Let us draw our lines and have this out!

A free man would have no such problems; he would not have finally to draw a line in their absurd conditions which he has disdained from the very beginning. The truth is that he would regard coercive sanctions as no different from the other destructive forces of brute nature, to be prudently avoided.

A free man, so long as he creates and goes by his clear and distinct ideas, can easily maintain in his soul many apparent contradictions; he is sure they will iron out; a loose system is the best system. But woe if at the same time he is persuaded into mere prejudices and coerced into mere habits: then one day he will have the agony of drawing the line.

Well! there is a boyish joke that I like to tell. Tom says to Jerry: "Do you want to fight? Cross that line!" and Jerry does. "Now," cries Tom, "you're on *my* side!"

We draw the line in their conditions; we proceed on our conditions.

May 1945

The *May Pamphlet* was written in May and early June 1945, except for "Revolution, Sociolatry, and War," which was written in October. Parts of it were published in *Why?, Retort,* and *Politics,* and the whole was collected in *Art and Social Nature,* New York: Vinco, 1946.

On
Treason
Against
Natural
Societies

We speak of the Society, with a capital S, as "against the interests of Society," as tho it were a unitary thing, more than the loose confederation of lesser societies which also admittedly exist. The unanimity of behavior in the industrial, economic, military, educational, and mass-entertained Society certainly justifies the usage. Some philosophers call the Society "inorganic," meaning that many of the mores, e.g. traffic-congestion, are too remote from biological functions and impede them; but in the classical sense of organism, namely that the least parts mutually cause each other, the Society is more organic than societies have ever been; every action, especially the absurd ones, can be shown to have social causes and to be a social necessity. Disease is no less organic than health.

Yet in some of the strongest meanings of social unity, the Society is almost chaotic; one such is the unanimity of moral judgments in the most important personal issues. Thus, ought a girl to be a virgin at marriage? Is there a single standard for husband and wife? Is theft within the law permissible? Is patriotism ridiculous?—It would be possible to collect millions of votes on either side of such questions. I have made a practice of asking various persons what would be their attitude to receiving an incestuous brother and sister as overnight guests, and on *this* issue got many diverse replies! the universal confusion and toleration in such matters is itself a sign of social unanimity: namely, that people have agreed to divorce (and disregard) intimate personal concerns and opinions from the public ritual that exerts social pressure. The resulting uniformity of dress, behavior, desire is at the same time intense and bloodless; and there is no longer such a thing as earnest speech.

Now with regard to the legal penalty for crimes, like theft, bigamy, incest, treason, murder, no such confusion and toleration exists. Once the case is brought to court, there is little diversity of judgment and punishment. Yet obviously the lack of moral pressure keeps many cases out of court, for there is no scandal; adultery, for example, is a crime that is never brought to court. Does not this put the criminal law in an extraordinary position, and reduce the work of juries—which ought to express the strength of social opinion—to the merely logical function of judging evidence, which a judge could do better?

But the discrepancy between the moral and the legal judgment of crime reveals the following situation: On the one hand the people, distracted by their time-table and their commodities, are increasingly less concerned with the passional temptations that lead to crime; these are suppressed, sophisticatedly understood rather than felt, partially abreacted by press and movies; they do not seem diabolic; the easy toleration of the idea goes with the total repression of the wish. But on the other hand, the brute existence of any society whatever always in fact depends on the personal behavior of each soul, and of a coercive society on instinctual repression. Therefore the Law is inflexible and unsophisticated. It is as though *the Society knows the repressions that make its existence possible, but to the members of the Society this knowledge has become unconscious. In this way is achieved the maximum of coercion by the easiest means.* The separation of personal and political and of moral and legal is a sign that to be coerced has become second nature. Thus it is that people are "protected from the cradle to the grave"!

Many (I believe most) of the so-called crimes are really free acts whose repression causes our timidity; natural society has a far shorter list of crimes. But on the contrary, *there is now an important class of acts that are really crimes and yet are judged indifferent or with approval by law and morals both. Acts which lead to unconcerned behavior are crimes. The separation of natural concern and institutional behavior is not only the sign of coercion, but is positively destructive of natural societies.* Let me give an obvious example.

Describing a bombed area and a horror-hospital in Germany, a Sergeant writes: "In modern war there are crimes not criminals. In modern society there is evil but there is no devil. Murder has been mechanized and rendered impersonal. The foul deed of bloody hands belongs to a bygone era when man could commit his own sins...Here, as in many other cases, the guilt belonged to the machine. Somewhere in the apparatus of bureaucracy, memoranda, and clean efficient directives, a crime has been committed." These have become familiar observations: the lofty bombardier is not a killer, just as the capitalist trapped in the market does not willingly deal slow death, etc. The system and now the machine itself! are guilty. Shall we bring into court the tri-motor aeroplane?

The most blessed thing in the world is to live by faith without imputation of guilt: having the Kingdom within. Lo, these persons have no imputation of guilt, and have they the Kingdom within?—riders, as Hawthorne said, of the Celestial Railway!

The crime that these persons—we all in our degree—are committing happens to be the most heinous in jurisprudence: it is a crime worse than murder. It is Treason. Treason against our natural societies so far as they exist.

Not all commit Treason to our natural societies in the same degree; some are more the principals, some more the accomplices. But it is ridiculous to say that the crime cannot be imputed or that any one commits it without intent and in ignorance. For every one knows the moments in which he conforms against his nature, in which he suppresses his best spontaneous impulse, and cowardly takes leave of his heart. The steps which he takes to habituation and unconsciousness are crimes which entail every subsequent evil of enslavement and mass-murder. The murder cannot be directly imputed, the Sergeant is right; but the continuing treason must be imputed. (Why is he *still* a Sergeant?)

Let us look a little at the horrible working out of this principle of imputation, which must nevertheless be declared just. We are bred into a society of mixed coercion and nature. The strongest natural influences—parental concern, childish imitation; adolescent desire to stand among one's brothers and be independent; an artisan's ability to produce something and a citizen's duty—all these are unnaturally exerted to make us renounce and forget our natures. We conform to institutions that up to a certain point give great natural satisfactions, food, learning, and fellowship—then suddenly we find that terrible crimes are committed and we are somehow the agents. And some of us can even remember when it was that we compromised, were unwisely prudent, dismissed to another time a deeper satisfaction than convenient, and obeyed against our better judgment.

It is said the system is guilty, but the system is its members coerced into the system. It is also true that the system itself exercises the coercion.

Thus: a man works in a vast factory with an elaborate division of labor. He performs a repetitive operation in itself senseless. Naturally this work is irksome and he has many impulses to "go fishing," not to get up when the alarm-clock rings, to find a more interesting job, to join with some other machinists in starting a small machine-shop and try out certain ideas, to live in the country, etc. But against these impulses he meets in the factory itself and from his fellow workers (quite apart from home pressures) the following plausible arguments: that they must band together in that factory and as that factory, and in that industry and as that industry, to fight for "better working conditions," which mean more pay, shorter hours, accident insurance, etc.; and the more militant organizers will even demonstrate that by this means they can ultimately get control of all industry and smash the profit-system. None of this quite answers the original irk of the work itself; but good! he commits himself to this program. Now, however, since no one has native wit enough to decide for a vast factory and industry, and all industry, what to demand and when to demand it, and what means are effective, our man must look to others for direction concerning his own felt dissatisfaction. He fights for more pay when perhaps he does not primarily care about improving his standard of living but wants to accomplish something of his own between the cradle and the grave; he fights for seniority, when in fact he does not want the job, etc., etc. The issues of the fight are now determined by vast, distant forces; the union itself is a vast structure and it is tied to the whole existing Society. Next he finds that he is committed not to strike at all, but to help manufacture machines of war. The machines are then "guilty"!

True, the impulses of such a man are vague, romantic, and what is called adolescent; even if realizable they would not lead to full satisfaction. Nevertheless their essence is deep and natural. A program is a crime that does not meet the essence of the industrial irk, the non-creative job, but shunts across it. The worker who does a coercive job is a traitor. When he is sidetracked into a good, but irrelevant program, he is a traitor.

I have chosen a hard example that will rouse opposition. Let me choose a harder that will rouse even more.

A very young adolescent, as is usual enough, has sexual relations with his playfellows, partly satisfying their dreams of the girls, partly drawing on true homosexual desires that go back to earlier narcissism and mother-identifications of childhood. But because of what they have been taught in their parochial school and the common words of insult whose meaning they now first grasp, all these boys are ashamed of their acts; their pleasures are suppressed and in their stead appear fistfights and violence. The youth grows up, soon marries. Now there is conscription for a far-off war, whose issues are dubious and certainly not part of his immediate awareness and reaction. But his natural desire to oppose the conscription is met by the strong attractiveness of getting away from the wife he is a little tired of, back to the free company of the boys in camp; away from the fatherly role of too great responsibility, back to the dependence on a paternal sergeant. The camp life, drawing always on a repressed but finally thinly disguised sexuality, cements the strongest bonds of fellowship amongst the soldiers. Yet any overt sexual satisfaction amongst them is out of the question: instead the pairs of buddies pick up prostitutes together, copulate with them in the same room, and exchange boasts of prowess. Next this violent homosexuality, so near the surface but always repressed and thereby gathering tension, turns into a violent sadism against the enemy: it is all knives and guns and bayonets, and raining bombs on towns, and driving home one's lust in the guise of anger to fuck the Japs.

What a hard thing it is to impute the crime of treason against natural society to these men who do not even consciously know what their impulse is. They know as boys; shall we blame boys? And even the adults, priests, and teachers who invidiously prevent the boys' antics, do it out of unconscious envy and resentment. But they at least could know better, or why are they teachers?

It is horrifying, though not useless, thus to impute treason to the particular persons and to trace the institutional crimes, which are but symptoms and results, back to the incidents of coercion and acceptance. The guilty ones turn out to be little children and dear parents, earnest radicals, teachers unconscious of their intent, and even ancestors who are dead. Thank God the libertarian does not need to think of punishments, for he knows—following Socrates of old—that the punishment of injustice is to be what one is. The persons who separate themselves from nature have to live every minute of their lives without the power, joy, and freedom of nature. And we, who apparently suffer grave sanctions from such persons, betray on our faces that we are drawing on forces of nature.

But in fact the case is like the distinction in theology between the Old Law and the New. In the Old Law all are guilty, in the New they may easily be saved. We see that in fact everybody who still has life and energy is continually manifesting some natural force and is today facing an unnatural coercion. And now, in some apparently trivial issue that nevertheless is a key, he *draws the line!* The next step for him to take is not obscure or difficult, it presents itself at once; it is even forcibly presented by the Society! Will he not soon develop, in contrast to the habit of coercion, a *habit* of freedom? And positive natural acts bloom like the flowers.—

Brothers! the slave within the heart is dead, there's nothing more to slay—can you not hear, already love is finding means; around the world are whispering creative voices and bravery blooms like the flowers.

May 1945

First published in *Retort* (Fall 1945).

A
Touchstone
for the
Libertarian
Program

*T*he political program of libertarians is necessarily negative, for positive goods are achieved by other forces than (coercive) political institutions. And the opposition program varies with the oppressions and restrictions. Libertarians must not fall into the trap of wasting force by still opposing what authority no longer proposes, while failing to see the new kinds of exploitation. The mass press and radio of the democracies are masters at stealing liberal thunder; what are the words and acts that can expose this verbiage, which is often indeed well meant? Thus, the industrial authority does not exercise the same forms of oppression when there is a technology of surplus as it used when there was a technology of scarcity. In scarcity, the chief means of profit for the exploiters consisted in the depression of the workers' standard of living to reproductive subsistence; in surplus, the problem is sometimes rather to compel and control an artificial "high" standard of living that will clear the shelves. This is again pure authoritarian compulsion, but exercised especially by psychological means, advertising, education, and rousing the spirit of emulation. The result is that men find themselves even more enslaved in their time, choice, invention, spontaneity, and culture than in the black days of want, when at least a man's misery was uncontaminated and might produce a natural reaction. Given a surplus of goods and mass media of misinformation, it is possible for authority to cushion all crises and allow "freedom of expression" (or even encourage it as a safety-valve) to a small eccentric press.

I should like to suggest a kind of touchstone for the right libertarian program in a period like the present when the corporate integration of the economy, morals, tastes, and information of the society is so tight: I mean when the press, the movies, etc., themselves commodities, generate an increasing flow of commodities. The touchstone is this: *to advocate a large number of precisely those acts and words for which persons are in fact thrown into jail.* (The grounds of distinction between those acts which should and those which should not be advocated, is made in the next paragraph.) We must proceed on the assumption that the coercive society knows well which acts are a threat to it and which are not; acts which in fact rouse a coercive reaction have libertarian force; those which, tho once coerced, are now tolerated, are likely to be stolen thunder that is not neutral but in fact coercive in its effects. Thus, it is no longer the case that the man who publicly speaks for the organized bargaining power of labor is jailed; on the contrary he is approved. But this is not because organized labor has grown so strong as to compel its toleration (if it were this strong it could compel much more). It is simply because, as every libertarian knows, the organization of labor is a means of social control; higher wages are a means of profit—especially when by price-controls the public market is becoming a company store; and it is increasingly convenient for labor to regard itself as a "participant" in the general corporation of production and consumption. On the contrary, the man who advocates a wildcat strike is thrown into jail, but not merely because the demands are dangerous to profits, but that he disrupts the ordered system, the due process. Again: the man who advocates (advertises or displays) moral vices that fit well into the commodity system is an agent of society; but the man who advocates (exemplifies) pleasures outside the system of exchange or that undermine the social discipline, is frowned on and jailed—thus, one may not steal, copulate in the park, or encourage the sexuality of children.

Concerning the "crimes" that are actually punished, the libertarian must ask himself: which of these is detrimental to any society, including even a more natural non-coercive society in which discipline is somewhat but not so deeply and widely grounded in (reasonable) successful repression; which "crimes," on the contrary, are precisely the acts that would undermine the present coercive structure? I think that the list of the former would be small indeed—an obvious instance is murder. With regard to the latter, many beautiful opportunities could be found for libertarian action. What I urge is not that the libertarian at once bestir himself to commit such "crimes"—I do not think, by the way, that our small numbers would inconveniently crowd the jails—but that he at once loosen his own "discipline" and prejudice against these acts. For most of us do not realize how broadly and deeply the coercive relations in which we have been born and bred have disciplined us to the continuation of these coercive relations. Once his judgment is freed, then with regard to such "crimes" the libertarian must act as he should in every case whatsoever: if something seems true to his nature, important and necessary for himself and his fellows at the present moment, let him do it with a moral good-will and joy. Let him avoid the coercive consequences with natural prudence, not by frustration and timid denial of what is the case; for our acts of liberty are our strongest propaganda.

It is often cited as an example of the barbarity of America that here no distinction is made between "political prisoners" and "common criminals," that the political prisoner is degraded to the level of the criminal; yet in fact the "common criminal" has, altho usually by the failure of repression and but rarely by reason and in full consciousness, committed a political crime.

Returning now to the starting-point, the need to change the libertarian program with the change of the coercive circumstances, I should like to make a criticism of the continued use of one of the darling words of anarchist literature, the word "personal," as in "personal freedom," "personal expression," etc. The fact is that at present it is exactly the aim of all the organs of publicity, entertainment, and education so to form the personality that a man performs by his subjective personal choice just what is objectively advantageous for the coercive corporation, of which further he feels himself to be a part. Because of their use of the terms "free personality," "personal spontaneity," "personal participation," the hogwash of psychologists like Fromm and Horney has won the praise of even such an excellent anarchist as Herbert Read; yet it is not hard to show that their psychology has as its aim to produce a unanimity of spirit in the perfected form of the present social system, with its monster factories, streamlined satisfactions, and distant representative government. This kind of subjective personality is an effect of coercion, acting in the unconscious; it is not a causal principle of freedom. Going back to Rousseau, let me suggest the substitution of the word "natural," meaning those drives and forces, on both the animal and human level, which at present act themselves out in defiance or the conventions that we and our friends all agree to be outmoded and no longer "natural conventions," but which in a free society will be the motors of individual excellence and mutual aid.

To sum up: the greater part of what are now called crimes are nature. Even libertarians acquiesce in these prejudices because their "free personalities" have been coercively formed and are subject to unconscious coercion. The internal repression of spontaneous natural forces is today more than ever, in our era of time-tables and standardized pleasure, the chief means of dispiritment and coercion. Let us work not to express our "selves" but the nature in us. Refuse to participate in coercive or merely conventional groups, symbols, and behavior. The freedom of the individual is the expression of the natural animal and social groups to which he in fact belongs. Re-examine the "crimes" which seem proper to yourself and see which are indeed not crimes but the natural behavior of natural groups.

May 1945

First published in *Why?* (June 1945).

Natural
Violence

I have reached middle age and have not attended, nor even seen, a man dying or a baby being born. As things are arranged in our city, it is impossible to come close to a violent or noisome disease, unless professionally. What one meets in our city is a kind of health, usually mildly ailing, and a vigor youthful enough to ambulate. Decrepit age is confined to its rooms. One is faced with plenty of neurotics but never a maniac. In rural places there is as yet much more dying and being born socially, of both men and animals; but the tendency is not otherwise than with us. Again, the bourgeoisie (and my own class, the lumpen bourgeoisie) is more protected against such experience than the proletariat; but giant strides have been made toward extending protection to all. In general, women in childbirth necessarily are unprotected, but it is the practice to anodyze this experience as much as possible.

Men protect themselves from the major conditions of life. I do not say the major concerns, but surely the value of our concerns, such as they are, is problematical when they are not potentially, in ready memory and anticipation, related to their major conditions. Infants and children, it seems to me, are universally less protected; they have close acquaintance with their creature-anxiety, *Angst der*

Kreatur. We others now successfully repress the creature-anxiety from recall.

(Primitive people, of course, attempt to repress it, but they have not the means. In theory their art should therefore be more powerful than ours and their neuroses, unless they have lucky institutions, more widespread.)

The facts of war revive the lost anxiety in a terrible way, but they are valueless for a natural culture. They are the breakdown of the Society, but the exposed sufferer does not then have other feelings and habits to help him use these terrible truths for inventive life. The mentally broken soldiers who return from fiery fronts do not readjust to unnatural conventions, but they rarely create natural conventions—individual symptoms are not valuable social conventions—for the most part they are really ill as well as ill in the eyes of the community.

An example of childish invention comes to mind: One morning at our country school some men butchered a cow, and strung it up and flayed it. It was the hour of recess for the smallest children and they ran and stood in a circle round the bloody sight and drank it in with lewd eyes, afterwards manifesting extreme fright, excitement, and nausea when meat was served them. But they invented a ritual game of flaying a cow, in which one of their number would put on a coat and the others strip it off. (Of course their fear and disgust at the original scene were already the results of previous unnatural coercion.)

A wise society ought to have a better expression of its major conditions than ritual games.

I confess that I have been so disciplined that I cannot spontaneously and from my own experience see a way thru our dilemma, yet it presents a crucial problem for libertarians. Let us contrast the rational medical approach to birth, disease, decrepitude and death, with the rational efficient approach to industrial production. Wherever so-called efficiency in production leads to stultified and one-sided habits of the worker, we confidently say that the efficiency is inefficient in the long run because the means destroys the end. But medical efficiency—e.g., hospital technique or the therapeutic attitude—seems *prima facie* useful for our lives altogether, therefore for our full lives. On the other hand, the necessary isolation of the non-professional leads to a sterilization of general social experience that conceivably itself makes life flat and increases the flight into illness.

Every one is baffled and saddened by the spectacle of doctors straining their art to heal the soldiers hurt in the battle in which they themselves take part. They are even willing to heal the wounds of both sides at the same time as they fan the rage of one side. What on earth is the psychology of divided loyalty at such a level? Must we not conclude that the present medical training and practice themselves isolate the meanings of birth and death from the other judgments of life? And we have everywhere proved that the separation of those things that are naturally related is the sign of coercion.

Certainly we others, unused to the primary facts of life, are easily coerced by the threat of bringing them into play—until the moment we recklessly plunge into disaster of our own accord, and beyond what is necessary.

Strange as the phrase may seem we may speak of such a thing as "natural violence" (just as previously we defined "natural coercion"), although all violence is precisely the destruction, inhibition, or forcing of natural motions. *Natural violence is the destruction of habits or second natures in the interests of rediscovering the primary experiences of birth, infantile anxiety, grief and mourning for death, simple sexuality, etc.* Such violence as a natural motion of the soul can be demonstrated in many critical actions. An obvious example is the violence sought by and done to a virginal or sexually timid person. Again, deeper than their fears, civilized people yearn for and welcome natural catastrophes like fires, hurricanes, and earthquakes, that will strip them of the encumbrance of their possessions and touch routine to the quick.

And so men also plunge recklessly into the war, relying on each other for mass hypnosis and social approval so that they may do it with a good conscience. We must believe that they are not dreaming of their death, a psychological impossibility, but of putting the established ego in peril in order to bring it back into subordination to the instincts. But the war destroys not only their conventions but their lives altogether; for those who survive, there is provided not new, more natural habits but social isolation and nervous breakdown; and for the society as a whole, the war does not liberate natural associations and release social inventiveness, but on the contrary reinforces coercive and authoritarian institutions. War is unnatural violence.

The people of the Middle Ages, as Huizinga has pointed out, lived in a welter of natural and unnatural violence. With us there is progressively less of natural violence: the unnatural violence is pent up until it bursts forth, as a great corporate institution, in these world wars.

In the state of nature no positive effect springs from a negative cause. Yet the free man is forever clearing the decks and seems to exert political pressure only by negation. This is natural violence. He habitually employs non-violent "passive resistance" in order not to complicate further, by material weapons and authoritative organizations, the situation which is already too encumbered. He sets up the vacuum in our learned follies, so that original forces can operate to our advantage.

Resistance—patience—firmness—duty; these are not negative nor even passive virtues; they are not the restraint of force; they are action of the more elemental forces of primary nature; of time and clinging to one's place.

The libertarian apparently seeks to create a political vacuum; but it is the fertile vacuum of Tao, where heavy masses fall of their own weight and the invisible seeds burst into bloom. He speaks a word that *heals* as it violates.

May-June 1945

First published in Art and Social Nature, 1946.

Revolution, Sociolatry, and War

I. A MISCALCULATION IN THE MARXIAN DYNAMICS OF REVOLUTION

*A*ccording to Marx and Engels, the dynamism of the people's revolution into socialism rises from the interaction of two psychological attitudes: (a) the spiritual alienation of the proletariat, because of extreme division of labor and capitalist productive relations, from man's original concern with production and from natural social cooperation; (b) the brute reaction to intolerable deprivation brought on by the falling rate of profit and the capitalist crises. To expand these points somewhat:

(a) To Marx and Engels the specific properties of humanity are the ability to produce things and to give mutual aid in production. But the sub-division of labor and the capitalist use of machine technology de-humanize production: a man makes only a part of a commodity sold on a distant market, and performing an automatic operation he employs only a modicum of his powers. Further, the conditions of bourgeois competition and wage-slavery isolate men from each other and destroy mutuality, family-life, comradeship. There is therefore nothing in the capitalist institutions to engage the deep interest or keep the loyalty of the proletariat. They are made into fractional people and these fractions of men are indifferent to the bourgeois mores and society.

(b) On the other hand they are not indifferent to starvation, disease, sexual deprivation, infant mortality, and death in war; but these are the results of the wage-cuts, imperialism, unemployment, and fluctuation inherent in the bourgeois need to counteract the falling rate of profit and to reinvest. At the level of resentment and frustration and animal reaction to pain, there is concern for a violent change, there is latent rebellion.

From these attitudes, the revolutionary idea emerges somewhat as follows: driven by need to consult their safety, and with understanding given by teachers who explain the causes of their hurt, and with their original human aspirations recalled from forgetfulness and already fulfilled somewhat by comradely unity, the proletariat turns toward a new order, new foundations, a socialism immeasurably improved yet in its main features not unlike original human nature. By contrast to this idea, the life of the bourgeoisie itself seems worthless. And being increased in numbers and with their hands on the productive machinery of all society, the proletarians know that they can make the idea a reality.

Psychologically—and even anthropologically and ethically— this Marxian formula has great power, if indeed all of its elements exist as prescribed. But on the contrary, if any of the elements is missing the formula is disastrous and takes us as far from fraternal socialism as can be. Now there is no question that point (b) is missing: that by and large over the last century in the advanced industrial countries the real wages of the working class as a whole have not lingered at the margin of *physical* subsistence and reproduction; they have advanced to a point where even revolutionary writers agitate for a "sociological standard of living" and cry out against "one-third of a nation" being ill-fed and ill-housed. (The reasons, of course, are the astounding increase in productivity, the need for domestic markets, and such gross profits that the rate of profit has lost paramount importance.) What has been the result?

The spiritual alienation of point (a) has gone even further, I suppose, than Marx envisaged. He followed the de-humanization of production to the last subdivision of labor into an automatic gesture, but I doubt whether he (being sane) could have foreseen that thousands of adult persons could work day in and day out and not know what they were making. He did not foresee the de-humanization of consumption in the universal domestic use of streamlined conveniences whose operation the consumer does not begin to understand; the destruction of even the free choices in the market place by mass-advertising and monopolistic controls; the segregation among experts in hospitals of all primary experience of birth, pain, and death, etc., etc.

Yet it is not the case that these fractional persons, alienated from their natures, are brought sharply to look out for themselves by intolerable deprivation. On the contrary, they are even tricked, by the increase in commodities, into finding an imitation satisfaction in their "standard of living"; and the kind of psychological drive that moves them is—emulation! The demand of the organized proletariat for a living-wage and tolerable working-conditions, a demand that in the beginning was necessarily political and revolutionary in its consequences, now becomes a demand for a standard of living and for leisure to enjoy the goods, *accepting the mores of the dominant class.* (What are we to say of "leisure" as a good for an animal whose specific humanity is to be productive?) Then if these persons have gone over to the ideals of another class, it is foolish to call them any longer "proletarians" ("producers of offspring," as Marx nobly and bitterly characterized the workers); but given the apparently satisfied alienation from concern in production—and where do we see anything else—it is also unjust to call them workers.

Marx saw wonderfully the emptiness of life in the modern system; but he failed to utter the warning that this emptiness could proceed so far that, without the spur of starvation, it could make a man satisfied to be a traitor to his original nature. What he relied on to be a dynamic motor of revolution has become the cause of treason.

Lastly, the scientific teachers of the masses are no longer concerned to recall us to our original creative natures, to destroy the inhuman subdivision of labor, to look to the bands of comrades for the initiation of direct action. On the contrary, their interest has become the health and smooth functioning of the industrial machine itself: they are economists of full employment, psychologists of vocational guidance, and politicians of administrative bureaux.

So far the psychology of the masses. But in the psychology of the bourgeoisie there is a correlated difference from what Marx envisaged. The Marxian bourgeois has the following characteristics: (a) Preoccupied with exchange-value, with money which is featureless, he is alienated from all natural personal or social interests; this makes all the easier his ruthless career of accumulation, reinvestment, exploitation, and war. (b) On the other hand, he embodies a fierce lust, real even tho manic, for wealth and power. The conditions of his role are given by the economy, but he plays the role with all his heart; he is an individual, if not quite a man. The spur of a falling rate of profit or of closed markets, therefore, drives him on to desperate adventures.

By and large I do not think that this type is now very evident. Partly, to be sure, it is that the owning classes adopt a democratic camouflage for their protection; but the fact that they are willing to do this already shows that they are different men. Other factors seem to me important: (1) In absentee-ownership there is an emasculation of the drive for maximum exploitation of the labor and the machine; the owner does not have the inspiration of his daily supervision; he is not approached by inventors and foremen, etc.; but the salaried manager is usually concerned with stability rather than change. (2) But even if the drive to improve the exploitation is strong, the individual capitalist is disheartened by the corporate structure in which most vast enterprises are now imbedded; he is embarrassed by prudent or timid confrères. (Government regulation is the last stage of this corporative timidity.) (3) Not least, it now seems that even in peace-time there is a limit to the falling rate of profit; technical improvement alone guarantees an annual increment of more than 2%; by deficit spending the state can subsidize a low but stable rate of profit on all investment; there is apparently no limit to the amount of nonsense that people can be made to want to buy on the instalment plan, mortgaging their future labor. And in fact we see, to our astonishment, that a large proportion, almost a majority, of the bourgeoisie are even now ready to settle for Plans that guarantee a low but stable profit. Shall we continue to call them bourgeois? they are rentiers.

The more dynamic wolf, on the other hand, is no longer a private enterpriser, but increasingly becomes a manager and administrator of the industrial machine as a whole: he is in the Government. He bares his teeth abroad.

II. SOCIOLATRY

With the conclusions so far reached, we can attempt a formal definition of the mass-attitude that we call *Sociolatry* (after Comte).

Sociolatry is the concern felt by masses alienated from their deep natures for the smooth functioning of the industrial machine from which they believe they can get a higher standard of living. The revolutionary tension of the people is absorbed and sublimated by the interesting standard of living; but this standard is not physiological (which would be potentially revolutionary) nor is it principally economic, a standard of comfort and luxury (which would slow down the machine by breeding idleness, dilettantism, and eccentricity); it is a sociological standard energized by emulation and advertising, and cementing a sense of unanimity among the alienated. All men have—not the same human nature—but the same commodities. Thus, barring war, such an attitude of alienated concern could have a long duration. I say "barring war"—but we must ask below whether the war is not essentially related to the attitude.

On the part of the political elite: sociolatry is the agreement of the majority of the bourgeoisie to become rentiers of the industrial corporation in whose working they do not interfere; and the promotion of the more dynamic bourgeoisie to high-salaried, prestigious, and powerful places at the controls of the machine. Sociolatry is therefore the psychology of state-capitalism and state-socialism.

III. WHAT MUST BE THE REVOLUTIONARY PROGRAM?

Still barring from consideration the threat of war, we must now ask: what is a revolutionary program in the sociolatry? (By "revolutionary" I here refer to the heirs of Rousseau and the French Revolution: the conviction that man is born free and is in institutional chains, that fraternity is the deepest political force and the fountain of social invention; and that socialism implies the absence of state or other coercive power.)

For if indeed, with the steady expansion of technical productivity, the attitude of the masses has for a century moved toward sociolatry and the attitude of the bourgeoisie toward accepting a low but stable rate of profit, then the Marxian program is not only bankrupt but reactionary. The Marxian economic demands (for wages and conditions) cement the sociolatry; the Marxian political demands (for expropriation of the expropriators by seizing power) lead to state-socialism.

It is with diffidence and sadness that I here openly dissent from statements of Karl Marx. When I was young, being possessed of an independent spirit I refused to embrace the social science of Marx, but proceeded, as an artist and human-being, to make my own judgments of the social behavior I saw about. And then I found, again and again, that the conclusions I slowly and imperfectly arrived at were already fully and demonstrably (and I may say, beautifully) expressed by Karl Marx. So I too was a Marxist! I decided with pleasure, for it is excellent to belong to a tradition and have wise friends. This has to do with Marx as a social psychologist. As regards political action, on the other hand, I do not see, it has not seemed to me, that the slogans of the Marxians, or even of Marx, lead toward fraternal socialism; rather they lead away from it.

Now (*still* barring the war!) there is a great advantage for the revolutionist in the existence of sociolatry and of even a tyrannical state-socialism. The "standard of living" and the present use of the machinery of production may rouse our disgust, but it is an ethical disgust; it is not the fierce need to act roused by general biological misery. We may therefore act in a more piecemeal, educational, and thorogoing way. The results of such action will also be lasting and worthwhile if we have grown into our freedom rather than driven each other into it. Our attack on the industrial system can be many-sided and often indirect, to make it crash of its own weight rather than by frontal attack. ("One of the Evil One's most effectual arts of seduction," says Kafka, "is the challenge to battle. It is like the fight with woman, that ends in bed.")

Nor is it the case that the absence of tension and despair makes it impossible to awaken revolutionary feeling. For we know that the society we want is universally present in the heart, tho now generally submerged: it can be brought into existence piecemeal, power by power, everywhere: and as soon as it appears in act, the sociolatry becomes worthless, ridiculous, disgusting by comparison. There is no doubt that, once awakened, the natural powers of men are immeasurably stronger than these alien institutions (which are indeed only the pale sublimations of natural powers).

On the one hand, the kind of critique that my friends and I express: a selective attitude toward the technology, not without peasant features, is itself a product of our surplus technology; on the other hand, we touch precisely the vulnerable point of the system.

Then, as opposed to the radical programs that already presuppose the great state and corporative structure, and the present social institutions in the perfected form of the Sociolatry, we must—in small groups—draw the line and at once begin action directly satisfactory to our deep nature. (a) It is essential that our program can, with courage and mutual encouragement and mutual aid, be put into effect by our own effort, to a degree at once and progressively more and more, without recourse to distant party or union decisions. (b) The groups must be small, because mutual aid is our common human nature mainly with respect to those with whom we deal face to face. (c) Our action must be aimed not, as utopians, at a future establishment; but (as millenarians, so to speak) at fraternal arrangements today, progressively incorporating more and more of the social functions into our free society.

1. It is treasonable to free society not to work at a job that realizes our human powers and transcends the inhuman subdivision of labor. It is a matter of guilt—this is a harsh saying—to exhaust your time of day in the usual work in office and factories, merely for wages. The aim of economy is not the efficient production of commodities, but cooperative jobs themselves worth doing, with the workers' full understanding of the machines and processes, releasing the industrial inventiveness that is in each man. (Nor is it

the case, *if we have regard to the whole output of social labor,* that modern technical efficiency requires, or is indeed compatible with, the huge present concentrations of machinery beyond the understanding and control of small groups of workers.)

2. We must re-assess our standard of living and see what parts are really useful for subsistence and humane well-being, and which are slavery to the emulation, emotional security, and inferiority roused by exploitative institutions and coercive advertising. The question is not one of the quantity of goods (the fact that we swamp ourselves with household furnishings is likely due to psychic causes too deep for us to alter), but that the goods that make up the "standard of living" are stamped with alien values.

3. We must allow, and encourage, the sexual satisfaction of the young, both adolescents and small children, in order to free them from anxious submissiveness to authority. It is probably impossible to prevent our own neurotic prejudices from influencing small children, but we can at least make opportunity for the sexual gratification of adolescents. This is essential in order to prevent the patterns of coercion and authority from re-emerging no matter what the political change has been.

4. In small groups we must exercise direct political initiative in community problems of personal concern to ourselves (housing, community-plan, education, etc.) The constructive decisions of intimate concern to us cannot be delegated to representative government and bureaucracy. Further, even if the Government really represented the interests of the constituents, it is still the case that political initiative is itself the noble and integrating act of every man. In government, as in economic production, what is superficially efficient is not efficient in the long run.

5. Living in the midst of an alienated way of life, we must mutually analyze and purge our souls until we no longer regard as guilty or conspiratorial such illegal acts as spring from common human nature. (Needless to say, I am here referring to ethical discussions not amateur psychoanalyses.) With regard to committing such "crimes," we must exercise prudence not of inhibition but such prudence as a sane man exercises in a madhouse. On the other hand, we must see that many acts commonly regarded as legal and even meritorious are treason against our natural society,

if they involve us in situations where we cease to have personal responsibility and concern for the consequences.

6. We must progressively abstain from whatever is connected with the war.

I am sensible that this program seems to demand very great initiative, courage, effort, and social invention; yet if once, looking about at our situation whatever it is, we *draw a line* (wherever we draw it!), can we not at once proceed? Those of us who have already been living in a more reasonable way do not find these mininal points too difficult; can those who have all their lives taken on the habits (if not the ideas) of the alienated society, expect not to make drastic changes? If we are to have peace, it is necessary to *wage* the peace. Otherwise, when their war comes, we also must hold ourselves responsible for it.

IV. THE WAR

The emergency that faces sociolatry and state-socialism is the War, and we know that this catastrophe of theirs must overwhelm us all. Is it a necessity of their system? Must one not assume, and can one not observe, that beneath the acceptance and mechanical, unspontaneous pleasure in the current social satisfactions there is a deep hatred for these satisfactions that makes men willing to rush off to armies and to toy with the idea of loosing explosive bombs?

(To put this another way: In a famous passage Freud pathetically justifies competitive capitalism as a means of releasing aggression without physical destruction. Now if, under improved economic arrangements of full-employment and non-competitive profits, this means of release is thwarted, how will the general aggression find an outlet—if the aggression itself is not moderated by small-scale fraternal competition, mutual aid, and instinctual gratification?)

We have defined a mass alienated from deep natural concerns, but occupying the conscious and pre-conscious with every manner of excitement, news, popular culture, sport, emulation, expenditure, and mechanical manipulation. Now let us draw from the individual psychology what seems to be an analogy, but it is more than an analogy.

When an ego-system is set up against the id-drives, rather than as the interpreter, guide, purveyor, and agent of those drives, then this ego is basically weak and "tends to destroy itself." Further, the more elaborate the distractions sought by the ego, the tighter is the defense and rationalization against the instincts, the greater the tension, the more suggestive and hypnotic the daily experiences, and the more inevitable the self-destruction. During the last years of his life, largely in order to explain the phenomena of war, Freud introduced into his theory the primordial death-wish. But whether or not, as is hotly debated among the analysts, such a drive is really primitive (in general a hunch of Freud is better than the clinical evidence of a lesser man)—nevertheless, to explain the tendency to self-destruction that we are here considering, no such primitive drive is required. On the contrary, the rebellion of the instincts against the superficial distractions of the ego is a healthy reaction: it is a healthy kind of violence calculated not to destroy the organism but to liberate it from inanity. To the ego, however, this desire to "burst" (Wm. Reich) might be interpreted as the desire for suicide—and if the ego can indeed control the movements of the body and the imagination, that is in fact the end of the organism.

Let us return to the real social context (for all individual psychology is an abstraction): we see on all sides an ill-concealed—concealed only to those who are expressing it—hatred for the social satisfactions. The most refined champions of our civilized arena, namely the technicians and practical scientists, seem almost the most inspired to feverish cooperative activity if once it has in it the promise of violence. Further, the people as a whole can the more cheerfully rush to the destruction of what they have and what they are, because, inspired to it en masse and suggesting it to one another, they release one another from the guilty restraint that each would feel by himself.

The behavior of the Americans during the last interbellum was terribly significant. On the one hand, people were almost unanimously opposed to the coming war; there was even a certain amount of successful pacifist agitation (such as the barring of military training from many colleges). On the other hand, one economic and political action after another was committed that led directly to a world-wide war; and these acts were acquiesced in by the people despite the clear, demonstrative, and thousand times re-iterated warnings from many quarters that the acts were heading towards a general war. It is absurd to claim that such warnings did not get a hearing, for the point is: why did they not? To me it seems that the public behavior was exactly that of a person in the face of a danger that he consciously wants to flee, but he is paralyzed because unconsciously he wants to embrace it: thus he waits and will not think of it.

But alas! this social violence that wants, not to destroy mankind, but only to get back to natural institutions, cannot be healthy, because it will in fact destroy us.

We others had better wage our peace and bring them quickly into our camp.

October 1945

First published in *Politics* (December 1945).

Unanimity

*I*n the mixed society of coercion and nature, positive political action is always dialectically good and evil. But nature underlies and coercion is imposed. Then we must act so as to avoid the isolation of a particular issue and the freezing of the coercive structure, but always to submit the issue to the dynamism of the common natural powers that nobody disputes. The defining property of free political action is potential unanimity, drawing on common nature and undercutting the conflict of interests. Our political action is the emergence of unanimity from natural conflict. Many conflicts are wholly *theirs* and may profitably be disregarded. In others, such as the class struggle, where there is a direct attack on obvious goods such as sustenance or time of life, the issue is clearly enough drawn and we lend all force to freedom, justice, and nature. But where there is a natural conflict, between natural forces, the free man must not subscribe to a compromise, but must invent a program, for natural conflict is solved only by invention, that introduces something new into the issue. If he cannot invent, it is likely that the conflict is internal in himself and inhibits his invention; then he must withdraw to the sure ground previous to the conflict where in fact he can invent.

I. DIALECTICS OF POSITIVE ACTION

It is unprofitable to strive, in coercive conditions, for a relative advantage in a situation that, even if the victory is won, is coercive. Thus, to demand a just trial when the law to be executed is unjust; or to exercise civil rights within the framework of the State. To demand higher pay when the standard of living that can be bought for money is unsatisfactory. To cry for military democracy when the war is unnatural violence. This is wasting one's strength and obscuring the true issues; it results in being frozen and trapped.

On the other hand, since the strength and the continuance of any society must depend on the naturalness of its conventions, it is profitable to defend the natural conventions even with scrupulosity—though scrupulosity is most often avoided by the wise. Thus, we appeal in the court as our court and enjoy the civil powers that were liberated by our own great men; we bargain because the marketplace has free choices; we demand a voice not for the soldier but the man. (Yes! and the next step is for the man to say "I quit.") This is essential to show that we are not alienated from society—if not this society, what society do we have?—but on the contrary, the Society is alienated from itself.

The ordinary man is baffled by social dilemmas; the free man must make social inventions that liberate strength. Nothing is more disheartening than to see an honest party or press, unwilling to lend itself to bad alternatives, that does not also continually produce a stream of good natural solutions. If a man cannot in fact invent a way out, what right has such a man to be libertarian on the issue at all? his negative criticism insults and disheartens the rest. Further, it is not sufficient to proffer as a solution a state of society and of institutions which is precisely not attainable by a man's present powers of action; he must invent an action which can be performed today. But indeed, those who draw on natural powers find it easy to be inventive—on natural issues; a man who finds himself usually constrained merely to veto all the presented alternatives is almost surely coerced by unconscious resistance to some possible solution.

In natural ethics there is no such principle as the choice of the lesser of two evils. Such a principle is self-contradictory, for any free action or abstention must draw on natural power and cannot depend on a negation. When a social issue has come to the pass of a choice between evils (as, conscripting an army to resist a tyrant), then we know that the citizens have long neglected their welfare; the free actions that we can then invent are all attended with great suffering. They must involve withdrawing utterly from the area of guilt, a painful sacrifice—and more and more painful till all the consequences work themselves out. The lesser evil is a sign that an interest has been allowed to develop in isolation until it now threatens even our lives. *It is the isolation of the issue from its causes that restricts the choice to the lesser evil.* Those who break the spell and again draw on all their forces will find other choices.

Thus, to resist the greater evil it is usual for well-intentioned men not to embrace the lesser evil but to form a "united front" with it; in the feeblest case, such a united front is called "critical support"; in the strongest case it is based on a program of "minimum demands," presumably relevant to the causes of the crisis. Now in principle, a united front is nothing but mutual aid itself; but in practice it is often the inhibition of precisely the natural forces whose exercise would overcome the evil lesser and greater both. The formula of critical support usually comes to be simple acceptance. Therefore Gandhi said, that by nature he was cooperative, but he could not acquiesce to conditions that made it impossible to cooperate.

The formula of the "minimum program" is in principle the same as Drawing the Line: relax coercion at this point and we will cooperate, the presumption being that then the issue is no longer isolated and our action is not necessarily evil. But in practice this often comes to freezing the situation into a new coercive compromise and inhibiting the dynamism of the next step (but drawing the line is inseparable from the dynamism of the next step). The very granting of the minimum demands proves to be the form of the new coercion—otherwise it would not have been granted; as, social legislation prepares the corporate state. But social invention is impossible when the situation is frozen. Thus, with the aim of doing justice to the untouchables, Gandhi fasted against what seemed to be the reasonable minimum program of granting them a certain number of sure constituencies in the Congress ("separate electorates"), because this would freeze their status as separate from the community.

In general, right action with regard to the lesser evil and the united front is part of what can be called "aggressive non-commitment" and "limited commitment":

Obviously a man cannot act rightly with regard to bad alternatives by simply not committing himself at all, for then he is in fact supporting whichever bad alternative happens to be the stronger. But the free man can often occupy an aggressive position outside either alternative, which undercuts the situation and draws on neglected forces; so that even after the issue has been decided between the alternatives, the issue is still alive: new forces have been marshalled that challenge the decision, except that now the challenger is not a bad alternative but an inventive solution. This is the right action when the presented alternatives are frozen fast in the coercive structure. On the other hand, when the situation is somewhat fluid or confused, the free man, "cooperative by nature," can make a limited commitment to a presented alternative, if (a) he can work to clarify the issue and (b) he can, if the issue crystallizes badly, withdraw still leaving the issue in doubt. He must retain considerable freedom of action; any free action, so long as it is exercised, will generate increasing power. The aggressively non-committal man and the man who retains freedom of action when he commits himself to a limited extent, will surely be effective and exert influence among those who are coerced, inhibited, and committed against their best nature.

But best of all is to act in situations where there is a natural unanimity and no need for either withdrawal or limitation, for such action inspires a man beyond his best judgment.

II. UNANIMITY

Fraternal unanimity is the social resolution of a natural conflict better than the ability, desire, or judgment of the separate conflicting persons. For the most part unanimity is found not by relaxing but by sharpening the conflict, without unnatural coercion, until the emergence of a new idea.

(I think it is preferable thus to define unanimity in terms of conflict and invention rather than in terms of the harmony of egos which, as I have argued against the revisionist Freudians, is narcissism and not a social relation at all.)

When the two parties to a conflict are in fact concerned for the common good, it is impossible that they should ever, unless for a temporary convenience, come to an electoral division and seek the majority. Each side will rather eagerly welcome rational opposition in order to perfect its own judgment. The conflict will generate a common solution, and the assent will be unanimous. This is of course a commonplace among bands of friends. When they are forced to a division and a vote, it is a sign that moral standards are at play which are outside the dynamism of the friendship. To be sure, in friendly groups many decisions become unanimous by default, when some of the friends are not sufficiently concerned to press their claim; but it is reasonable that those most concerned should win the decision.

Primitively the rule of the majority was, I suppose (without evidence), a tacit agreement not to fight the armed battle that the majority would win anyway. As such it is an obvious coercion that soon, moreover, becomes unconscious under the cover of an illusion of justice, fair play, etc. Some philosophical color of justice could be given the majority by the utilitarian calculus, that the satisfaction of many is better than the satisfaction of few, if only it were the case that the majority opinion generally turned out to their own satisfaction; but on the contrary, often the smaller the minority the more deeply considered its opinion. It is impossible that other things should ever be so equal that there is more wisdom in six heads than in five. Luckily most of the coercive conflicts that come to a vote are so nicely weighted with evils against each other that tossing a coin would also give a just decision. In practice, of course, the few are most concerned—either about the issue or just getting elected—and they have their way; the many default but regard themselves as uncoerced because they say Aye.

The general notion of a division and a vote would be ultimately justifiable only if there could in fact be irreconcilable natural forces or interests (then the agreed coercion would be better than the death-struggle). But no such thing exists in psychology, and in social ethics it is a self-contradiction, for any free society springs from common humanity, and any natural interest is not accidentally but essentially related to this common basis. And what free man would rest easy if he thought that his friend had a value that he absolutely could not share, at least in sympathy?

"But," it is objected, "even if we agree that there cannot be any ultimately irreconcilable natural conflict, in practice there is always a temporary irreconcilable conflict: therefore we have de facto an irreconcilable conflict and consult the majority rather than the force of arms." Where such a de facto conflict really exists, then certainly the conclusion follows. But in fact it rarely exists; almost always an inventive solution is at hand or close at hand. It is an illusion that in the kind of issues that arise in practical communal problems a *long* time, more than a few weeks or months, is required to hit on an inventive solution rather than a compromise or a bad powerful alternative (as if these were spiritual problems in which the soul must be tried before it comes to know); but it is precisely because the majority knows it will have its way that it inhibits invention and will not wait a single day. Was it the case, for instance, that in 1775 the Parliament did not have an inventive solution at hand?

Of unanimity itself, there is the natural and the coercive. Coercive unanimity is a political evil especially of modern times, though it has always had every kind of religious and military manifestation: it is the coercion of habits and unconscious forces so that the judgment of the ego comes as if spontaneously to assent. The classical instance is the hundred deep thinkers who explain in identical irate language that socialism would destroy their individualities. Natural unanimity relies also on unconscious ties—the creative power of fraternity goes beyond the abilities of individuals; but these are kept in a natural relation with the judging ego as their interpreter, informant, and guide. Bursts of uncontrolled social enthusiasm are also no doubt salutary, purgative and inspiring, and approximating the relaxation of the total orgasm; but—Lord!—not the settled and monotonous hypnosis, that both sustains and is sustained by many of our institutions of industry and entertainment—and often indeed without a personal hypnotist, so that coerced and coercer walk in one trance!

III. POSITIVE POLITICAL ACTION

We have been speaking of positive political action. Now I hope that I have not deviated from the essence of libertarian thought except to add to it some notions of the psychoanalysis; but it must be admitted that at least the word "politics" is anathema in anarchist writing. "Politics" is equated with coercion by the state apparatus and as the business of the group that is both the executive committee of the economic exploiters and practices exploitation on its own. This restriction of the term is unwise. For the fact is that throughout history, especially the best ages and many of the best men have spoken of themselves as political, and politics along with art and theory has been the noble activity of free men, not coercers. Let us try to define politics as a free act, therefore belonging to free societies.

Anarchist writers often speak of "politics," the coercive functions of the state and the struggle for perquisites, as degenerating in free societies to mere "administrative functions." But in the first place, we can see today that it is precisely through administrative functions that the most poisonous features of state coercion come to express themselves. Secondly, it is false that such degeneration would occur or would be desirable. *Any measure of social initiation whatever, that is not routine and that faces initial opposition and must win its way to acceptance, is political.* Precisely a free man in a free society will often initiate new policies, enter into conflict with his fellows, and coerce them; but this is natural coercion.

A property of free political action is to be *positive,* in the legal sense of imposing a new convention. Here too the anarchists, true to their false intuition, condone only negative or abstaining political action, and they are justified by the centuries of unnatural coercive conventions. But it is not the case that out of day to day economic and domestic existence there arises any great thing without the imposition of a positive, naturally coercive, yes even aggressive, idea. Consider the Zionist movement—to take an example from our coercive society: great cities have sprung up (some of them stupidly located), gardens have bloomed in deserts, and tribes of men have been set at rifle-point; and all this is the effect of a mere idea in the mind of a journalist, working on prepared potentialities.

A free positive idea could be said naturally to coerce social forces into action—this is natural politics. A coercive positive idea will invariably inhibit or destroy natural forces—this is unnatural politics.

The alternative to natural politics is not no politics but coercive politics, for men will not cease to innovate positive social action. On the contrary, just the sentiment of routine and "administrative functions" invites bad innovations. Therefore we must speak of "waging the peace," just as we say "waging the war." The sense in which a free artist can speak of "arts of peace"—who knows what manner of peace one has with one's art!

Let me quote the great sentence of Michelet: "Initiation—education—government: these are three synonymous words."

To its initiator a positive idea seems at first coercive; then he recognizes it, perhaps only by acting it out, as the expression of his deeper powers, or sometimes of forces too deep to be properly called his own at all. If it is an idea that requires social cooperation, his fellows in turn will regard it as coercive. If then, as happens most often, the idea is erroneous—it is perhaps peculiar to his own nature or situation—their free judgment will safely resist him, especially since there are other positive ideas in the field. But if indeed he has a better reason, they must perforce again be naturally coerced; they are his pupils.

IV. A WRONG NOTION OF UNANIMITY

Just as there are terms unwisely rejected by our authors, so there are philosophers. (In principle it is unwise to reject any philosopher, for what they say comes to pass anyway.) And the most rejected is Nietzsche. Nevertheless it is just the notion of Nietzsche that we are a bridge for who is better that can give salt to our concept of mutual aid. If freedom is the exercise of natural power we cannot avoid coming to speak of natural aristocracy; to do so would be precisely internal fear and, as Nietzsche would have said, resentment. Therefore we must say, "mutual aid *and* individual excellence"—and a moment's reflection will show that this is the same as saying, "waging the peace."

All honor to our fraternity that has more than its share of eccentrics! But what a pity if free societies failed to transmute strong eccentricity into exemplarity, but instead absorbed it. This would be the wrong kind of unanimity.

Strong eccentricity is the result in a coercive society of exercising any simple power too strong to be repressed. Since the system of coercion is organic and oppresses his power at every turn, hypocritically bringing it into "irreconcilable conflict" with other natural interests, the eccentric soon comes to deny that even plain goods are good. Thus we see that the gift of fearless speech, or strong animal lust, or common sense, all make eccentrics.

But in free society the strong power finds its relation to other forces; it tries to impose on them its positive idea; and it becomes exemplary of its own character. When the peace is waged, when there is individual excellence and mutual aid, the result is exemplarity: models of achievement.

V. ANOTHER WRONG NOTION OF UNANIMITY

A favorite saying of mutual aiders is "Happy is the people that has no history"—no wars, no dynasties, no need to rebel; and what is there in the round of sensible human existence, always springing from the same needs, to make a theme for history? Yet I should like to question this saying and distinguish coercive history from free history.

If we have regard only to the potentialities of human beings, it could be argued even that there has been no history, coercive or otherwise. In the thousands of years there is no sensory, scientific, ethical, or even technical capability that has evolved or been lost. It is always a common human nature.

(Indeed, the existence of a common unchanging human nature is an a priori principle of historical research—it is the true analogue, sought by Henry Adams, of the principle of the conservation of energy; it is by this regulative principle that the historian is confident that when he consults the documents they will prove explicable. If there had been changes in human nature, he would not recognize them anyway, except by lacunae in his understanding; but the justification of the principle is that in fact very few records turn up that defy some explanation or other in our terms, and further and more important, that the more faithful he is to the letter of the records, and the more he renounces "modern" preconceptions, the more recognizable the ancients become. By the same principle we also recognize our kinship to the lions and the bears.)

But now, returning to the anarchist saying that the people is happy etc., supposing we ask: what *is* this natural existence, what *are* these human powers, needs, and satisfactions that free society fosters? Then we see that we know them, in their fulness, only through history. History is the actuality of the human powers, and we infer the power from the act. It is Homer and Sophocles that demonstrate that we can be poets. From the peculiar character of an epoch we infer that certain powers, elsewhere actually expressed, were inhibited by the institutions; etc.

In the end, *it is only free positive action that makes history,* revealing the depths of our common powers. (So Marx, restricting himself to the consideration of man in class bondage, declared that history had not yet begun.) For in all the empires, systems of exploitation, and first, second, third world wars that make up coercive history, there is a deadly sameness: everywhere the inhibition of most of the forces of life and always the expression of the same trivial force. It is startling—and therefore their wars possess a certain melancholy interest—that even the Greeks, those inventors and sons of the morning, could not improvise anything better than this. But proofs, poems, heroic and saintly deeds, though there be many thousands of each, and thousands of each species of each, have all a difference and inventiveness.

June 1945

First published in *Art and Social Nature,* 1946.

Jail and blows, being a coward,
I dread, but I am inured
    to be misunderstood,
    because the common reason, God

communes with me. Let them refute
the propositions I have put
    with nail and hammer on the door
    where people pass, upon the square.

II

Some
Practical
Proposals

Notes
on
Neo-Functionalism

Author's Note: The esthetics of Functionalism is in many ways an expression of capitalist industrialism and a system of efficiency for profits. By extending the functionalist criterion, however, to cover the ends *of production as well as the* means, *it is possible to come in sight of a more humane style. This extension I have called "Neo-Functionalism."—P. G.*

*F*unctionalism is design of the means simply for the end. Such design cannot fail to have a certain beauty, of either directness or of ingenuity, and always the beauty of clarity. But these beauties are consequences of functionalist designing; they are not implicit in the artificial object itself; indeed we may often turn away from the object—once we see how it works—in boredom or disgust. But beauty is a resting in the experience of the object.

In functionalist design, the experience of the means leads us directly to the end or use, but there is no reciprocal relation by which the experience of the ends turns us back to the renewed experience of the means. The form expresses the content; the content never expresses the form: it is not a content formal in itself.

To be sure, no true functionalist ever leaves the use of end or content uncriticized. On the contrary, the practicers of this method of design are perhaps too intensely social-conscious to have the playful freedom that is the prerogative of art. But the criticism of the end is in terms of the grand social utility, efficiency, and satisfaction; it is not immediately and directly turned back on the production itself of the object, but only comes to this indirectly thru considering the health, labor and happiness of all the working class; but then we are far from the easy, immediate satisfactoriness of art.

The neo-functionalist goes further and reciprocally criticizes the end in terms of its producing means: Is the use, he asks, as simple or ingenious or clear as the efficient means that have produced it? He insists on a much closer scrutiny of the utility of the ends than does the functionalist; he keeps his eye more immediately on the object itself and asks, is it worthwhile? Obviously his scrutiny is much too close for our complicated civilization which requires that almost everything be overlooked a little, that is to say, judged in terms of final ends that are too indirect and distant to be looked at at all, by the eyes or the intellect.

Yet even on political and ethical grounds, our friend is not such a fool, for he asks (a little quizzically): If the usefulness of your immense productive machine is the happiness, the pleasure, the welfare, and the intellect of all mankind, why not start here now with this man making, using, and experiencing this object that we are considering? (In character the neo-functionalist man seems at the same time crotchety and easy-going: he takes exception to the much that is universally accepted; he stops to praise many things universally disregarded, such as the custom of sitting on slum sidewalks with or without chairs. Some persons interpret his tastes as simple laziness; but he sees no reason to be busy so long as he is not bored.)

This esthetics which asks both for the efficiency of the means toward the end and of the human appropriateness of the end to its means, is the trained feeling of the truth that in ethics one cannot ultimately distinguish means and end, for the means also consumes one's time of life, and the end of life is to live well also during that time. Any end is *prima facie* suspicious if its means too do not give satisfaction.

Meantime the neo-functional object stands before us expressing an humane appropriateness thru and thru: an *easy* body for the breath of the creator spirit to bring alive.

THE UNIFORMS OF NURSES

At a great municipal laundry in New York is done the washing and ironing of all the city's hospitals. Now it comes out on investigation that most of the work is done by a small part of the labor and machinery, but the small remainder of the work requires all the rest of the labor. This is the kind of situation that at once puts our neo-functionalist friend on the alert.

He finds that most of the labor goes into ironing the uniforms of the doctors and nurses, but especially into ironing the frilly aprons and bonnets—for all the washing and the flat-work is done by machine and mangle, but these require hand-finishing.

Now if these nurses' uniforms were made of seersucker, for instance, they would not have to be ironed. If the hats were in the form of colored kerchiefs they would equally well indicate the school from which the nurses have graduated.

These considerations are presented to the city-fathers who decide that they are impractical, but who at the same time want a functional laundry to be designed.

THE MUSEUM OF ART

And suppose that a number of mighty masterpieces of painting and statuary (we mean such works from which the creator spirit speaks in a kind of universal and timeless language, and why should he not one morning therefore speak also to you or me?)— suppose they were *decentralized* from their museum and placed one in this neighborhood church and one on this fountain in a local square, wherever there is a little quiet or a place to pause. A few of the neighbors would soon come to have a friendly acquaintance with, and a somewhat proprietary feeling for, their priceless masterpiece. What! They are not to be trusted so close with such a treasure?

These pieces of thread and dust do not exist except one by one in the soul of a man, no matter how much you heap them up together before a crowd.

A stranger, who has heard from afar of the fame of this work and already he loves it in prospect, will come to visit the local square where he would otherwise never have adventured.

THE THEORY OF PACKAGES

In general, when the consumption of a product is far removed from its production—removed by the geographical distance between factory and home, removed by the economic distance of sale and resale up to the retail, and removed by the temporal distance between making and use—the product is encased in a series of Packages. There is the shipper's crate and the wholesaler's case and the middleman's carton and the retailer's box, and the waterproof airtight cellophane wrapper that must be kept inviolate and intact except by the ultimate bridegroom, the eater.

These packages are the career of the physical goods as a saleable commodity; *and once the last wrapper has been broken, the commodity is destroyed,* it is no longer marketable. It has been corrupted by all the moisture and air and germs of life; it has been corrupted by the passionate fact that some one actually desires the thing enough to dare to touch it rather than sell it. Economically then, this is the sacramental moment, when the man or woman brutally breaks the wrapper and takes the bread out of circulation. (From any point of view, the first insipid taste is less important.)

The theory of Packages is a corollary of Ralph Borsodi's blanket principle that: As the cost of production per unit decreases by mass production, the cost of distribution increases because of the intermediary services involved in mass distribution. From this principle he derives the paradox of Prosperity and Insecurity, for the apparent copiousness of commodities entails the subordination of the consumer to a vast economic machine which can become deranged in many of its parts and leave him without the most elementary necessities. But Borsodi's principle must be closely interpreted or it is obviously fallacious: It must not be taken to mean that machine-production and labor-saving devices are humanly inefficient in themselves, but only when they become too geographically centralized, instead of tending to become community appliances or domestic appliances; and only when the machines become foreign to and unworkable by the citizens, who are then helpless if they are deranged. Borsodi himself is an enthusiast for the domestic machine and for home-industries, but he does not seem to be aware of the possibility of a reasonably large community of integrated industrial, agricultural, cultural, and domestic life such as we have been describing—where the efficiency of machines can be exploited without their inefficiency.

TIME

In the present economy, a man's time of life is also put into packages; and we speak, as George Woodcock pointed out in the October (1944) *Politics*, of "lengths of time as if they were lengths of calico." And he concluded that the clock, and especially the time-clock that the worker aggressively punches, is the chief machine of industrial exploitation of the capitalist regime, for it enables human labor to be quantified and priced as a commodity in the calculation of the cost and the surplus-value of the other commodities on the market.

This commodity-time is the time of not-life that people step into when they take leave of their hearts and their homes and their time of life, early in the morning. It is the time of the secondary environment ruled over by the inner and forgotten but still authoritative voice of parents who seemed to wish (so children get to think) to deprive one of pleasure and simple ease. Especially in the morning at 20 to 8, and late in the afternoon at 20 after 4, the fatherly face of the clock is frowning, deeper first on the right side, then on the left.

THE THEORY OF HOME FURNISHINGS

The theory of Home Furnishings is that the furniture limited to a private house expresses, in its quantity and kind, a certain division of the concerns of the soul; and that in different community arrangements this division will fall in different places.

On the principle of neo-functionalism, the place where the chief material outlay is made should give the chief satisfaction of the soul. If this rule is neglected, the material outlay will be a dead weight, discouraging both by its initial cost and its continuing presence any satisfaction that could be gotten elsewhere.

Now in the communities we see everywhere in our country (except in the most isolated wilds), the chief material outlay is the public city itself with its services. But these streets and squares and public highways do not pretend to compete in satisfaction with the private homes or the theatres of fantasy. They are a dead weight on these other satisfactions: one emerges from the theatre into an environment that is not more but less exciting, and one emerges from home into an environment that is completely impersonal and rather uninteresting. Even where, by exception, the streets and squares are beautiful, they charm the eye, they do not arouse the energies of the soul. Yet, given our economy and politics, it is always necessary to emerge, not as if one were a medieval baron or a farmer on a relatively self-subsistent farm.

Let us rather take a lesson from the Greeks, who were most often practical in what concerned the chief end, and did not complicate their means beyond what was animating. An Athenian (if free and male) experienced in the public places of the city—the market-place, the law-court, the porticoes, the Gymnasia—many of the feelings of ease, intimacy, and personal excitement that we reserve for home-gatherings and private clubs; he lived in the city even more than at home; and these feelings had for their objects the affairs of an empire as well as the passions of private friendship. There was no sharp distinction between private affairs and public affairs.

Correlated with this, both as its cause and its effect, and also being the very same thing, was a system of direct democracy, in which each man participated personally, not thru representatives —in vast legislative bodies and mass juries.

On these civic places and public institutions they lavished an expense of architecture, mulcted from an empire, which with us would be simply deadening—but the thousands of free men were there, as if at home, personally making political decisions (such as they were) for that empire.

An Athenian *home* was not, therefore, the refuge, the asylum of a man's personality; leaving it he did not cease to be himself. It did not therefore have to be so filled with the furniture, the mirrors, the keepsakes, the curiosa, the games, that are the comfort and distraction of a soul pent-up.

But a bourgeois gentleman, when he is about to leave his home in the morning, kisses his wife and daughter; then he steps before the mirror and adjusts his tie; and then, the last thing before emerging, he puts on his public face.

The most curious examples of these heavily furnished homes that are the insane-asylums of the spirit frozen and rejected in the city-square, can best be found among the middle-classes at the beginning of the present century. And the most curious room of this most curious home is not the bedroom, the dining-room, or the parlor, where after all there existed natural and social satisfactions, but the master's *den,* the jungle and the cavern of his reveries.

"PUBLIC FACES IN PRIVATE PLACES"

It is always a question whether the bourgeois den is worse or better than no personal home at all, this latter being the norm of those states ancient and modern wherein men are public animals and homes dormitories or barracks.

But it has remained for our own generation to perfect the community arrangement that is incontestably the worst possible: namely, the home of the average American. This home is liberally supplied with furniture and the comforts of private life; and these private things are neither made nor chosen by personal creation or idiosyncratic taste, but they are made in a distant factory and distributed by irresistible advertising. At home they exhaust the energy by their presence (the energy that a bare cell would at least force back inward into sublimation); and they print this experience with a public meaning. But if we turn to read this public meaning, we find that the only psychological aim of the society is the provision of private satisfactions, called "the standard of living." It is not in politics or humane culture or even war; aims which are genuinely public. This is remarkable! The private places have public faces, but the public faces are supposed to imitate private faces. Where can anything salty or characteristic accidentally happen in this booby-trap? But boredom will set us free.

First published in *Politics* (December 1944).

Two Points of Philosophy and an Example

*I*n principle, technology, the use of instruments, is a branch of moral philosophy, subject to the criteria of prudence, efficiency, decency, and so forth. I need not demonstrate, in 1967, that those who abuse our technology at present are not interested in moral philosophy, are certainly not being prudent and decent, and are only in a narrow sense careful of efficiency and costs—they altogether neglect social costs. But even if we are interested in moral philosophy and want to use our technology prudently and decently, there are modern dilemmas that are hard to solve. So here let me make two small points of philosophical analysis that are usually overlooked.

In the first place, as technology increases, as there is a proliferation of goods and as civilization becomes more complex, there is a change of the scale on which things happen. Then, if we continue to use the concepts that apply to a smaller scale, we begin to think in deceptive abstractions. There are certain functions of life that we think we are carrying on, and that *were* carried on on a smaller scale, but which now on a larger scale are only seemingly being carried on. Sometimes, indeed, because of the error in our thinking, we get an effect opposite from that which was intended.

Consider penology, a poignant example. When some fellows sat in stocks in the town square and people passed by and jeered at them or clucked their tongues, it is possible, though the psychology is dubious, that the effect might have been reform or penitence. (In my opinion, public confession on the square was more likely to lead to penitence and social integration.) But the Tombs in New York, a jail for many thousands locked up in cages, obviously has no relation whatever to penitence, reform, or social integration. In fact it is a school for crime, as is shown by the rate of repeaters who come back on more serious charges. This kind of penology on this scale has the opposite effect from that intended: it produces crime. Yet we have come by small steps from the fellow in stocks on the town square up to the Tombs or San Quentin. It seems to be "penology" all along the line, but there has been a point at which it has ceased to be penology and has become torture and foolishness, a waste of money and a cause of crime. And even the social drive for vindictiveness, which is probably the chief motive for punishment, is not satisfied; instead, there is blotting out of sight and *heightening* of social anxiety.

The change of scale has produced the same contrary effect in schooling. When there was academic instruction for many for a short time, or for a few for a longer time, it is possible that some academic education occurred. To be sure, most education for most people happened by means other than schools. Society functioned very well and many people became very expert and learned without going to school—in 1900, 6 percent graduated from high school and less than half of 1 percent went to college. Now, however, 100 percent are forced to go to high school and last year 75 percent graduated. Nearly 40 percent now go to college and by 1970 we are planning for 50 percent. On this scale, it is my observation as a reporter, very little education is occurring. For academic purposes, we might do just as well if we closed all the schools, though of course they serve for baby sitting, policing, and so forth. We could surely provide all the academic instruction that is achieved by far simpler and cheaper methods. Yet by small steps we have come to the present, using the same framework of administration and the same language, although the reality has entirely changed with the change of scale.

Take communications, as it is called. Newspapers, public speaking, and vaudeville meant one thing when they occurred in a simpler context, with the means of communication generally available to all. They mean another thing when we have mass media, semimonopolist broadcasting, licensed channels. The effect, by and large, has been homogenization and brainwashing—that is, precisely to prevent communication. We speak of our mass media as communications, yet they are importantly the preventing of communication. There is certainly very little talk back. Indeed, since television time is so expensive and by law the networks must give equal time on "controversial issues," the inevitable effect has been to avoid controversy altogether.

Grimly, the same damaging abstraction has been occurring in medicine. Since the doctors are swamped, there is a tendency in urban medicine to deal in vital statistics rather than health. I was recently at a conference in San Francisco concerned with the contraceptive pill. The doctors agreed that the pill was a heroic means of contraception and in private conversation they were dubious about its use because of the different effects on different women. Most of them felt, however, that since the pill's contraceptive effects were sure and since there was population pressure and economic pressure among the poor, it was a good policy publicly to promote its use. Classically, though, medicine was primarily concerned with the health of each individual. I am sure each of us is very much concerned about his own health. Vital statistics and the welfare of society 10 years from now are other kinds of questions, also very important, but because of the change in scale of operation, medicine has begun to lose its classical function and practice begins to have only an approximate relation to that function. This process can go very far, as it has already done in schooling. For instance, hospitals that are very large because of technological advantages may come to be run for administrative convenience even to the disadvantage of patients.

To conclude with a global example that includes the previous ones, we now see that city planning has turned into something called "urbanism," planning for urban areas. In this planning there is no such word as "home," but only dwelling units and housing. Yet it is a real question whether it is possible to have good housing, to provide people with homes, if we slip into thinking of dwelling units. It is a question whether urban areas are governable as cities, or whether just this way of thinking does not worsen anomie. Historically, when the city's functions occurred on a smaller scale and with smaller bureaucracies, an average citizen could understand their integration, even when he did not control it. There was shape and style, something to belong to and be loyal to. Vandalism and neglect were not indifferent. It was not possible for large segments of the population just to drop "out of society." And the sense of citizenship is indispensable for the high culture that is one of the most interesting functions of cities. Florence in its heyday had a hundred thousand inhabitants, Athens about the same; Goethe's Weimar had twenty-five thousand. In New York, a metropolitan region of fifteen million, I doubt that there are more than one hundred thousand who take part in the city with the feeling that in some sense it is theirs, that they understand its integration and control it or try to control it. The others just live there.

But of course there *are* changes in scale, brought about by new technologies and increased populations. How to cope with these? One suggestion has been that instead of pretending to education, communication, health, and so forth in a mass context that makes these things impossible, it would be better if we began to provide two entirely distinct sets of services: the old (and indispensable) professions with a personal responsibility to clients, and the disciplines of social engineering (a term I here use uninvidiously) working mainly on background conditions and treating persons in respects where individual differences are unimportant and personal response is not called for. Our present procedure, however, both destroys the old professions and embarrasses forthright social engineering. Thus, the ancient academic ritual of text, examination, and commencement, that made sense with academic types in a community of scholars, makes no sense in mass universities; yet we also cannot forthrightly use teaching machines and television for brute instruction and provide other means of usefully occupying the time of the nonacademic. Physicians are not trained for home visits, family medicine, and preventive psychiatry, and the conditions of medical practice become more and more routine; yet we cannot forthrightly provide mass routine checkups, and it is only a few specialists in Public Health who show any medical concern for the background conditions of physical and mental disease.

Architecture and neighborhood planning are determined by bureaucrats according to abstract standards rather than the preferences of inhabitants, and all planning is subordinated to highway planning: yet we do not use our technology to clean the air and the rivers or rationalize transportation.

Local and competing newspapers have lapsed, town meetings and ward politics have lapsed, political oratory is ghost-written and not subject to cross examination, there is no vaudeville or local live theater except in a few metropolitan centers. Instead, we have packaged opinion and bland controversy on the mass media. Yet with these, there is no effort either to raise the cultural level by high-standard fare or to open the media to searching extremes that question the usual premises. The mass media can be used only to discuss mass-acceptable options, and then no new wisdom can enter the arena. For instance, instead of the usual spectrum from doves to hawks in a television panel on Vietnam, we ought to consider the views of those who think we have entered the phase of a universal American empire that should regulate the world and, on the other hand, of those who hold that the entire structure of sovereignty and power is long outmoded and unworkable.

I have spoken of the "disciplines of social engineering... working mainly on background conditions." This brings me to the second philosophical issue I want to raise. In fact, at present we do not really have these disciplines. The social-psychological, anthropological, and ecological studies that are necessary for good social engineering and the right use of new technology are not sufficiently developed. We do not know the remote effects of what we institute in education, medicine, or urbanism; I have given a few examples to show how the remote effects might be the opposite of our intentions. We may use computers to estimate requirements, costs, and benefits, but in the fields we are discussing the theories on which the programs are based are puerile.

Let us suppose, however, that we do have better studies and better programs. There then arises the philosophical question: can we directly apply our best theories to human and social situations? I think not, for to preplan too thoroughly is to kill life; and the more subtle the theory, the more dangerous the attack. This is the invidious sense of "social engineering." Prudence and science are one thing, determining how people are to live and breathe is quite another. It is probably best just to open a space in which they can live and breathe in their own way. That is, we should aim at decency, not excellence. We cannot draw the lines a priori, but in every case there is something to plan for and much to refrain from planning for. This often means when to technologize, to achieve a decent background, and when not to technologize, to achieve freedom.

Contrast an ideal forest preserve with a real State park. The forest preserve would be a kind of museum. We would put a hedge around a piece of the past, the antiquity of the globe untouched, saying that this place is not to change. You would come there by car but enter on foot. You may camp where you choose but there are no campsites and you don't need a permit—only be prudent and don't set the trees on fire. The forest preserve would be a kind of wilderness area with no rules whatever. But the State park is part of the urban complex; it is an extension into the green places of the rules of the city. You need a permit to camp and must camp at the specified places. This has advantages; you have a platform, and wood and water are provided. The fee is nominal, but there *is* a fee.

When I was young, we could freely pitch a tent on Fire Island Beach and freely build our fires or build a shack and squat. Because of the pressure of real estate developers, this has been forbidden and you now cannot squat in the sun and wind; many more cops patrol the beach and it is part of their duties to see that you do not. One feels trapped. One must make social arrangements and pay rent. But it is not the money that is onerous, it is that one has to obey their rules. They have planned for us, no matter how benevolent the plan.

The possibility of an escape into freedom from social rules is, of course, the pastoral ideal, as well described by Leo Marx. But the pastoral ideal can apply also in urban places. (Some of my novels have been called urban pastorals, and so they are.) One of the objections to much recent architecture and public housing is that it presents an impenetrable glass front; there are no holes and basements to creep into for games and sex. The waterfront has been improved into a concrete wall or a lovely promenade; there are no railroad yards or abandoned piers where one could hide from truant officers or fish. It is interesting that Jane Jacobs, who is a zealot against the new architecture because she wants to preserve neighborly sociability, nevertheless balks at the pastoral ideal of dark places and nooks. She wants everything bright and public, for safety. And to be sure, urban life has become more dangerous than the jungle. But I doubt that safety can be assured by architectural design or doormen. People who feel trapped and powerless will follow you home or finally assault you in public.

The philosophical point I wish to make is that there must be a kind of constitutional limit to planning, even at the expense of efficiency and the "best" solution. An analogy is the protection of freedom of speech in the Bill of Rights. In the interpretation of the "absolutists," Justices Black and Douglas, freedom of speech is not to be balanced in terms of its social aspects, it is anarchic, prior to law—you can say what you damned please, up to the limits of actual emergency, however troublesome, violent, or conflictful your speech may be. And as a writer, let me say that unless I have this freedom of speech, I do not have freedom at all. I cannot know beforehand what words will come to me, and if I feel that there is a limit to what I can say, then nothing new will ever come to me.

A realistic method of guaranteeing freedom from excessive physical planning and social engineering is to condone or even encourage people's resistance to them. I say "realistic" because there is in effect a rising wave of popular protest in the country. The courts can encourage resistance by a tolerant attitude toward sit-ins, certain kinds of trespass, and civil disobedience. Bureaucratic control can be largely delegated away to "black power," "student power," etc. And it would be advantageous to replace many bureaucratically-run social services with a guaranteed income, which would enable powerless people to form their own cooperatives and suit themselves. These countervailing factors would then have to be taken into account in the programs of the social engineers. At present, needless to say, politicians who have to cadge votes are acutely conscious of inarticulate popular resistance and do draw the line. But planners disregard it because it is inarticulate, and since they—organized, rational, and well-financed

—have more staying power than the populace, there is steady encroachment on freedom.

Another method of guaranteeing freedom from excessive planning brings me back to my first point, the revival of old-fashioned professionals responsible to clients and the immediate community rather than to society and social trends. Unless people become things, they will always live in the small scale as well as the big scale, and more intensely in the small scale than in the big scale. It is the role of their professionals, whom they ought to be able to hire and fire, to articulate, interpret, and design for them their small-scale needs in education, medicine, law, and housing. These will inevitably include spontaneity, individual differences, personal response, local options, and the need for freedom. Big-scale planners and social engineers will then have something articulate to cope with.

With this much introduction, let me launch into some remarks on rural reconstruction as interpreted in modern conditions. I want to propose a new look at rural-urban symbiosis.

It is important to understand that the present urbanization throughout the world is not a result of technological advance. Indeed, the thrust of modern technology has been against urbanization; consider electrification, power tools, telephone, radio and television, the automobile. And automation implies, if anything, the concentration of a great plant in a small space with a few workers, and the freedom of location of the programmers and the managers. Patrick Geddes assumed that with electrification the cities, amassed around steam power, would cease to grow. Ralph Borsodi thought that power tools would lead to dispersal, and Frank Lloyd Wright thought that the automobile would do it. Marx and Engels and Kropotkin blamed excessive urbanization on the power structure and looked to a better rural-urban symbiosis.

As has always been the case, our present urbanization is the consequence of a policy of enclosure. Poor people and farmers never leave home willingly. The young leave the land for adventure and bright lights; the especially gifted have to seek out the centers of culture and opportunity. But the mass of country people stay as long as they can make a living. Enclosure takes place in various ways. In the 18th century they shut off the commons to raise sheep;

at the same time the city factories were developing and needed cheap labor, so there was a place for desperate farmers to find work, beginning at age nine. This combination of the "squire-archy" and the new capitalists is described in *The Deserted Village* and by Wordsworth. In our own century, during the 70 years that we have had control in Puerto Rico, we have destroyed this beautiful and fertile land by another classical method; old-fash-ioned mercantilism of the genre of George III. We have forbidden the Puerto Ricans to ship and travel directly without touching at United States ports, we have imposed severe quota restrictions on the processing of Puerto Rican sugar, we have ruled out coffee, and we have sequestered the more fertile plain for industrial use. Thus we have destroyed the agricultural base. But in the past two decades we have imposed on the top a thin crust of high technology and now the country is ravaged. Thirty-five percent of the popula-tion is on relief. People flee a thousand a week to New York, and flee back a thousand a week to the slums of San Juan. In other parts of the world, for example the Virgin Islands or Latin America, enclosure occurs by the importation of some industry, e.g. oil or hotels, with a wildly inflationary standard. A few natives are paid $70 a week where the average cash income was $70 a year. Then the *campesinos,* in sheer self-respect must flock to the city where there is no provision for them; they settle in thousands in tin shacks and die of cholera. Meantime, there is no effort to subdivide the land and get rid of feudal landowners; when there is such an effort, we dispatch the Marines.

Our American enclosure—the rural population is now 6 percent actually farming—has come about through cooperation in the American cash style amounting virtually to a conspiracy among chain-grocers, big plantations, suburban developers, and highway bureaucrats, steadily abetted by public policy. It is said to be efficient, and, indeed, one farmer can now feed thirty. Neverthe-less, the price of food has *not* fallen (during the war in Vietnam, of course, it has risen), although the farmers' take has declined by about 8 percent a decade. Nor indeed do the retailers make much— at A & P wages are low and still the profit on store sales is 1 percent; 11 percent of A & P's 12 percent profit goes to their own middlemen, packagers, processors, transporters, jobbers. Thus it seems clear that the new "agrindustry" is not all that efficient. At present, 70¢ of the food dollar is spent in national chains and, naturally, food technology has been developed according to this pattern. If the technologists had put their wits to intensive agriculture by small growers, as in Holland, no doubt that method too would have become much more efficient.

The result has been depopulation of vast areas of the country at the same time that there are evident signs of overpopulation in the urban areas. As John Calhoun puts it, there are too many social signals in the urban centers, so that the circuits are clogged and normal development is impossible; there is not enough social space for trying out, there is too much noise, there is no solitude to develop personality, all experience is preprocessed, there is no relief from chronic anxiety. Of the million Negroes in New York, more than half came during the last 20 years as a result of the failure of southern sharecropping. Seven hundred thousand Puerto Ricans have come to New York City in the past 30 years. Of course, since New York has a housing shortage, it is necessary to provide public housing. This costs $20,000 a unit—which money could have been spent to keep the immigrants in the country. Clearly if the Negroes had wanted to come north, they would have done so 40 years ago, for they were not well treated in Mississippi and Alabama.

At present, however, or certainly during this generation, there is no chance of rural reconstruction on an agricultural base; indeed, the skills are rapidly vanishing. Possibly there may be a revival of specialized intensive farming, selling fresh food to nearby cities, if people can begin to demand a quality standard of living. This cannot occur in the ring surrounding the cities, for that has been suburbanized, but conceivably it might happen in the next ring.

But there is a chance of rural revival on a different principle: to help solve urban problems that are not easily or cheaply soluble in urban conditions. Such a principle would bring the country into the mainstream of modern problems, which are urban, and it would channel urban cash into rural areas now depopulating. Consider some possibilities.

It is advantageous for city children to spend a year or two at a country school and live on a family farm. Something similar is not uncommon for the upper middle class, but it would be profoundly awakening for slum children who have not, by age 13, been half a mile from home. Cost per child in a New York School is $850 a year; for little more than this sum one could help support the failing rural school and provide worthwhile cash for a farmer (perhaps three children to a farmer, who need merely feed them well and not beat them). The Farmers' Union and the 4-H clubs have offered to administer such a program.

It is advantageous to allow urban welfare money to be used for living in a rural neighborhood. Twenty-five hundred dollars buys destitution in a big city, but in a depopulating area, where one can also farm for part of subsistence, it provides a very decent life, including running an old car. Indeed, if we had a rational world, it would be possible for welfare recipients to use urban welfare money in foreign regions which have noninflationary prices, e.g., parts of Mexico, Crete, Sicily.

In our present system of enclosure, country vacations in motels and resorts have become part of the urban system. It would be advantageous to try to revive something more like the old visiting of country cousins at the farm.

The majority of patients in big mental institutions are harmless but cannot cope, or would hurt themselves and stop traffic, in urban environments. Very many are really getting no treatment and are just rotting away, though at great social expense. For the same money they could be boarded with rural families, and there is evidence that in such conditions there would be more remissions.

In functions like these, I am drawing on the classical pattern of regionalism, the capital and its country in symbiosis, each with a contrasting but complementary set of conditions and functions. This is, of course, the opposite of our homogenizing "conurbation" and regional planning. And the meaning of contemporary endless suburbanization is that one is never really in the city or in the country. The center becomes blighted and decays; the country is depopulated and returns to swamp. In the conurbation, regional planning means highway planning, smog planning, or efforts to equalize taxation; these are necessary, of course, but hardly sufficient for human needs.

The symbiotic conception of an urban-rural region requires

administrative changes, e.g., to use New York City school money or welfare money in Vermont, central Pennsylvania, or the northern counties of New York. Or to use urban public housing money for improving farms in Mississippi or Alabama.

Rural reconstruction on this basis could well be culturally administered by revived Land Grant colleges, whose functions have now entirely been perverted to teaching urban know-how (usually in a second-rate fashion). Likewise there ought to be a renascence of local newspapers, which are now nothing but advertising and gossip sheets. And there ought to be established numerous local radio and TV stations—each region can have 17 television channels, of which usually only two are in use. There cannot be rural reconstruction unless one's home place stands for something and is worth remaining in; but there are ways to strive for this.

In conclusion, let me repeat that I do not think there can be a significant cutback in urbanization in this generation. Nevertheless, the kind of rural reconstruction proposed can alleviate urban problems in terms of 2 percent of this and 5 percent of that. More important, it recreates options in an increasingly monolithic society. And finally, the pattern of rural subsistence with sources of cash from providing useful social services is tranquil and beautiful in itself.

"Two Points of Philosophy and an Example" was first delivered as a paper at the Smithsonian Institution Annual Symposium in February 1967, and then printed as the lead essay in *The Fitness of Man's Environment,* Washington, D.C.: Smithsonian Institution Press, 1968.

The
Present
Moment
in
Education

I.

*I*n every society, the education of the children is of the first importance. But in all societies, both primitive and highly civilized, until quite recently most education occurred incidentally. Adults did their work and other social tasks. The children were not excluded. The children were paid attention to and learned to be included; they were not "taught."

In most institutions and in most societies *incidental education* has been taken for granted. Incidental education takes place in community labor, master-apprentice arrangements, games, plays, sexual initiations, and religious rites.

Generally speaking, this incidental process suits the nature of learning better than direct teaching. The young experience cause and effect rather than pedagogic exercise. Reality is often complex, but every young person can take that reality in his own way, at his own time, according to his own interests and own initiative. Most importantly, he can imitate, identify, be approved, be disapproved, cooperate, or compete without suffering anxiety through being the center of attention.

The archetype of successful incidental education is that of an infant learning to speak, a formidable intellectual achievement that is universally accomplished. We do not know how it is done, but the main conditions seems to be what we have been describing: Activity is going on involving speaking. The infant participates; he is attended to and spoken to; he plays freely with his speech sounds; it is advantageous to him to make himself understood.

Along with incidental education, most societies also maintain institutions specifically devoted to teaching the young, such as identity rites, catechisms, nurses, pedagogues, youth houses, and formal schooling. I think there is a peculiar aspect to what is learned through such means, rather than what is picked up incidentally.

Let me emphasize that it is only in the last century that a majority of the children in industrialized countries have gotten much direct teaching. Only in the past few decades has formal schooling been generally extended into adolescence and further. For example, in the United States in 1900, only six percent of the youngsters went through high school, and only one quarter of one percent went through college. Yet now, formal schooling has taken over, well or badly, very much of the more natural incidental education of most other institutions.

This state of affairs may or may not be necessary, but it has had consequences. These institutions, and the adults who run them, have correspondingly lost touch with the young; and on the other hand, the young do not know the adults who are involved in their chief activities.

Like jails and insane asylums, schools isolate society from its problems, whether in preventing crime, or in curing mental disease, or in bringing up the young. To a remarkable degree, the vital functions of growing up have become hermetically redefined in school terms. Community service means doing homework. Apprenticeship means passing tests for a job in the distant future. Sexual initiation is high school dating. Rites of passage consist in getting a diploma. Crime is breaking the school windows. Rebellion is sitting in on the Dean. In the absence of adult culture, the youth develop a sub-culture.

Usually, there has been a rough distinction between the content of what is learned in incidental education and what is learned in direct pedagogy. Teaching, whether directed by elders, priests, or academics, deals with what is not evident in ordinary affairs; pedagogy aims to teach what is abstract, intangible, or mysterious. As the center of attention, the learner is under pressure. All education socializes, but pedagogy socializes deliberately, instilling the morals and habits which are the social bonds.

There are two opposite interpretations of why pedagogy seeks to indoctrinate. In my opinion, both interpretations are correct. On the one hand, the elders instill an ideology which will support their system of exploitation and the domination of the old over the young, and they, the elders, make a special effort to confuse and mystify because their system does not recommend itself to common sense.

On the other hand, there is a vague but important wisdom that must be passed on, a wisdom which does not appear on the surface and which requires special pointing out and cloistered reflection. The champions of the liberal arts colleges maintain that, one way or another, the young will pick up contemporary know-how and mores, but that the greatness of Mankind—Hippocrates, Beethoven, Enlightenment, Civil Liberties, the Sense of the Tragic—all will lapse without a trace unless scholars work at perpetuating these values. I sympathize with the problem as they state it; but, in fact, I have not heard of any method whatever, scholastic or otherwise, of teaching the humanities without killing them. I remember how at age twelve, browsing in the library, I read *Macbeth* with excitement; yet in class I could not understand a word of *Julius Caesar,* and I hated it. I'm pretty sure this is a common pattern. The survival of the humanities would seem to depend on random miracles which are becoming less frequent.

Unlike incidental learning which is natural and inevitable, formal schooling is deliberate intervention and must justify itself. We must ask not only whether such schooling is well done, but is it *worth* doing? *Can* it be well done? Is teaching possible at all?

There is a line of critics from Lao-tse and Socrates to Carl Rogers who assert that there is no such thing as teaching either science or virtue; and there is strong evidence that schooling has had little effect on either vocational ability or on citizenship. Donald Hoyt, in *American College Testing Reports* (1965) found that in any profession, college grades have had no correlation with life achievement.

At the other extreme, Dr. Skinner and the operant-conditioners claim that they can "instruct" for every kind of performance, and that they can control and shape human behavior much as they can the behavior of animals who have been sealed off from their ordinary environment. But it is disputable whether children are good subjects for such instruction in any society we might envisage.

The main line of educators from Confucius and Aristotle to John Dewey hold that one can teach the child good habits in morals, arts, and sciences through practice. The art is to provide the right tacks at the right moments; and Froebel, Herbert, Steiner, Piaget, etc., have different theories about this. But sociologists like Comte and Marx hold that social institutions overwhelmingly determine what is learned—so much so, that it is not worthwhile to be concerned with pedagogy. My bias is that "teaching" is largely a delusion.

In every advanced country, the school system has taken over a vast part of the educational functions of society. The educationists design toys for age two, train for every occupation, train for citizenship, train for sexuality, and explain and promote the humanities.

With trivial exceptions, what we mean by *school*—curriculum, texts, lessons, scheduled periods marked by bells, teachers, examinations, and graded promotion to the next step—was the invention of some Irish monks of the seventh century who thought to bring a bit of Rome to wild shepherds. It has been an amazing success story, probably more important than the Industrial Revolution.

No doubt it was a good thing, at first, for wild shepherds to have to sit still for a couple of hours and pay strict attention to penmanship and spelling. The imposed curriculum was entirely exotic and could only be learned by rote anyway. Mostly, of course, it was only aspiring clerics who were schooled.

By an historical accident, the same academic method later became the way of teaching the bookish part of some of the learned professions. There is no essential reason why law and medicine are not better learned through apprenticeship, but the bookish method was clerical, and therefore scholastic. Perhaps any special education based on abstract principles was part of a system of mysteries, and therefore clerical, and therefore scholastic.

The monkish rule of scheduled hours, texts, and lessons is also not an implausible method for giving a quick briefing to large numbers of students, who then embark on their real business. Jefferson insisted on universal compulsory schooling for short terms in predominantly rural communities, in order that children might be able to read the newspapers and be catechized in libertarian political history. During the following century, in compulsory urban schools, the children of immigrants were socialized and taught standard English. The curriculum was the penmanship, the spelling, and the arithmetic needed for the business world.

At present, however, the context of schooling is quite different. The old monkish invention of formal schooling is now used as universal social engineering. Society is conceived as a controlled system of personnel and transactions, with various national goals depending on the particular nation. And the schools are the teaching machines for all personnel.

There is no other way of entry for the young. Teaching aims at psychological preparation in depth. Schooling for one's role, in graded steps, takes up to 20 years and more; it is the chief activity of growing up; any other interest may be interrupted—but not schooling. The motivation for a five-year-old's behavior is thus geared 15 years in the future.

In highly productive technologies like ours which do not need manpower, the function of long schooling is to keep the useless and obstreperous young *away* from the delicate social machine. The function of the school is to baby-sit the young and police them.

Yet the schools are not good playgrounds or reservations either. The texture of school experience is similar to adult experience. There is little break between playing with educational toys and watching educational TV, or between being in high school and dating, or between being in college and being drafted, or between being personnel of a corporation and watching NBC.

Since the trend has been to eliminate incidental education and deliberately to prepare the young for every aspect of ordinary life through schooling, we would expect pedagogy to have become functional. Yet radical students complain that today's schooling is ideological through and through. The simplest, and not altogether superficial, explanation of this paradox is that scholastic mystery has transformed adult business. It is society that has become mandarin.

None of this works. Contemporary schooling does not prepare for jobs and professions. For example, evidence compiled by Ivan Berg of Columbia shows that on the job dropouts do as well as high school graduates.

Nor has today's education made for peaceful baby-sitting and policing. Instead of an efficient gearing between the teaching machine and the rest of the social machine, the schools seem to run for their own sake. There IS a generation gap. Many youngsters fail; many drop out; others picket.

Predictably, the response of school administrators has been to refine the process; to make the curriculum more relevant, to start schooling earlier, to employ new technologies in teaching, to eliminate friction by admitting students to administrative functions.

But the chief objection to engineering in education is that it is inefficient. It tries to program too much, to pre-structure syllabi and lesson-plans. But human behavior is strong, graceful, and discriminating only to the extent that, in concrete situations, it creates its own structures as it goes along. Things can be learned securely, quickly, and naturally only through coping. As John Holt has pointed out, the teacher wants the child to learn the lesson according to the teaching plan; but the child quickly learns how to con the teacher, for getting a passing grade is the child's *real* problem of the moment.

It has frequently been said that human beings use only a small part—"just two percent"—of their abilities. Some educators therefore propose that much more demanding and intellectual tasks be set at a much earlier age. There is no doubt that most children can think and learn far more than they are challenged to. Yet it is likely that by far the greatest waste of ability occurs because a playful, hunting, sexy, dreamy, combative, passionate, artistic, manipulative, destructive, jealous, magnanimous, selfish and disinterested animal is continually thwarted by social organization—and perhaps especially by schooling.

If so, the main purpose of pedagogy should be to counteract

and delay socialization as long as possible. For our situation is the opposite of the situation in the seventh century. Since the world has become overly scholastic, we must protect the wild shepherds.

Current high thought among schoolmen, for instance those of the National Science Foundation and those of the Harvard School of Education, is that the contemporary syllabus is indeed wasteful and depressing. But they would expand the schools and render the programming more psychological. Since the frontiers of knowledge are changing so rapidly, there is no use in burdening children with data that will be outdated in ten years, or with skills that will soon be better performed by machines; rather children must learn *to learn*: their cognitive faculties must be developed; they must be taught the big Ideas, concepts like the conservation of energy. This is exactly what Robert Hutchins was saying 40 years ago.

Or more daringly, the children must not be *taught,* but be allowed to *discover*. They must be encouraged to guess and to brainstorm rather than be tested on the right answers.

In my opinion, in an academic setting, these proposals are never bona fide. As Gregory Bateson has noted with dolphins and trainers, and as John Holt has noticed in middle class schools, learning to learn means picking up the structure of behavior of the teachers, becoming expert in the academic process. In actual practice, the young discoverers are bound to discover what will get them past the College Board examinations. Guessers and dreamers are not free to balk and drop out for a semester to brood and let their theories germinate in the dark, as proper geniuses do.

It is a crucial question whether "cognitive faculties" does not mean the syntax of school performance. There is an eccentric passage in an early work of Piaget where he says that children in the playground seem to be using intellectual concepts, e.g. causality, a couple of years earlier than they are "developed" in the classroom, but he sticks to the classroom situation because it allows for his "scientific" observation. Yet this might mean that the formal routine of the classroom has hindered the spontaneous use of the intellect, and that the "concept" which is developed in the classroom is not an act of intellect grasping the world at all, but is a method of adjustment to the classroom, the constricted seats, the schedule, the teacher's expectation, the boring subject-matter to which one must pay attention.

II.

Progressive education is best defined as a series of reactions to a school system that has become rigid. Progressive education aims to include what has been repressed; it aims to right the balance.

Moreover progressive education is a political movement; progressive education emerges when the social problem is breaking out. To put it more positively, an old regime is not adequate to cope with new conditions; new energy is needed. The form that progressive education takes in each era is prophetic of the next social revolution.

Rousseau reacted to the artificiality and insincerity of the royal court, and the parasitism, the callous formalism, and the pervasive superstition of the courtiers. The establishment of his day had simply become incompetent to govern. A generation later, it abdicated.

John Dewey reacted to a genteel culture that was irrelevant in an industrialized society. Dewey reacted to rococo decoration, to puritanism that denied animal nature, to censorship, and to rote performance imposed on children. Again, after a generation (by the end of the New Deal) Dewey's moral vision had largely come to be. In his lifetime, most of the program of the Populists and the Labor Movement had become law; education and culture (among whites) had become utilitarian and fairly classless; the revolution of Freud and Spock was well advanced; censorship was on its way out; and there was no more appliqué decoration.

A.S. Neill's Summerhill School, a recent form of progressive education, was likewise a reaction against social-engineering. Neill reacted against the trend to 1984 as Orwell came to call it, against obedience, authoritarian rules, organizational role-playing instead of being, the destruction wrought by competition and grade-getting. Since going to class is for children in the immutable nature of things, Neill's making of attendance a matter of choice was a transformation of reality; and to the extent that there was authentic self-government at Summerhill and to the extent that small children were indeed given power, the charisma of all institutions was challenged.

Progressive education has been criticized as a middle-class

gimmick. The black community, especially, resents being used for "experiments." Poor children, it is claimed, need to learn the conventional wisdom so they can compete for power in the established system. Black parents demand "equality education" and expect their children to wear ties.

In my opinion, this criticism is wrongheaded. The scholastic evidence shows that the more experimental the high school, the more successfully its graduates compete in conventional colleges.

Black communities should run their own schools, and they should run them on the model of Summerhill. This has indeed been the case with the sporadic Freedom Schools which have been influenced, directly or indirectly, by Neill.

I don't agree with the theory of *Head Start* that disadvantaged children require special training to prepare them for learning. I find nothing wrong with the development of their intellectual faculties; they have learned to speak, and they can make practical syllogisms very nicely, if they need to. If they have not learned the patterns by which they can succeed in school, the plausible move is to change the school. But, as Elliott Shapiro has suggested, the trouble might be that these children have been pushed too early to take responsibility for themselves and for their little brothers and sisters as well. The trouble is that their real problems have been all too insoluble. It's not that these children can't reason; the fact is that pure reason is of no use to them in their coping with their all too real difficulties.

What these kids need is freedom from pressure to perform. And, of course, they need better food, more quiet, and a less impoverished environment to grow up in—AT THEIR OWN PACE. These things are what the First Street School on the Lower East Side in New York, which was somewhat modeled on Summerhill, tried to provide.

Nevertheless, we must say that progressive education has been almost a total failure. The societies that have emerged after fulfilling their programs, were not what the visionaries had hoped for. French or American democracy was not what Rousseau had in mind. Dewey's social conceptions have ended up as technocracy, labor bureaucracy, and suburban conformity. The likelihood is that A.S. Neill's hope, too, will be badly realized. It is not hard to envisage a society in the near future in which self-reliant and happy people will be attendants of a technological infrastructure over which they have no control whatever, and whose purposes do not seem to them to be any of their business. Indeed, Neill describes with near satisfaction such success-stories among his own graduates. Alternately, it is conceivable that an affluent society will support its hippies like Indians on a reservation.

How to prevent these outcomes? Perhaps Neill protects his community a few years too long, both from the oppressive mechanistic world and from adolescent solitude—it is hard to be alone in Summerhill. Moreover, it seems to me that there is something inauthentic in Neill's latitudinarian lack of standards. For example, Beethoven and Rock 'n Roll are considered equivalent (though Neill himself prefers Beethoven). We are not only free organisms but parts of a mankind that historically has made strides with great inspirations and through terrible conflicts. We cannot slough off that accumulation of cultures, however burdensome, without becoming trivial. It seems clear to me that the noisy youth subculture of today is not grown-up—which is to the good—but also that it can *never* become grown-up.

Generally, the young of today have strong feelings for honesty, frankness, loyalty, fairness, affection, freedom and the other virtues of generous natures. They quickly resent the hypocrisy of politicians, administrators, and parents who mouth big abstractions, but who act badly. But the young themselves—like most politicians and administrators and many parents—seem to have forgotten the concrete reality of ideals like magnanimity, compassion, honor, consistency, civil liberty, integrity and justice— ideals which maintain and which re-create Mankind. Naturally, without these ideals and the conflicts they engender, there is no tragedy. Most young persons seem to disbelieve that tragedy exists, they always interpret impasse as timidity, and casuistry as finking out. I may be harsh, but though I am often astonished by their physical courage, I am not often impressed by their moral courage.

III.

My own thinking is that:

(1) Incidental education (taking part in the ongoing activities of society) should be the chief means of learning.

(2) Most high schools should be eliminated. Other kinds of youth communities should take over the social functions of the high school.

(3) College training, generally, should follow—not precede—entry into the professions.

(4) The chief task of educators should be to see that the activities of society provide incidental education. If necessary, government and society should invent new useful activities offering new educational opportunities.

(5) The purpose of elementary pedagogy through age twelve should be to protect and nourish a child's free growth, since both the community and family pressure are too much for a child to withstand.

IV.

Let me review the arguments for this program:

We must drastically cut back schooling because our extended tutelage is against nature and actually arrests growth.

The effort to channel growing up according to a preconceived curriculum discourages the young and wastes many of the best of our powers to learn and cope.

Schooling does not prepare for real performance; it is largely carried on for its own sake. Only the academically talented, only 10 to 15% according to Conant, thrive in this useless activity without being bored, and without being harmed.

Our system of education, isolating as it does the young from the older generation, alienates the young.

Yet it makes no sense for many of the brightest and most sensitive of our young to simply drop out or to confront society with hostility. This state of affairs does not lead to social reconstruction. The complicated and confusing conditions of our times require fresh thinking, and therefore, what we need is participation, particularly by the young.

Young radicals seem to believe that political change will solve our chief problem. Or that our problems will solve themselves after political change. This is a delusion. Our novel problems of urbanization, technology, and ecology have not heretofore been faced by any political faith. The fact is that the educational systems of other advanced countries are no better than ours.

It has been my Calvinistic and Aristotelian experience that

most people cannot organize their lives without productive activity. Of course, this does not necessarily mean paid activity. The professions, the services, industries, arts and sciences are the arena. Radical politics and doing one's thing are careers for only a very few.

As things are, American society either excludes the young, or corrupts the young, or exploits the young. I believe we must make the rules of licensing and hiring more realistic, and we must get rid of mandarin requirements. We must design apprenticeships that are not exploitative.

Society desperately needs much work, both intellectual and manual, in urban renewal, in ecology, in communications, and in the arts. All these spheres could make use of young people. Many such enterprises are best organized by young people themselves, like the community development and the community action of "Vocations for Social Change." There are also excellent apprenticeships open for the brainy at think-tanks like the Oceanic Institute at Makapuu Point, or in the Institute for Policy Studies in Washington, both of which are careless about checking diplomas. Our aim should be to multiply the paths of growing up. There should be ample opportunity for a young boy or girl to begin his career again, to cross over from one career to another, to take a moratorium, to travel, or to work on his own. To insure freedom of option, and to insure that the young can maintain and express their critical attitude, adolescents should be guaranteed a living. Giving a young person the present cost of a high school education would provide enough money for a young person to live on.

The advantage of making education less academic has, of course, occurred to many school people. There are a myriad of programs to open the school to the world by: (1) recruiting professionals, artists, gurus, mothers, and dropouts as teachers' aides; and (2) granting academic credit for work-study, for community action, for the writing of novels, for service in mental hospitals, for spending one's junior year abroad, and for other kinds of released time.

Naturally, I am enthusiastic for this development, and I only want it to go the small further step of abolishing the present school establishment, instead of aggrandizing it.

There is also a movement in the United States, as there is in Cuba and China, for adolescent years to be devoted to public service. This is fine if the service is not compulsory nor regimenting.

It *is* possible for everyone's education to be tailor-made according to his own particular developing interest. Choices along the way will often be ill-conceived and wasteful, but such choices will nevertheless express desire, and will therefore immediately coincide with reality. Such choices will, therefore, converge to find the right vocation for a young person more quickly than through any other method. One's vocation is what one is good at and can do. Vocation is what employs a reasonable amount of one's powers. The use of the full power of a majority of the people would make for a stable society which would be far more efficient than our own. In such a set-up, those who have peculiar excellences are more likely to find their way when they have entry by doing something they can do well, and then proceeding to their more particular interests, and by being accepted for *what* they can do.

Academic schooling, of course, could be chosen by those with academic talents. Obviously, schools would be better off if unencumbered by sullen uninterested bodies. But the main use of academic teaching should be for those already busy in the sciences and the professions, who need academic courses along the way to acquire further knowledge. Cooper Union in New York City used to fulfill this function very well.

Of course, in such a set-up, employers would themselves provide ancillary academic training. In my opinion, this ancillary schooling would do more than any other single thing to give blacks, rurals, and other culturally deprived youth a fairer entry and a chance for advancement. As we have seen, there is no correlation *on the job* between competence and prior schooling.

This leads to another problem. Educationally, schooling on the job is usually superior to academic schooling, but the political and moral consequences of such a system are ambiguous. At present, a youth is hired because of his *credentials,* rather than for his actual skill. This system allows a measure of free-market democracy. However, if he is to be schooled on the job, he must be hired essentially for his promise. Such a system can lead to company paternalism like Japanese capitalism. On the other hand, if the young have options and they are allowed to organize and to criticize, on-the-job education is the quickest way to workers' management which, in my opinion, is the only effective democracy.

University education—liberal arts and the principles of the professions—should be reserved only for adults who already know something, and who have something about which to philosophize. Otherwise, as Plato pointed out, such "education" is just mere verbalizing.

To provide a protective and life-nourishing environment for children up through age twelve, Summerhill is an adequate model. I think Summerhill can be easily adapted to urban conditions. Probably, an even better model would be the Athenian pedagogue touring the city with his charges; but for this to work out, the streets and the working-places of the city will have to be made safer and more available than it is likely they will be. The prerequisite of city-planning is that children be able to *use* the city; for no city is governable if it does not grow citizens who feel that that city is theirs.

The goal of elementary pedagogy is a very modest one: a small child should be able, under his own steam, to poke interestedly into whatever goes on; and he should be able, through observation, through questions, and through practical imitation, to get something out of such poking around. In our society this is what happens at home pretty well up to age four; but after that, such random poking around becomes forbiddingly difficult.

V.

I have often spelled out this program of incidental education, and I have found no takers. Curiously, I get the most respectful if wistful attention at teachers' colleges, even though what I propose is quite impossible under present administration. Teachers *know* how much they are wasting the children's time, and teachers understand that my proposals are fairly conservative.

However, in a general audience the response is incredulity. Against all evidence, people are convinced that what we are now doing must make sense or we wouldn't be doing it. It does not help if I point out that in dollars and cents it might be cheaper—and it would certainly be more productive—to eliminate most schools and have the community itself provide more of the education. Yet the majority in a general audience are willing to admit that they themselves got very little out of *their* school years. Occasionally, an old reactionary businessman agrees with me enthusiastically that book-learning isn't worth a penny.

Among radical students, my proposals are met by a sullen silence. They want Student Power, and for the most part, they are unwilling to answer whether they are authentically students at all. I think they're brainwashed. Naturally, it makes no difference to them if they demand "University Reform," or if the University is shut down altogether.

Instead of Student Power, what they should be demanding is (a) a more open entry into society, and (b) that education money should be spent more usefully, and (c) that licensing and hiring should be handled without consideration of irrelevant diplomas; and so forth. Youth Power can make the authentic demand for the right to take part in initiating and deciding the functions of society that concern them, as well as the right to govern their own lives—which are nobody else's business. Bear in mind that I am speaking of youths between age 17 and 25. At all other times in man's history, these individuals would already have found their places in the real world.

"The Present Moment in Education" was first published in the *New York Review of Books* (April 10, 1969). The version printed here was first published in *Summerhill: For and Against,* New York: Hart Publishing Co., 1970.

Pornography
and
the
Sexual
Revolution

One kind of "utopian thinking" that rouses anxiety in people is the suggestion simply to stop doing something hard and useless; for instance, to stop repressive efforts that do not work and that indeed increase the evil that they are supposed to prevent. "I am unimpressed," says William Sloane of Rutgers, "with the record of repressive legislation in this country. The laws against narcotics, for example, are supporting a large criminal class and leading to large-scale corruption of our youth. The laws against off-track betting are supporting a large criminal class and leading directly to police corruption. No set of laws will prevent the bootlegging of pornography." Yet the bother with this good sense is that, in these cases, people apparently cannot simply leave off, for these laws and prosecutions are psychological means of keeping down their own confused panic.

The case of pornography, however, is peculiarly interesting, for here both sides of the public ambivalence are now on the surface. It is not the case any longer that the pornographic is "obscene," shocking to society's conception of itself. The sexual is now, in an important sense, quite acceptable; yet at the same time the sexual is guilty. This puts the courts in an embarrassing position. Not only to protect vital liberties, but also to express existing public sentiment, the higher, more intellectual courts stand out against censorious police, postmasters, and popular prejudice; yet since they don't dare tell the whole truth, the issues are never settled. And worse, the courts lend themselves to the sexual prejudice which, at this moment in our history, creates the very "hard-core" pornography that is objected to. That is, the court corrupts, it helps the censors to corrupt. Nevertheless, perhaps precisely in this issue of pornography and censorship, "utopian thinking" *can* avail, since instead of simply "stopping" and becoming panicky, people can busy themselves with something practical, namely, the real problems of the sexual revolution.

We are faced with the dilemmas of a society in transition. In discussing censorship, it is impossible to make good sense and good law without sociological and psychological analysis; rehashing the statutes and precedents will not do. But it is no secret that in this field earnest authorities angrily clash on the most material issues (this is a sign of transition). Take the most undoubted sadistic pornography, socially worthless and sold at a criminal profit: one psychologist will say that its effects are disastrous, it causes "sex crimes" and juvenile delinquency; yet another psychologist will flatly assert that no such connection has ever been proved, there is no clear and present danger to warrant legal action. Now, in this particular difficulty the courts seem to have a convenient out: since admittedly the dubious object has no social merit, since its associations are unsavory and the purveyor is a racketeer, why shouldn't the court go along with the censorship? No real freedom is impugned. But here is a dilemma: what if the censorship itself is part of a general repressive antisexuality, which creates the need for sadistic pornography sold at a criminal profit? We must remember that the tone of the censorship, *and* of the usual court decisions, is vindictive and anxious; it is not the tone of a simple prudential choice in terms of broad social policy. The censoring is a dynamic and emotional act, with novel and perhaps unthought-of effects. The social question is not the freedom of a venal purveyor, though the case is always argued in his terms since he is the one brought to court; the question is whether the sexual climate of the community is perverted by the censorship.

The censorship justifies itself as protection of children and adolescents. But consider this issue in terms of an accepted commonplace of contemporary pedagogy, that we must provide the child a "structured permissiveness" to grow in: permissiveness so that he can act without fear, shame, and resentment, and learn by his mistakes; and a structure of firm *parental* morals and culture—"how we behave" not, "how you must behave"—with which he can identify when, in his anxiety and confusion, he needs security and guidance. A good parent rarely sees a situation as a clear and present danger (of the level of swallowing poison or being hit by a car). Most dubious associations and behaviors of a child outgrow themselves in his ongoing career in a moral and cultural environment. And indeed, this ongoing career is the only real solution for him; whereas a "protective" parental attitude will almost surely communicate the parents' anxieties and complicate things further.

If this is a correct analysis, then the recent "liberal" decision on *Lady Chatterley's Lover* is inadequate. It is not permissive in the right way and it does not provide a firm moral and cultural support. Therefore I am urging the court to re-examine its anxieties, decide that the pornographic is not in fact, in our times, obscene, and give light and moral leadership.

I.

Judge Bryan's exoneration of *Lady Chatterley* takes its doctrine from Woolsey on *Ulysses* (1933) and Brennan in *Roth vs. United States* (1957). Let us consider these in turn.

In clearing *Ulysses,* Judge Woolsey's method is first to equate the obscene with the pornographic, as "tending to stir the sex impulses or to lead to sexually impure and lustful thoughts," and then to show that the book does neither, but "is a sincere and serious attempt to devise a new literary method for the observation and description of mankind." Let us postpone the literary criticism till the next section, but here stop short at the definition of obscenity.

The notion that sexual impulse or stirring sexual impulse is a bad thing comes from an emotional climate in which it was generally agreed that it would be better if sexuality did not overtly exist, at a time when people bathed and slept fully clothed, and a bull was called a he-cow. Then anything which was sexual in public—as the publication of "detailed representation in words and pictures"—violated society's self-image and was certainly obscene. In our times such a notion is absurd. The pornographic is not as such obscene. As Judge Jerome Frank pointed out in 1949, "No sane man thinks that the arousing of normal sexual desires is socially dangerous." We live in a culture where all High Thought insists on the beauty and indeed hygienic indispensability of sexual desires, and where a vast part of commerce is busy in their stimulation. Nevertheless, Judge Bryan on *Chatterley* finds himself compelled to repeat the precedent of *Ulysses,* in 1960! This leaves us in utter confusion. For consider: Bryan goes on to define the "prurient . . . that is to say, shameful or morbid interest in sex"; but if the stirring of desire is defined, and therefore treated as, obscene, how can a normal person's interest in sex be anything else *but* shameful? This is what shame is, the blush at finding that one's impulse is unacceptable. Only a brazen person would not be ashamed. So the court corrupts. It is a miserable social policy. I would rather have Lawrence condemned than defended by such reasoning.

But it is Woolsey's second clause, "leading to lustful thoughts," that is the more interesting, for this is the likely and immediate effect of literary or pictorial stimulation. Bluntly, "lustful thoughts" means incitement to masturbate. I guess that in the overwhelming majority of cases this is the chief use of pornography. Let us again look to history. In the nineteenth century, all sexual facts were suspect, but masturbation was a mortal sin and the prelude to insanity. Let me quote from a great, good-natured, and liberal man, the prince of the Enlightenment: "Nothing weakens the mind as well as the body so much as the kind of lust directed toward oneself. It is entirely at variance with the nature of man. We must place it before the youth in all its horribleness," etc., etc. (Immanuel Kant, *On Education*.) Now contrast with this a philosopher of our own day: "Left to itself, infantile masturbation has, apparently, no bad effect upon health and no discoverable bad effect upon character; the bad effects which have been observed in both respects, are, it seems, wholly attributable to attempts to stop it." (Bertrand Russell, *Education and the Good Life.*) And this is pretty nearly the identical opinion of Benjamin Spock, M.D., in his book on *Child Care,* which is, I suppose, in every middle-class home in America (more than twelve million copies of the paperback have been sold). Also, since the connection between pornography and juvenile delinquency is much touted, let me quote the identical opinion of a revered criminologist: "Masturbation is a habit without deleterious effect in itself, yet a source of behavior difficulties because of strong social disapproval." (Donald Taft.)

My point is not that this habit is good; it is morally otiose. But when the court says that stirring to masturbate is obscene, certainly the court corrupts. Let me specify the damage. According to sexologists, the dangers in masturbation come from (1) inhibited performance, holding the body rigid, holding the breath, keeping silent; (2) guilt and shame of performing the act; and (3) guilt about the accompanying images. Our public policy obviously worsens the first two conditions, but it is also importantly responsible for the guilt-inducing images, for it associates lust with punishment and degradation and so creates sado-masochistic thoughts.

It is claimed that the court must judge according to public sentiment; but there is plenty of better public sentiment. Why must the police and the courts follow the worst part of the population instead of leading with the best? A more enlightened court would not solve these problems any more than it has created integration in the South; but by the same example, a good decision is not irrelevant.

This brings us to the doctrine of *Roth vs. United States.* The standards to be applied in determining obscenity, Bryan quotes Judge Brennan, are "whether to the average person, applying contemporary standards, the dominant theme of the material taken as a whole appeals to prurient interest." Bryan then uses part of this sentence, "the dominant theme taken as a whole," to exonerate *Lady Chatterley* by proving that it is a "serious" work, following the tactics of Woolsey. Again let us defer the literary criticism, and here stop at "applying contemporary standards," which is an attempt on the part of the court to cope with the changes in emotional climate that we have just been discussing. As Judge Bryan puts it, "Much of what is now accepted would have shocked the community to the core a generation ago." But I do not think this is a sufficient account of the sexual history of recent times.

As one reviews the many cases, one is struck by how, year after year, this theme of changing standards recurs in the decisions. "What was regarded as indecent in the days of the Floradora Sextette, is decent in the days of the fan dance." But what is most striking is that in the long chain of decisions over two generations, the standard becomes increasingly broader in almost every respect: the bathing suits more scanty, the four-letter words more tolerable, the descriptions of the sexual act more realistic, the "unnatural" themes more mentionable. It is just this tendency through time that the courts fail to take into account as they judge each case. Therefore they are always behind, they miss the essential nature of the phenomenon they are judging, and this has consequences.

The essence is that our generations are living through a general breakdown of repressive defenses, increasingly accelerating, and therefore a deepening social neurosis. Freud's doctrine, let us remember, is that it is not repression (total amnesia) that causes neurosis, but the failure of repression, so that repressed contents return in distorted guise. This process is irreversible. Our culture has experienced too much of the emerging content to ban it, or will it, or frighten it, out of mind. Therefore the only recourse is to try to get, as methodically and safely as possible, to the end of the line, to undo the repressive attitude itself, so that the drives can reappear as themselves and come to their own equilibrium, according to organism self-regulation. It is in just this that our high courts, like the Lords in England, could be excellent social counselors. With expert advisers they could try to forecast, and guide toward, a sane sexual policy. Instead, they cling to an outmoded concept of obscenity and they prevent outmoded statutes from becoming dead letters. Yet at the same time they are forced to cede to changing public taste and to relax standards. Now, this must lead to social chaos—the pornography is only an example—for so long as the attempted repressing continues, the repressed contents must continually emerge in more and more distorted forms. And of course we also get legal chaos, as the court twists and turns to avoid the outmoded statutes.

For a writer like myself, there is a bitter irony in Bryan's statement that the previously shocking is now acceptable. Yes it is—because Flaubert, Ibsen, and Wedekind, and Dreiser, O'Neill, and Joyce paid their pound of flesh to the censor. They opened the ever new sensibility and were punished for it. Probably this is inevitable, and any advance worth having is worth suffering for; but it is a bitter proceeding. And now *Lady Chatterley* is accepted as a community art-work just when it has ceased to be a living art-work. Lawrence has explicitly told us that he wrote it ''in defiance of convention''; that defiance and the awkward rusticity of the book were its life. Now we are left merely with a rather neurotic fantasy of a frigid woman and a class-resentful ''dominating'' man. The court's lagging acceptance of bygone classics for the wrong reasons makes it difficult for a living classic to be accepted and exert an influence in the living community.

In the breakdown of repression, the artists do their part by first dreaming the forbidden thoughts, assuming the forbidden stances, and struggling to make sense. They cannot do otherwise, for they bring the social conflicts in their souls to public expression. But the court does not do its duty; and the critics (I will mention no names) go along with the court's convenience, and lie and lie.

The court's duty, as I see it, is to set aside the definition of pornography as obscenity—just as it set aside the doctrine of separate but equal facilites—and to clarify and further the best tendency of the sexual revolution. In my opinion, as I shall argue later, such a policy would indeed tend to diminish pornography, make it not a big deal.

As it is, for well-known historical reasons, we live in a stimulating, unsatisfying society midway in transition; and while the liberal court hedges in embarrassment and the critics lie, the police and the administrators lurk to get convictions on any grounds. The police make wholesale raids against girlie magazines, they entrap a harmless old man for collecting postcards, the postmaster bars Lawrence from the mails, and the Drug Administrator burns the books of Wilhelm Reich as ''labels'' for a contraband commodity. Only a wiser policy can restore order.

II.

Let me proceed to a philosophical question raised by these decisions, which is, in my opinion, even more important for our society than the sexual matter: What is the nature of speech and art? To protect their "serious" books, the courts attempt to distinguish speech as communication of an idea or even as talking *about* a subject, from speech as an action that does something to its speaker, subject, and hearer. This is the tactic of Woolsey when he devotes most of his opinion to Joyce's "new method for the observation and description of mankind" and of Bryan when he says that the plot of *Lady Chatterley's Lover* "serves as a vehicle through which Lawrence develops his basic . . . philosophy. Most of the characters are prototypes." The judges reason that if something like this can be established, a book can be protected under the Bill of Rights' guarantee of freedom to communicate opinion. Yet, although this is a useful distinction for some kinds of speech—e.g., scientific reporting and conscientious journalism—it simply does not apply to common speech, and it is necessarily irrelevant to art, for one essential function of art is to move the audience. If Joyce and Lawrence felt that all they had done was to convey ideas, they would have considered themselves failures.

Naturally the decisions themselves, based on an unphilosophical distinction, have been notoriously inconsistent. For example, *The Well of Loneliness* was banned because "it seeks to justify the right of a pervert . . . it does not argue for repression of insidious impulses . . . it seeks to justify and idealize perverted ideas." Yet these are merely the ideas of the author. But contrariwise, Justice Stewart defended the film of *Lady Chatterley* by saying, "The picture advocates an idea—that adultery under certain circumstances may be proper behavior. The First Amendment guarantee is freedom to advocate ideas." Jerome Frank has wryly commented that if an "idea" is eloquently argued, it is in danger; if it is dully argued, it is safe.

Here is an example of the legal doctrine at work. At Marble Arch in London, crowds gather to listen to popular orators vent their grievances and longings on every topic under the sun: freedom for Nigeria, a subscription for the Irish Republican Army, the ethics of deceiving one's wife, the nearest way to salvation. Like Bernard Shaw, the orators test their repartee against a powerfully insolent audience. All is strictly legal. But if a man comes within twenty-four inches of the speaker, he is at once hauled off by a guardian bobby! A man can say anything, but he mustn't do anything; he can listen to anything, but he mustn't let himself be aroused. Freedom of speech means freedom to talk about. Speech is not saying-as-an-action. The limitations are clear. If there were incitement to riot, the freedom would cease. "Fighting words" are forbidden because they lead to fights. Pornography is forbidden because it is in the nature of detailed sexual reporting that it leads to physiological reactions and likely acts. Blasphemy and obscenity are forbidden because they are acts as such, they break a taboo in their very utterance, as well as presumably undamming what is held in repression by the taboo. Also, there are even particular topics, like the subject of *Lolita,* where merely to treat them at all in some public way is tantamount to sanctioning their existence in the universe. Here speech becomes magic, to name the Name creates the thing.

Jefferson and other revolutionaries who insisted on the Bill of Rights probably had a more risky notion of freedom of speech than our courts, as they did of political action in general. But if to them freedom of speech meant merely freedom to communicate opinions, they could not have intended the First Amendment to apply to belle-lettres at all, for the neoclassical esthetic doctrine of their time held that the function of art was to move and instruct, to instruct by moving. In our modern esthetics, the legal embarrassment is extreme; we pay less attention to imitating reality and lay all the more emphasis on speech as action. To Freud, the art-act alleviates a repressed conflict by daring to express and publish it (this is Lawrence's "defying convention"). In advance-guard art, where the artist is reacting to and vomiting up something intolerable in society, the art-act cannot help being offensive. Since the nineteenth century, the naturalists have meant to defy and shame when they stripped away the mask of hypocrisy. The primary aim of Dada is to shock. In his *Theater of Violence,* Antonin Artaud declares that theater is precisely not communicating ideas but acting on the community, and he praises the Balinese village dance that works on dancers and audience till they fall down in a trance. (For that matter, the shrieking and wailing that was the specialty of Greek tragedy would among us cause a breach of the peace. The nearest we come are adolescent jazz sessions that create a public nuisance.) The "poetry readings" of the Beats try to give us their "existent situation," usually drunken, and the audience copes with it as best it can. I could continue a long list.

To these facts of modern art, the doctrine of Woolsey, Brennan, and van Pelt Bryan is not adequate. Such art cannot be defended as communicating ideas, and anything objectionable in it (there is much) must condemn it. Indeed, the arguments of the censoring customs officer or postmaster betoken a more genuine art-response, for they have been directly moved, although in an ignorant way, by the excitement and inner conflict of Joyce and Lawrence. Their experience is ignorant and low-grade because they are unwilling to let the sexual excitement belong to a larger world of experience, and this is why they excerpt passages. But at least they have been made to feel that the world is threateningly sexual. As the British Magistrate Mead said, on paintings by Lawrence, "Art is immaterial . . . Obscene pictures should be put an end to like any wild animal which may be dangerous." And so Justice Manton, in his dissent on *Ulysses,* "Obscenity is not rendered less by the statement of truthful fact," for it is precisely the fact, the nature of things, that is obscene to the censor.

Woolsey's doctrine is insulting to the artist. He says that the book did "not tend to excite lustful thoughts, *but* the net effect was a tragic and powerful commentary" (italics mine). Surely the author wants to say, "It is lustful among other things, and *therefore* its net effect is tragic."

In our culture an artist is expected to move the reader; he is supposed to move him to tears, to laughter, to indignation, to compassion, even to hatred; but he may not move him to have an erection or to mockery of public figures making a spectacle of themselves. Why not? By these restrictions we doom ourselves to a passionless and conformist community. Instead of bracketing off the "classics," as especially the British courts do—indeed, the legal definition of a classic seems to be a "nonactionable obscenity"— let us pay attention to the classical pornography and we shall see that it is not the case, as the court feels obliged to prove, that a work has a "net" social use despite its sexual effect, but rather that the pornography, in a great context and spoken by a great soul, *is* the social use. Aristophanic comedy was still close enough to a seasonal ritual to encourage rebelliousness and lead to procreation. Rabelais is disgraceful, like a giant baby, and this *is* the Renaissance. Catullus teaches us the callous innocence of high-born youth, free of timidity and pettiness; and Tom Jones is a similar type, with a dash of English sentimentality. If we may believe their preludes, both the *Arabian Nights* and the *Decameron* are cries of life in the face of death; and in our times Jean Genet, one of our few fine writers, is pornographic and psychopathic because only so, he tells us, can he feel that he exists in our inhuman world. But apart from these lofty uses, there are also famous pornographic books made just for fun, since sex is a jolly subject.

To explore the nature of speech as action, consider the other forbidden topic, the mockery of sacred public figures. In our country we suffer from a gentleman's agreement that is politically and artistically disastrous. For instance, our recent President could not frame an English sentence, and according to some observers his career as the head of a great university was dismally hilarious. "Dwight Eisenhower at Columbia" is a title to rouse an Aristophanes. In the eighteenth century Ike would have been richly mauled. But our satirists on stage and TV avoid such subjects. Then there cannot be great comedy, for if you dare not mock the pink elephant looming in the foreground, you can't mock anything. Instead, our satire consists of isolated gags that do not add up to an explosion. But satire is an essential of democracy, for how can we expect our leaders to be anything but front-figures if they do not take any personal risk and cannot be stung?

The court is not philosophical. It does not see that lively speech is active speech. Sexual action is a proper action of art. The question is not *whether* pornography, but the grade of the pornography. To sting powerful figures into personal engagement is a proper action of art, otherwise we sink in a faceless swamp. What the more intellectual court does do is to protect exceptional cases against vulgar prejudices and police busywork. (But often, as in the astounding case of the revocation on moral grounds of Bertrand

Russell's appointment at New York's City College, the matter never gets to a better court.) This is not enough to improve the cultural climate. In principle, the living writers are not exceptional and famous cases. Rather, it works out as follows: publishers will not publish what will get them into trouble; authors cease to write what will not be published, or what the lawyer censors the heart out of; soon the public has lost the authors at their best, and the authors have lost the common touch. The actual situation is that there is little that is published, and perhaps not much that is written, that does or would get into trouble with the censorship, except precisely the hard-core pornography. Why is there so little? If the publishers and authors were doing their duty, the courts would be battlegrounds. Instead, the void is soon filled with safe entertainers, gag men, pap journalists. Advertising is the chief public art. The community hears no ideas.

III.

It has become the fashion to say that the esthetic and libertarian matters we have been discussing have no relation to the actual police problem of hard-core pornography; let the police be careful not to encroach on serious writers, and let the writers leave the police to their raids and entrapment. This schizophrenic theory is false. We are one community, and the kind of high culture we have and the kind of low culture we have are opposite faces of the same lead quarter. But let us look at the hard-core pornography in itself.

I have been arguing that not only is there innocent and useful pornography that ought not to be censored, but the method of censorship helps to create the very kind of harmful pornography that we should like to see checked. The case is similar—and not causally unrelated—to the social creation of juvenile delinquency by social efforts to control it. When excellent human power is inhibited and condemned, it will reappear ugly and dangerous. The censorious attitude toward the magazines and pictures is part of the general censorious attitude that hampers ordinary sexuality and thereby heightens the need for satisfaction by means of the magazines and pictures. It is said that the pornography artificially stimulates, and no doubt this is true—though there is no evidence that there can be such a thing as "too much" sex—but it is not so importantly true as that the pornography is indulged in because of a prior imbalance of excessive stimulation and inadequate discharge. Given such an imbalance, if the pornography heightens satisfaction, as it probably does in many cases, it is insofar therapeutic. This is an unpleasant picture of our country, but there is no help for it except to remedy antisexuality. I have argued that the revolution is irreversible, and the attempt to re-establish total amnesia must lead to more virulent expressions, e.g., still less desirable pornography.

Let us consider two aspects of poor pornography, its mere sexuality or "lust," devoid of any further human contact, drama, or meaning; and its very frequent sado-masochism.

The experience of mere "lust" in isolation is a neurotic artifact. Normally, affection increases lust, and pleasure leads to gratitude and affection. The type neurotic case is the sailor ashore, who seeks out a "pig" and works very hard *not* to get emotionally involved. Why should he behave so strangely? An explanation is that his promiscuity is approved by his peers but, more deeply and morally, it is disapproved by himself. If he regarded the woman as a person, he would feel guilty and hate her, and sometimes he manifests this as brutal violence, really meant for himself. More decently, he restricts his experience to bare lust, though this is not much of a *sexual* experience. I choose the example because it is a fair analogy of the attitude of a large population in America, not unknown in middle-class suburbs. We accept the naturalness of sexuality in an abstract and permissive way, but we have by no means come to terms with its moral, family, and pedagogic dilemmas during a hard period of transition. There then occurs an isolated "sexuality" which at its best is hygienic and at its worst comes to mate-swapping, disowning the sexuality of those we love. Finally, I would suggest that this is the style of much of what the court elegantly calls "dirt for dirt's sake," the sexually stimulating without dramatic, plastic, or other artistic value. Necessarily this must be limited to a few stereo-typed anecdotes and a few naked poses; and it must soon become boring.

The sado-masochistic pornography, however, that combines lust and punishment, torture, or humiliation, is the darker effect of a more restrictive and guilty-making training, for example, certain kinds of religious upbringing. There are comparatively few real life sado-masochists, but all the more do the smash hits of popular culture cultivate fantasies that proceed in guilt and end in punishment, genre of Tennessee Williams. This calamitous requirement, that the lust be punished, used to be a standard of legality employed by learned judges. How stupid can grown men be! For the consumer, such fantasies have a dual advantage: they satisfy both the need for righteousness (sadistic super-ego) and the "weakness" of giving in to pleasure; they embody an exciting conflict. But the bother with such images when used privately as pornography is that they are socially disapproved and enhance individual guilt; the excitement proceeds against strong resistance, and mounting fear, and often dies; and there is a tendency to raise the ante. It is said that this kind of pornography creates juvenile delinquents; the likelihood is rather that the type of delinquent who has a need to prove his potency has a hankering for such pornography, all the better if it can be combined with cerebral know-how, as in hipster literature. Nevertheless, it doesn't do him any good, for, on balance, it increases tension.

From even so rudimentary an analysis, it is clear that we can differentiate the moral quality of various pornography and make a rough rating of useful, indifferent, damaging. The social question would be how to improve the first and eliminate the last. But police courts and administrative officers, and even jury courts and high courts, are not the right forum for important and subtle moral debates. Expert opinion doesn't agree either—I could quote a crashing dissent to most of the propositions I have been making. Still, I am even less impressed by the bellow of J. Edgar Hoover that the police cannot wait for the experts to make up their minds; for one of the few things that *is* demonstrable is that ignorant suppression is wrong.

Yet I do not think that moral problems are private problems and can be left alone. Here I must dissent from my bold and honest classmate, Judge Murtagh, who wants to leave most such issues to a person's conscience before God. On the contrary, it is because moral problems are so publicly important—sexual practice is crucial for family, courting, friendship, education, and culture—that they must be ongoingly decided by all groups, as well as individuals; and they are so subtle that only the manifold mind of all the institutions of society, skirmishing and experimenting, can figure them out and invent right solutions. In this essay, I have been proposing to the judges a particular public experiment, a "firm morals and culture" and "permissiveness" in which there might be both the progressive solution of social evils and, more important, a growth into a more living culture. Let us speculate about it. Suppose that the courts altered their previous doctrine, as I have suggested, and now decided that it was not obscene to stir sexual desires and thoughts. What might occur?

An immediate effect of this drastic change would be to open to the legal public media a very large, and I think soon preponderant, part of the traffic that is now subterranean and culturally uncontrolled. This is an advantage, for the traffic can now meet open evaluation, the appraisal of critics, the storm of angry letters that frightens advertisers.

In principle anything might now be shown, from the hero beginning to have an erection when he sees the heroine across the street, to the drama of the sexual act itself. Since the change-over would be so drastic, the court might aim at a deliberate slowness, and the mass media would wisely want to meet and agree on a prudent rate of change. The test of proper deliberateness would be that, *regarded as mere isolated and excerpted pornography,* there would be little difference of effect on the audience between showing the hint and showing the coition. (In between these extremes, it is hoped that there would develop the habit of treating sexual facts as the common part of life which they are.)

Artistically, of course, there is a vast difference between a hint and the showing of a sexual act. It requires a setting of powerful passion and beauty, or ugliness, to make artistically workable so vivid a scene as a couple copulating. And indeed, one of the most salutary and hoped-for effects of the proposed change would be the radical diminution in sheer quantity, and the improvement in variety and quality, of the hundreds of shows that a person exposes himself to every year. Since at present the stimulation is low-grade, the repetition is chronic; perhaps if the experience were fuller, there would be less need to repeat. Perhaps we could have something other than the endless westerns, crime stories, and romances, if there were more animal satisfaction and not merely the symbolic stereotyped satisfactions that these genres offer, with the sex climaxing in shooting, which for some reason can be shown. As it is, the public never gets beyond sex and violence. Culturally, the greatest curse of censorship is that it produces too many and too trivial art works, all of them inhibitedly pornographic.

The aim is to establish a principled general policy. The states and localities could continue to enforce whatever censorship they please, so long as they do not risk a national suit and are content to do without some of the national culture. The situation, as I envisage it, is somewhat the opposite of the school-integration decision; for the federal court is not intervening in any region, but is insisting that national policy must provide intellectual and historical leadership unhampered by local prejudices; yet as far as possible it will keep hands off to allow for regional experimentation. This is not the effect of the court's present policy—e.g., in opening the mail to *Chatterley*—for that does violence to local sensibilities, necessarily, in order to give some scope for mature experience. But if these were a more principled general policy and the courts were not continually obliged to fight, a generation too late, a rear-guard action against morons, the nation could allow the localities to be even more restrictive and self-defensive; in order to protect local option they could even uphold the postmaster. In a federal system, it is possible to decentralize the cultural climate. This allows for experiment and for citizens to have a freer choice of the life that suits their needs; but there must be freedom to experiment here and there. Now we have the worst of the contrary situation: a degenerate centralism, a conformist mass made of the lowest common denominator of the narrow provincial multiplied by the venality of Hollywood and Madison Avenue.

Legalized pornography would, naturally, deplete the criminal market. (As Morris Ernst has speculated, the price of dirty postcards would drop from three for a dollar to three for a nickel.) In my critical opinion, a first effect would be that the great publishers, newspapers, networks, and film producers that now righteously keep their skirts clean and censor the prose and poetry of their moral and intellectual betters, would eagerly cash in. But a fairly quick effect, one hopes, would be that as a genre such isolated pornography would simply become boring and diminish, just as women's short skirts today create not a flurry.

Finally, there would be immense cultural advantages. Less embarrassment, a franker language, and a more sensual feeling would magnify and ennoble all our art and perhaps bring some life to the popular culture; and conversely, the exposure to such art would help to humanize sexuality and break down the neurotic compartment of "mere lust." In the difficulties of our modern sexual transition—where we do not know the best form of the family, the proper attitude toward pre-marital and extramarital sex, nor even what physical behavior is "normal"—we certainly can profit from the treatment of these subjects in lyric and tragic art. And not least, any social change in the direction of permissiveness and practical approval, which integrates sexual expression with other ordinary or esteemed activities of life, must diminish the need to combine sex with punishment and degradation. To increase the possibility of satisfaction in real situations is to make unnecessary the hipster struggle for violent and apocalyptic experiences.

My argument is a simple one: a more principled high-level policy on obscenity, which realistically takes into account the tendency of our mores, would facilitate the moral and cultural structuring that can alone solve the problems of hard-core pornography; and it would also have beautiful cultural advantages. Whereas the present attempted repression by the police, administrators, and lower courts not only must continue to fail, but in itself keeps creating the evil it combats. I suggest a remedy that many earnest people might consider worse than the disease. They would perhaps prefer to muddle along. But I doubt that we can.

First published as "Pornography, Art, and Censorship" in *Commentary* (March 1961); the version printed here is from *Utopian Essays and Practical Proposals*, New York: Random House, 1962.

Television:
The
Continuing
Disaster

*F*rom its inception in this country, TV has been considered ostensibly as a broadcasting medium. In fact (like network radio but more so) TV has itself been the chief program and product, as well as a peculiar kind of existence; the audience watches TV. The normal concept of a medium is that there is something needful, useful, or excellent to be conveyed, and the medium conveys it. But mostly the formats, ritual, and personalities of TV are what has been conveyed, to some as a way of life, to others as a subject of bile and satire, of which there is a considerable literature. When TV was a technological novelty, this was to be expected, but the continuance of the situation is a disaster. It fills the environment with a monster composed of distractions, lulling routines, and prestige-winners, to enlarge the number of TV-watchers as such, who are then sold to the sponsors like so many pounds of beef.

"The show was pretty good for TV," or "There are good things on TV," or "TV is lousy, how can it be improved?"—people do not seem to realize how extraordinary this form of sentence is. Obviously they do not mean TV but the world of NBC, CBS, etc. It is said there is not enough serious drama on TV or there is too much violence on TV. But the complaint is never posed as a naive question: "We need serious drama as part of our way of life; how can our TV medium be used to broadcast it?" or, "Since large numbers of people like to watch violent shows, what can we do to solve the psycho-sexual problems of the country?" It is taken for granted that TV is not ours, and of course, as it has been parcelled out, it isn't. In discussion, the needs of life, society, and art are shunted to the background, but how to cope with "TV" is a subject of lively debate.

Correspondingly, "TV is improved" not by freeing it as a medium to use, but by removing the blemishes of the monster—sex, violence, and puerility—and by making it a more comely monster, better rounded, more generally appealing, higher-toned. Thus, according to a recent homily of General Sarnoff, the present aim of NBC is "to set new standards of program diversity and balance while maintaining a strong competitive position in over-all popularity....Our concept of a balanced and diversified schedule springs from the conviction that a medium addressed to the total public must try to engage the interests of all parts of the public." But is the medium of TV (broadcasting images that somebody might want to see or send) indeed "addressed to the total public," or is it that NBC has cadged so many stations and potential watchers? And what does he propose for that diverse totality? General Sarnoff does not seem to be saying "Here are some important things, rose-gardening, lasers, the Night Court, the debate in the UN; broadcast them." He is saying, "attract as many groups as possible to swell the number of TV-watchers. (Is there a *sub rosa* implication that the present audience is getting bored?)

Naturally NBC and the other semi-monopolists who have captured big domains of TV time, equipment and staff regard TV as a self-subsisting proprietary world, to be protected, expanded, and made profitable. It is a commodity (sold by the hour) to be pre-planned, styled, and packaged so as to avoid criticism and be consumed by the widest audience. This proprietary interest is understandable. But somehow TV is *also* a medium for broadcasting the contents of the real world. It is photogenic and can communicate immediate current reality. What happens when a "total public," expecting to be seeing the real world through a medium, sees instead the domain of General Sarnoff, etc.? Inevitably, for many, the TV world begins to exist ambiguously as a replacement for the real world. And unfortunately there are even people who do not believe that an event is real if they see it on the street. It becomes real when seen on a TV screen with an official warrant for existence given by General Sarnoff, etc., as part of "balanced and diverse" experience.

Let me put this another way by comparing and contrasting the present state of TV with some comparable media. There are newspapers because there is news and people wish to know it. Not otherwise than TV networks, the different papers and syndicates try to increase circulation by various features and departments to appeal to the mothers, the kiddies, the sportsmen; and there is no doubt that, like TV-watchers, a vast number of newspaper-readers take in their favorite papers as a ritual, without a lively need to be informed about a particular something or to learn what's new. Yet nobody would dare say that news as such is a product to be styled and pre-planned. The ideology is still the scoop, the front page emphasis on the reality of the day whatever it happens to be, the coverage, the accuracy of the reporting. Journalism is a profession because it has a proper subject, the news.

In the publishing of books, every effort is made by the modern publishers, the clubs, the paper-back series, to condition the public to accept a format as if it were a book; there is the Publishing Business just as there is the TV Industry. Nevertheless, the ideology and the tone of book advertising are still that the subjects and authors are what publishing is about. Magazines, of course, have always been strongly colored little worlds of their staffs, whether *The Saturday Evening Post, The New Yorker,* or *Blast;* they offer different hypotheses of reality. But they are many, and new formats can enter the field. One would not say, "It's pretty good for *Cosmopolitan,*" but would usually just not read *Cosmopolitan,* unless an article was called to one's attention. It is only when we come to *Life, Look, Time,* and *Newsweek* that the product begins to seem like television, addressed to a potential total public and blandly replacing reality with an official reality.

The history of the movies has been somewhat the reverse. Almost from 1915, American movies have thrived on presenting a self-subsisting world, Hollywood and Beverly Hills and their fabulous inhabitants, with an esoteric literature of movie-magazines and ambassadorial press-releases. The cinema has not often been a medium for conveying reality and art, but has been used to help create the reality of the Movies. Nothing else was ever pretended. "The Movies are where your dreams are made." Yet in the films, there has been a continual rebellion—experimental films, documentaries, shoe-string ventures, foreign films, simply to use film as a medium for conveying some other reality than the Movies.

Broadcasting has been cursed by the worst trends of these other media. Economically, it is a great centralized Industry before it has ever been a number of little supply-and-demand businesses. It involves a concentration of investment that must protect itself and exploit its capital-goods and organization no matter whether the products are needed, creating artificial demand and cadging new audiences with gimmicks and slickness, yet remaining unbelievably conservative lest there be four angry letters. Because it deals mainly in formats rather than real thought or creative invention or audience excitement, TV exhausts and discards talents quicker than any other medium, yet gets the most superficial audience response. Like Hollywood, it has been dominated by the dreams of its moguls and is their artificial world; but since there is not even a box-office in contact with the audience, the dreamers are intensely insecure about their image and they draw in their horns because of signs and portents, ratings, the rumblings of possible regulation. Unlike in Hollywood with its extravaganzas, on Madison Avenue the fantasies even of foolish men are levelled to inanity. Although TV pretends to be a medium of news, information, and entertainment, it programs in terms of its own image and a putative audience response, as if the truth of things might not strongly displease audiences and as if creative genius were predictable one way or the other. By a miserable fatality, TV has had the misfortune to develop among a confused and passive populace, starved for stimulation but out of touch with its needs and tastes, many of whom crave any official picture of reality and gobble it up, and most of the rest of whom feel they are powerless to get anything else and take what they get.

This is too beautiful a medium to be thrown away like this. It offers opportunities for the frequent spontaneous emerging of plastic and poetic invention, the rapid dissemination of radical ideas, many kinds of training and instruction, the expression of folk needs, and the development of folk culture. None of this can occur under the present auspices. Regulation can only worsen the disease, making the networks more self-censoring and more self-conscious of their images. It cannot get them into touch with the real, for they are not set up for that. It is evident that the present top-down decision-makers have no notion whatever of what a free medium is.

The best is simply to get rid of them, break up the networks by a complete new deal in the franchises, and decentralize control as much as possible, on any plausible principle, to municipalities, colleges, local newspapers, ad hoc associations. With many hundreds of centers of responsibility and initiative, there will occur many opportunities for direct local audience demand and participation, and for the honest and inventive to get a hearing and try to win their way.

This was one of the series of TV columns Goodman wrote for the *New Republic* (January 26, 1963).

When our demonstration was a dozen
in front of Danbury jail
we furtively collected
—and made a brave loud noise!
—and slipped away in different directions.

When our demonstration was five hundred
in front of the City Hall
we were a resolute band
as we took our stand.
We wouldn't go underground.

When our demonstration was twenty thousand
far up Fifth Avenue as we could see
oh! I was astonished
and had the heady feeling
of being the sovereign people.

Now this demonstration is half a million.
I listen to it on the radio.
The speeches are lousy, they are half-truths.
Somebody I'm afraid has political intentions.
I'd thank them not to plan my future for me.

I'll find out two or three
and picket on the other corner.
I hope, I hope
never to walk alone.
But I'm not getting any younger.

III

Activism

Vocation
and
"Public
Conscience"

With regard to the war, the draft, and sedition, it is absurd to look for a personal formula for action other than the next step following from each man's past, just as the society itself has merely taken its next step into the war.[1] Those who concurred in the social ideals, took satisfaction in the social rewards (whether or not they got them) and were willing to cooperate in their production, and who adopted as their own coloration the general social style, such men are unlikely to dissent now, unless, by a strange ignorance, a want of feeling for the horrors long present, they did not realize where they were headed and now undergo a late revulsion. Others who, dissenting from the society, nevertheless thought the people were persuasible to a more or less imminent political change, can now hardly begin to see social values where they saw none before, and where certainly there are fewer to see; if they still hope to work politically, they are

[1] By the war I do not mean something subsequent to the attack on Pearl Harbor, but the activity of decades which has adapted itself with such astonishing smoothness to the present world-wide national unities. It is said that in America "everything is changed," when on the contrary "everything" seems to be coming precisely into its own. And by "our" war I do not mean America's side in the war, but the fact that all peoples have long involved themselves or allowed themselves to become involved. What I write here is grounded completely on a sense of this continuity between the past and present and of this world-wide interdependence.

committed to sedition; but if they think the odds are at present too great, they will lie low in waiting—whether inside or outside the army, or legally or illegally, makes no difference in principle. No difference in principle precisely because such political personalities are accustomed to subordinate the power of merely personal action, which exerts itself only in the very short, or, if inspired, in the very long run; their job is rather to find the next mass step to alleviate the disaster.

But those lastly, like myself—and I hope I speak for many educators, artists, and religious persons—who so strongly dissented from authoritative institutions and mores that they despaired even of political persuasion and pitched their work, their hopes, and their reward in a human, at best future-social rather than present-social, environment—these, it seems to me, will try to carry on their work and preserve their freedom to work in conditions which now involve either (a) civil disobedience or (b) legal or illegal evasion. (This is a group which has always been unwilling to accept a cleavage between private duty or desire and the limited kind of brotherhood possible in the immediate political environment, between the primary and secondary environment; but just for this reason it is emboldened and obliged, in a social catastrophe of such magnitude to make much of private values proved by lifelong testing.)

Let me distinguish (a) and (b) in principle: Those whose lives are given not so much to concrete works as to the purity of their principles and moral agitation and their devotion to the best in a bad world (I speak especially of moralists and religious persons) will find a worthwhile exemplary device in just standing out against the Goliath of social error, and will therefore embrace public civil disobedience, e.g. by refusing to register. Those on the other hand who sacrifice themselves to free works, living privately for the good of all, will seek just to go their own way, employing cunning, fraud, or flight as will best serve. (By "their own way" I do not necessarily mean in isolation, but in the same hole-in-corner institutions as previously.) From both groups, in the nature of the case, you will hear seditious utterances, tho it is only the first group that can have an interest in their publicity. But the main thing is not to cooperate day by day in the extreme of activity which, when it was more moderate, was day by day avoided.[2]

In these tight circumstances, the meaning of our persistent non-commitment becomes clear. It is the opposite not of revolutionary faith that holds its own, however the social temper may vary or be manipulated; in the long run it is even a form of such faith; but it is the opposite of the attitude of the boys who have been going "all out," again and again, in lecture and signature— on contradictory crusades—as opportunity presents.

It cannot be kept too firmly in mind that persons of this kind have always lived in the society more or less as in a state of nature, accepting the social conventions only pro tem and conditionally. Now when the social events have so far deteriorated that life and liberty themselves are in jeopardy, it is their duty to criminally do their best for themselves and their work. So Hobbes taught. But what of the other famous philosophic decision, whereby Socrates accepted the erroneous verdict of the court? He was right to do so, the error was just, in so far as he concurred in the social ideal *as proved by the fact that he did his work in Athens*. In such a case we could not speak of Socrates as "alienated" from the Athenians, but rather as teaching *them*. (I would not refer to such fundamental cases if the issue were not so terribly urgent.)

It is customary to use the term "alienation" and to refer to ourselves as "alienated," and I myself have spoken in this way. Now, however, when the social labor and acquiescence—that prepared the war in order to wage it—have so subverted the natural order of goods that one doubts of their sanity; and have frozen into a style that is nausea to the taste[3]; it becomes a kind of flattery to use a term that implies that these also represent a human standpoint from which one withdraws merely to take another human standpoint. *But disaster and general disgust will make us all brothers again.* Until that day we have an obligation to survive

---

[2] I hope the reader will see that this attitude is neither callous nor Olympian. Who would dare to take this attitude if he did not see his friends going to die against their better judgment! And what attitude must we take towards a society that has developed such an estrangement between its grandiose policy and the interests of its members that it cannot rely on their better judgment but must resort to force?

[3] Let me cite a headline from the conservative *N.Y. Herald-Tribune*, June 3, 1942, p. 2: "Bombardiers' View of Essen, No. 2 in the RAF Hit Parade."

intact! Even if the war were indifferently good, we should have to stand apart from it; there are plenty of others to approve what authority approves. And what if the "total war" were a mistake, and no one were left?

I say nothing here about the political nature of the war itself because I lack the study, experience and inventiveness of a political person. (My opinions, for what they are worth, I give them only to be ingenuous, are that: Almost all prepared the war by their arduous corporate labor; any considerable group might at any time have prevented it by following at home or against an invader the tactics of Mohandas Gandhi; since no such group could control its interests to this extent, the exploited masses, who were getting the least rewards and would suffer the worst penalties, might have alleviated the war in their own interests; and since even this recourse is at present in abeyance, it would be best if neither warring side had the opportunity to exploit a victory, if only the peoples by then had a bellyful.) But the point I am here laboring is that the personal action of each man will follow not his opinions but the life that he has in fact been leading. It is unlikely that the crimes I have been describing will be committed by those who have striven to make money or disciplined their time in offices, who have watched the Hollywood movies without puzzlement or worn the usual clothes without discomfort. Each habit has its own judgments and people will again act out what they have thought, or been tricked or compelled into thinking, worthwhile. But what I find contemptible are those hypocrites who up to a certain time saw only worthlessness in the usual ways, of commercialism, advertising, adolescence, and then the next day were eager to be the social spokesmen; how was this possible? Or how does a friend of literature like John Ransom, dare to write[4]: "The mentality of sensitive and mature writers is such as to oblige them to be citizens as well as artists. There is good evidence that the writers as a group have more of public conscience than other professional groups, not less. They take part in the military effort. Or if they are not wanted here, they take an interest in it; an interest so absorbed that it becomes difficult to manage the detachment, or the innocence,

[4] "Publication and War," *The Kenyon Review,* Spring 1942, p. 217.

which literary work exacts." Here is a disgracefully careless set of fallacies! Does not the history of great letters show enough men who were willing to be human beings before they agreed, as "citizens," to follow those whom it was their duty to lead? He speaks of the "innocence" of artists as if some other persons, presumably the Office of Facts and Figures, knew better what we ought to do. (It is curious that during the economic crisis he chastised artists for being too much citizens, when their citizenship was nearer to elementary humanity.) Are artists a "professional group"? then no doubt they have a public conscience as well as a public face! But it is clear that the artists he is referring to have been *hitherto at peace*; they are therefore distracted by the war. I for my part have never heard of such artists! What he calls the detachment of art, which they manage—which they *manage!!!*—is nothing but Victory, not without despondency and madness, in a permanent war.

I am reminded of Schumann who in the days of '48 (*there* was a war!) stole off to another town to escape the firing; and in his "detachment" he wrote—*Manfred*. . . .

June 1942

This is the original text of Goodman's own "declaration of conscience" written in the early months of World War II. The *Partisan Review* printed it, after first censoring it heavily, as "Better Judgement and Public Conscience" (July-August 1942). It was the straw that broke the camel's back in relations between Goodman and the *Partisan* editors.

"Dear
Graduate . . ."

*T*he congress is still squirming about deciding to extend the draft act, in the face of opposition of labor unions, farmers, religious organizations and other bodies of voters that seem to retain a little sanity on this direct personal issue though they cooperated with the war in their manufactures, taxes, dishonest sermons, and general compliance. The recalcitrance of the public and the congressmen's fear of losing their jobs have put it up to the Army to offer added inducements to volunteers, in case the draft lapses. That is, unable to persuade the minds of adults, the Army turns its appeal to the immature graduates of high school, who in school have learned nothing of the facts of our social life and who, immured in their homes and schools, have had no chance of learning anything by direct experience.

The truth is that the inducements for a youth to volunteer are indeed persuasive; the Army has a good case. A good case to entice a young man into an unproductive waste of his years, subservient to ignorant officers, dedicated to a purpose admitted to be universally disastrous, and in a status that up to now in American peacetime history has always been regarded with contempt by the citizens. Nevertheless the Army has a good case! What an indictment of the state of our institutions if even the Army has a good case!

111

THREE MAIN CAUSES

Omitting the prospect of being drafted willy-nilly, there are three main causes, interdependent on each other, that bring young men to volunteer: (a) The pressure of making a living and finding a job. (b) The fear of responsible independence. (c) The need to escape from home. On all those three counts the Army seems to provide the best solution available in the institutions—unless the young man opens his eyes, frees himself from the fear of authority, and joyfully works to change those institutions.

(a) I have before me a crude mimeographed circular distributed by the Army Recruiting Station, 29 East Fordham Road, The Bronx, New York. It begins:

Dear Graduate, Congratulations upon your successful completion of High School. You are now standing at the crossroads of your world.

And the circular then presents a diagram of 3 roads:

1. Career Road: To Security! Career! 20-year Retirement with Army.
2. Education Avenue: To College! Five Years free after 3 years in regular Army.
3. *Doubtful Lane? Civilian Job. No Security. Career Questionable. Retire—when? Education—Maybe.*

Doubtful Lane?! Such is the breakdown of the system of "free enterprise" that up to now has been the chief apology for American capitalism!

"Let's face facts," the circular goes on. "Millions of veterans are coming back into civilian life. They need jobs and have first priority, etc."

What gall!! to dare to argue from these "facts"! It is precisely the top of the hierarchy of this Army that has persistently withstood every struggle to improve economic conditions; this Army that has broken strikes when strikes were not yet controlled by the labor-bureaucracies, and that will again break strikes; this Army that must be filled in order to protect American "commitments" abroad, and the commitments are nothing but the interests of the very class and the very State that maintain the conditions of "no security, career questionable, education maybe." The Army helps to create and maintain the facts and then says face the facts. Is not this form of persuasion known as extortion?

I am myself academically trained, and I am astonished and ashamed to see how the colleges and the universities have grasped at these Army subsidies and fees. It is the end of free research and liberal education, for he who pays the piper calls the tune. The technical training of which the Army boasts will, for a time, invent new weapons, but it will not advance science.

(b) Even so, this economic argument of the Army circular would not be persuasive if it were not for the attitude of timidity, lack of self-confidence, and general lack of cultural and social interest with which it is received by the young men; for no independent and intellectually active youth would sacrifice during these exciting years of his life his freedom to explore and take his chances. But the pressure of parental economic anxiety has long since created in the child's mind the feeling that it is impossible to make a living; the young man, bullied and beaten at home, secretly believes that he is worthless and could never make a go of it. Further, he is secretly afraid to be economically independent, for such independence implies also sexual independence and perhaps marriage, but long deprivation and coercive taboos have invested this idea with terrible anxiety and guilt. Fundamentally, to go it alone means to dare to take father's place and even perhaps to become a father; but the child has long observed that father himself could not fulfill the responsibility in our society; how much the less can he, whom father has so often banged down and called a fool? Furthermore, years of mis-education have by now stifled every impulse of curiosity, cultural interest, and creative ambition that normally arises in growing boys; in his schooling no natural bent has been encouraged; now, consequently, every human activity seems impenetrably mysterious—the youth is sure that wherever he turns he will make a fool of himself; his ego resists the challenge with all its might.

But behold! the Army solves all problems. It imposes in an even stricter form the parental discipline and punishment, that the soul craves; and in a better form, for there is at least no admixture of love. At the same time it releases one from all responsibility; the Army provides every safety as it prepares its members for the moment of extremest danger. In the Army the young man has a disciplined irresponsibility. In the endless hierarchy of the Army it will even be possible for the young man to bully some one in turn, for there is always a newcomer with one less stripe.

(c) And to get away from home! Really away and far away! This also the Army provides. But apart from the Army, as things are in our society, even if the young man finds a job he will still have to remain for several years within the accursed parental walls, his new contribution merely creating a new friction. If his family is what we can observe nine out of ten families to be, it will forever be impossible for the children to grow up to regard their parents as equal human beings for whom one has a special affection. The relations have become strained. It is forever impossible for the youth to express the love that is at the bottom of his heart; it is equally impossible to express the rage that is boiling up from the bottom to the top, and knock the old man down. Therefore the best thing is to get away quick, because the next battle will be worse than the last one—but in the Army one can fight guiltlessly against foreigners and anarchists.

These are, I think, the main reasons that lead the young men to volunteer. Of course there are many corollaries that spring from one or another of them; the pride of uniform, the camaraderie of the other fellows in the same boat, travel, the feverish fantasy of sexual license in strange towns etc., etc. I should be much surprised, however, if among these motives there often occurred a false sentiment of patriotism. The Americans are not yet so co-ordinated as to imagine that there is a need for this Army.

What then? I hope I have filled out the case of the Army circular so as to present their offer in its full attractiveness. I hope that a few young men who might see this will have a small feeling of shame at their plight, and then a great burst of laughter.

Young men! you are indeed at the crossroads—the circular is right. On the one hand are the specious and lying and not unchangeable "facts" that they tell you and that you perhaps inwardly fear. On the other hand is the simple truth: that you are not worthless, you have great powers in you; the world is full of interesting possibilities, creative jobs, crafts, arts, and sciences that are not impenetrable mysteries; we need each other's mutual aid and no one is unappreciated or isolated; sexual love is guiltless and therefore not far to seek. You need money enough for health and happiness, not to buy what is pictured in advertisements and the movies, and if on our rich earth you can't get this much without going into the Army, you ought damn well seek out who's stopping you.

The inducements of the Army are not very different than extortion. Help us to change the "facts," to free yourselves and set each other free!

First published in *Why?* (April 1946).

To
Young
Resisters

Dear friends,

Let me make a few personal remarks to you young men in the throes of deciding *how* to resist the war and the draft. (That we must resist them is not in question.) A friend of mine has just again been put in jail for avowed non-registration, and I am concerned about you others who are likewise set on "enlisting in jail," as it seems to me—as if you approved more highly of penal institutions than the army. I have heard the arguments for such public affirmation of principle, but they do not strike home to me. Now the alternative modes of resistance are devious and flexible and do not thrive on publicity. What I say here is not about the alternatives, nor about any objective political or historical advantages or disadvantages; it is addressed to you personally. You may find these remarks presumptuous and offensive, but I do not have the right not to proffer them. I am ashamed to have to discuss in a newspaper, however, what should be discussed individually.

You are set on willingly accepting heavy penalties because of principle. Most of you, I think, do not have the right to hold such hard principles nor willingly to accept such heavy penalties. Right principles are the statements of deep impulses, intuitions, insights into our underlying natures; they come from deeper than our ordinary practice, and therefore we conform our practice to principles to help us realize our deeper natures. Now young men like yourselves have not had the chance to mature and test the principles to live by. It is only independent accomplishment that tests one's principles (the test is, "are they working in me?")—you have not had the time to accomplish enough of your own. What you take to be your principles are largely borrowed ideas, or the expression of various passionate attitudes towards your elders and teachers, or at best the fruit of reasoning. Excuse me, these are harsh sentences, but you will agree it is not a sweet subject.

On the other hand, willingly accepting heavy penalties, *you are violating your primary duty as young people: to seek for animal and social satisfactions and to plunge with youthful enthusiasm into work interesting to you.* You do not have the right to postpone these satisfactions and explorations. To the extent that the State or anything else tries to make you postpone them, you must fight for them by force, cunning, recalcitrance, camouflage, playing dead, flight, etc., like any other healthy creatures we observe in nature.

Again, you prematurely assume a public role. In your "principles" there is always, is there not, a guess at a certain public expectation of you: what people think of you and by reflection what you therefore think of yourselves. This public opinion is disastrous: it gives you a false assurety of rightness and courage when your hearts are really torn by doubt and fear. In general, when in doubt the wise course is delay, avoidance, not to have to make a commitment on the doubtful issue; but on the contrary, to throw oneself all the more into good activities that are not at all doubtful, one's life-work, or love, or the quest for them. Now what is the case at present? The vast states of the entire world are embarked on obvious folly, long proved calamitous to mankind. This we must resist. But how possibly can untried young citizens know with inner conviction how to cope with such colossal problems? You do not know; you know you must resist (this a child can grasp) but you do do know how; therefore, to avoid the tension, you embrace "principles" that give you a public picture of yourselves, that let you know what is expected of you as resisters. Then you throw yourselves in jails as sacrifices. No no, go softly; since you are torn by doubt, first rather exhaust every possibility of delay, avoidance, non-commitment; and meanwhile, to relieve the tension, throw yourselves fervently into what you are sure of, interesting work, sociality, love. *It is not necessary for you to be verbally consistent as yet: do not allow yourselves to be public figures. Your own kind of consistency can only emerge with experience and accomplishment; your public force will exert itself with the realization of your inward powers.* Therefore, loosely follow every positive impulse, avoid cooperating with obvious stupidity and evil, and postpone other issues. Have the courage to say to yourselves, "I don't know; I am afraid."

The penalties you think of willingly accepting are disproportionate to your actions as yet; you do not have the right to them. If a young man is a fiery revolutionary, a great champion, then such heavy penalties (one, three, five years in jail) have a certain fitness and beauty: he is a grave offender, a great champion, he runs great dangers, he suffers grave penalties. But most of you have so far done little, you have struck only weak blows for freedom against stupidity and authority. When you are penalized, the feeling is not noble, but ugly: a sense of pity for you, a sense of insensate cruelty of the oppressor. To give color and proportion to its blind fury, the State's attorney tries to elevate you into public enemies, symbols, examples. Do not lend yourselves to this convenient lie. *You are yourselves, not symbols. Your fact is that in our society there are horrible difficulties and obstacles, threats to your joy and creativity; this is your fact, act with your eyes on this.* Certainly there are deep causes underlying this fact, causes to be faced with principled behavior, the principles you live by and may die for as great champions, but you do not yet know them as your own. Do not let either your enemies or your friends prematurely assign "your" principles to you. Stubbornly work for the personal goods that you do know and desire, and your underlying principles will emerge; then will be the time to stand witness to principles.

I have been basing this personal argument on moral considerations of "rights"—your rights to hard principles, to accept punishment, to deserve such heavy penalties—because these considerations are obviously very important to you. I am passing by the considerations of practical effects—whether your mode or other modes of resistance would be most effective for peace—because I do not know how to estimate these quantities: it seems likely to me that the way of symbolic publicized witnessing and suffering fits more with the present character of people and therefore could have a wider superficial effect, but that the mode of fighting for real (millennial) satisfactions can effect a deeper change. But I cannot omit, finally, the most important matter of all, the state of your feelings.

In feeling, your position and your decision are enviable (I envy them); tho doubtful and fearful, you have occasion to be nearly bursting with pride and joy: and this is the wonderful flooding of life. For you can perform a definite act in a crisis, with justification: approved by your good conscience, cutting loose from the prudential ego that drags us down, and by-passing the animal desires that, as we are brought up, are freighted with guilt. Rarely indeed does the life we lead give us a moment of tears, dread, and glory! Then what kind of envious and spiteful moralist am I to try to dullen your definite act and tarnish your justification?

Good, I challenge you! You are prepared for jail and for worse (the history of other young men proves it). Is it not then just you who, not turning away from your resolution but going beyond it, is it not *just* you who can act with unexampled freedom, energy, and daring in our society that never sees these things and is hungry to be moved by them? Your crisis is the means of releasing wonderful powers of nature, because you have faced what is awful. (What is there now to fear; say lightly, "We are living on velvet!") To use these powers, releasing still new powers in yourselves and us, not in the infertile place of a jail, but in our general world productive of opportunities for life.

Whichever way, may you thrive in the creation of the heavens and the earth.

By the time this was published, *Why?* had a new name and format, but its anarchist editors were the same. The new draft act of 1948 was now in force, and a young friend of Goodman's had just been sentenced to a year in jail for refusing to register. *Resistance* (March 1949).

Declaring
Peace
Against
the
Governments

I.

*T*he unique situation of the world-wide Cold War must involve a revision and extension of basic juristic and political ideas. The following are a few broad philosophical considerations that have led me to be a "sponsor" of (be answerable for), and to take part in, the recent "Worldwide General Strike for Peace." This apparently pompous name is quite unhistorical, yet it is not inappropriate to the new circumstance.

Let us assume first a contractual, rather than an organic, theory of fundamental law: In this ideal model of rational persons making free choices, people submit to the rules and restrictions of Society and cooperate with one another in the agreed framework, in order to protect their lives and liberties and to avoid disorder and unnecessary conflict. As a decentralist and community anarchist, I of course believe that these rules are too numerous and the sovereignty of Society is too strict; indeed, if we had fewer and less coercive laws we should need them less, since the laws themselves create much of the disorder. Nevertheless, in any complicated community, the institutions and objective customs are the way by which people understand and accommodate to one another and work together: they are the "social compact." The opposite condition, called the "state of nature"—mythically, for there is no people in such a condition—will not be chosen for in it, life would be, as Hobbes said, nasty, brutish, and short.

But if the institutions of society become themselves dangerous to life and liberty, then the social compact is dissolved, it has lost its justification. For example, according to Hobbes again, if a man is imprisoned (and so the social compact is dissolved), he has a moral duty to try to escape, as a natural animal. The same reasoning has been used to justify revolution, when institutions are intolerable. A kind of proof of intolerability is given when people in fact do not tolerate them and succeed in replacing them.

The emergency of the Cold War is, unfortunately, rapidly becoming a black-and-white case of dissolution of the social compact. The poisoning of the atmosphere by nuclear testing; the accelerating accumulation of armaments that, by intention or not, will surely explode; and the tantrum diplomacy that must hasten the debacle, threaten imminently to destroy life, not to speak of liberty. If we may judge by the morality of the tommy-gun-defended private fallout shelters of last year, our life is becoming worse than nasty and brutish, and will not even be short. We are thus driven to think of refusing to cooperate with institutions of society so irrational that they undermine the basis of any society whatever.

This society-destroying property of war is not new. Certainly World Wars I and II, with their attack on civilians and massive bombings, have brought us to our present lawlessness. War of this kind is not a political policy; it has no pros and cons for persuasion. But the Cold War, finally, confronts us with an absolute biological emergency. The only response to it is the rational-animal response of saying, No. We won't go along with it. Stop it.

The term "general strike" used to refer to an all-embracing power-conflict short of violence, in a showdown between classes or parties for political control. In the face of nuclear war, however, the showdown has become a chronic acute emergency. We are forced to act, though few, as if it were a showdown in the minds of many; for it is in fact a showdown for everybody. Also, there is not, primarily, a conflict for political control. Everybody is equally threatened; the powerful are made powerless by the clinch of the danger. So the general withdrawal of cooperation is not, essentially, a weapon against the dominant power in order to replace it, but an act of common reason and imagination against the whole political structure, to relax the danger, *even though no rival structure is clearly envisaged.* (Let me return to this later.)

We have been assuming a contractual theory of society. It is more realistic, however, to assume a more "organic" theory: that people exist in society by bonds of animality, fellowship, and obedience that are broader and "deeper" than rational choice. Nevertheless, in the biological emergency of the Cold War, these bonds also are loosed, by revulsion, fear, and indeed a sense of the eerie. It is impossible, for instance, to hear a group of professors and scientists discussing war-game-theory and mega-corpses, without feeling that they, although rational men, are moving in a paranoid system, toward which the only therapeutic stance is a kindly but firm negative. Their institutions have become altogether alienated from any natural community. The massive reaction to the testing a few years ago, which led to the great initial success of organizations like SANE, was certainly due to the revulsion against poisoning. But even more significant of the weakening of the social fabric is the spontaneous and highly *dis*organized formation of small protest groups everywhere, thousands of ordinary people finding courage in their friends and neighbors to perform acts of non-conformity.

The belief of people in their official leaders is unable, over many years, to bear the strain of their patent fraudulence. When 353 sessions of experts cannot decide on an inspection procedure and break up in flat failure, one must conclude that there is no will to succeed and agree. And besides these complicated negotiations, there are several simple ways to relax the Cold War. The ingenious scheme of Charles Osgood to relax distrust and tension; Stephen James' dumb-bunny proposal to revive the medieval exchange of hostages—such things have the virtue of calling the bluff; they would safely and cheaply bring peace; there is no necessity for armed "deterrence." But the governments do not will peace. Even worse in arousing disbelief, the evident scientific quackery of our government in its shelter pronouncements and manipulation of the "safe" fallout levels, can have no other meaning than the wish to deceive our own people.

II.

In the world community—of communications and travel, technology and industrialization, and the responsibility to help backward regions—the national sovereignties are a baroque hangover. There might be some shadow of a reason for the transient existence of the new sovereignties of Africa and Asia in their emergence from colonialism; but on the whole this imitative evolution is an absurdity. Our own President and his associates are in principle little different from Louis XIV, and the Russian regime still reminds one of Peter the Great, unchanged, in this respect, by the October revolution. Naturally, in their senility the states exaggerate their worst archaic features, the cult of personality, the dead weight of bureaucratic routine, the tendency toward monopoly. The arts cannot lie; the newer official buildings of Washington, Moscow, or London give one a sense of crashing futility—worse than the positive ugliness of the Hohenzollerns and Hitler or the childish grandiosity of Victor Emmanuel and Mussolini. This idea can no longer renew itself.

The very futility of the States, however, commits them rigidly to the Cold War. Without it, it is doubtful if the great sovereignties could survive with anything like their present personnel, vested interests, motivations, and ideology. Their one function seems to be to continue a clinch and hinder the evolution of the world community. In our own country, our sovereignty prevents trade, hinders travel, corrupts foreign aid, forbids feeding the hungry, censors communication, destroys the open and universal tradition of science. And of course, domestic and economic policy are swallowed up by the Cold War. The President is angry because the labor unions want shorter hours and are "irresponsible." Civil rights for Negroes are regarded not as social justice, but as enhancing our Image in Asia and Africa. There is no money for the education bill, but nearly a billion a year for "defense education." Twenty per cent of the gross national production is devoted more or less directly to armament, a rise of more than twenty-five per cent over the previous administration.

The case is not different in Russia, except that Russia can afford it less. American statesmen eagerly wait for the Russians to crack under the strain: they point out (truly) that a declaration of peace would be to Russia's advantage. The Russian leaders, on the other hand, seek out and foment troubles anywhere in the world, in order to fish in muddy waters.

Such a rigidifying and already almost absolute, commitment to the Cold War cannot be altered by ordinary political means. In our country, petitions are ignored or lied to; the official parties, and the mass-media, put forward rival candidates who are equally Cold Warriors, so voting is meaningless. Thus people must engage in actions like this strike. We are doing so. Sporadically—in neighborhood walks and trainloads of mothers; in the anti-war use of class time by a hundred young instructors and a protest signed by a thousand senior professors; in the refusal of shelter-drills by children, the ingenious trouble-making of "nonviolent youth," and vigils by the conscience-stricken. These events become more frequent. The numbers involved become greater. There is a remarkable spontaneity. Organization is never more than ragged and usually it is *ad hoc.* A biological and moral reaction and good sense seem to be enough to arouse people, once it is suggested, and if they encourage one another in small groups.

Like the community itself, the nuclear danger is worldwide, and the protest is worldwide. There have been great popular protests in England, Scandinavia, and Africa. About the Soviet bloc we do not know, but the government had to try to keep its recent testing secret from the Russian people. If there is testing in the southern hemisphere, from Christmas Island, we can expect protests from the Anzacs, Indians, Indonesians, and South Americans. But of course the people of the United States have a peculiar mission to lead this movement; the bomb was our baby and we first made it mighty. Conversely, the almost uniquely American talk of shelters must rouse universal disgust.

III.

The peace movement is at present astoundingly negative: "strike for peace" means merely "refuse the Cold War." The most popular slogan is Ban the Bomb, and there is a rising realization that Peace Must Come from the People. But the idea of positively waging peace—in acts of community-forming, new culture, political reconstruction, economic conversion—seems not yet to take hold of the popular feeling. Yet it is psychologically and sociologically evident that the war spirit is energized by profound frustrations and anxieties of moral and civil life; that the extraordinary apathy of the vast majority to their danger is a result of institutions that have fragmented community and made people feel powerless; and that the only economy possible, under the present control, is the Cold War economy. Really to relax the Cold War requires withdrawing energy from its causes. Hard thinkers in fact propose real satisfactions, more practical institutions, a productive use of technology, and so forth. Yet these ideas are not importantly part of the peace movement. Apparently it is first necessary, at least in America, for hundreds of thousands of people to break loose, by merely negative action, from the mesmerism of affluent powerlessness. The decision-makers in our society, whether in the economy or in politics, seem to be simply in the grip of greed, stupidity, and timidity; and everybody, including the decision-makers, is in the paralysis that comes from wishing for a liberating catastrophe. All, then, deny their personal impotence in fantasies and enjoy the cheap excitement of being actors in the dramatic front-page battle of the Giants, We and They. This impotence *is* the Cold War.

To the extent that the refusers have escaped from this mesmerism and this fantasy, and returned to normal fear and sense, they have already done a lot of positive psychic and social work.

In the course of time, so much spontaneous action as we see occurring must also generate a political idea. But the attempt, e.g. by Leo Szilard, to create a political party for peace as such seems to be irrelevant, since the movement grows anyway. My guess is that a more positive political idea will begin to occur to people when the strike finally begins to reach the labor unions and to be a serious threat to important parts of the economy. For when it becomes clear that we will not continue to organize our purpose, work, and livelihood as at present, we shall think how we ought to organize them. Naturally, my own hope is that, having gotten a bellyful of centralized managerial capitalism and mass-media democracy, people will rally to decentralized economy and politics and communitarian ideals. But although the peace movement cuts across class-lines, color-lines and national-lines, and is non-conformist and raggedly organized, I do not as yet see that it presages any particular political shape.

IV.

Perhaps there is a spiritual travail still to be undergone before people can conceive a creative idea, just as after a loss, it is necessary to go through mourning-labor before one can again think of living on.

It is twenty years since we—I speak as an American—prepared and then dropped the bombs on Hiroshima and Nagasaki. Quite apart from the question of the right or wrong strategy of those acts, the fact remains that now we and the rest of the world exist in anxiety and danger because of them. From the aspect of eternity, it is impossible not to see this arc of events as a tragic retribution. He that takes the sword will perish by the sword.

It is not to be expected that the plight in which we have plunged ourselves can be evaded by game-theory or negotiations. It requires deep mourning, thoughtfulness, and hard labor to undo. There will have to be important changes. What is to be mourned for and thought about and undone, is how we live and what it has brought us to. By and large we have not been happy, and we live in fear.

In these twenty years, we have not heard such mourning begun by Mr. Truman, Mr. Eisenhower, or so far by Mr. Kennedy. We have not heard it from the churches or universities. But evidently many of the people of the peace movement, especially the older ones, have been mournful and thoughtful, and all are engaged in the hard labor to undo.

The Worldwide General Strike for Peace was the idea of Goodman's friends in the Living Theatre, Julian Beck and Judith Malina. On March 3, 1962 several thousand "strikers" gathered in Times Square to protest Kennedy's decision to resume atmospheric testing of the H-Bomb; mounted police charged the crowd with clubs, sending several to the hospital unconscious. Goodman described the event in his novel *Making Do*. "Declaring Peace Against the Governments" was published in *Liberation* (March 1962).

Berkeley
In
February

I.

The dominant system of society is critically dependent on the schools, especially the universities. Schools provide the brainpower for the scientific technology. They are wistfully expected, beginning with age 3, to bring everybody into the mainstream of economic usefulness; and more realistically, they process the professional personnel to control the increasing scores of millions useless to the economy, the out-caste poor, displaced farmers, people over 65, unemployable adolescents who must be regimented. Just as part of the Gross National Product, I have heard the estimate that more than 40% of the cash is in the Knowledge business.

The organization of all this, however, is calculated by the powers-that-be amazingly without regard to the thoughts or feelings of those who are to be "educated." (50% of the total population is under 25.) Establishment forecasts of the future almost never mention the response of the young as a factor; yet that response, whether as anomie or as insistence on more freedom and meaning than the system allows will be crucial. And if we take it into account, we see that the dominant system is probably unviable. Simply, it is not moral enough to grow up into.

The education has become mere exploitation—the abuse of the

abilities and time of life of school youth for others' purposes. As I have put it elsewhere, it is the first time in history that a dominant class has imposed on its free children the discipline of slaves. And the exploitation itself is of a peculiarly difficult and deadly kind, for it involves not merely forced time and labor, but active intellectual participation by the exploited, in learning and even in being original and creative under duress.[1] This is not viable. There must be both breakdown and revolutionary break-through; and recently I have come to hope that *freedom and meaning will outweigh anomie.* Needless to say, I am in love with that, and with Berkeley in February.

In my opinion, the situation at Berkeley is historical and will not be local. The calm excitement and matter-of-fact democracy and human contact now prevalent on the Berkeley campus are in revolutionary contrast to our usual demented, inauthentic, overadministered American society. This ordinary freedom had to be won by risky commitment, finding solidarity, living through fear; and its ferment will spread not only to other campuses but finally to other institutions of society.

The movement of the Negroes and their wise white friends, mainly youth, has been encouraging toward change; and probably our society cannot incorporate its out-castes without revolutionary changes in structure. Nevertheless, the shape of reconstruction cannot, in my opinion, appear among marginal groups; they do not have enough culture, science, and technique to work a good modern society, though plenty of spirit and justice. But the rising of students and of professors recalled to manhood occurs in the best of the middle-class itself and in the center of the economy; the shape of reconstruction *can* appear here. Not accidentally, the movement for the outcaste has sparked and energized this more central revolution, and we will finally come to the real issues: the

---

[1] I am using the word "exploitation" strictly. It is hard for people in the labor movement to understand this term as applied to students. Harry Bridges, e.g., seems to feel that the Berkeley students were pampered brats; they never had it so good. We would do well to recall Marx's description of the 9-year-olds picking straw, not because this was economically valuable but as training in work-habits. Besides, we must notice that nearly 50% of the young are now kept in schools till 21 and 22 years of age; previously most of them would have been in factories, etc., for 4 or 5 years by that age.

revival of democracy, the human use of technology, and getting rid of war.

As a University man, let me put it this way: Our society has been playing with the fire of mass higher learning; it is our duty to let it feel the blast of University truth.

II. CALM EXCITEMENT

During their troubles last winter, Berkeley students kept phoning me—at 3 a.m. Eastern time—in various states of fever, alarm, and despair; but then after a single shout of "Victory!" after the Faculty Senate decision in their favor, I heard nothing further. (Except for a New Year's Eve visit from Steve Weissman, one of the most thoughtful leaders of the Free Speech Movement, who was now interested in "University Reform.")

My expectation, on visiting in February, was that there would be deep depression. They had won their demand to advocate political action, like any other citizen. The Civil Rights energy, which had obviously been strong, could hardly continue animating them, since it was not essentially a campus issue at all. The election being over, Senator Knowland had subsided. And most important, they seemed to have no future goal to grow toward, to inspirit them. Indeed, reading the FSM's voluminous broadsides and pamphlets, I was appalled at the low level of analysis by such bright people. There was little ideology—which was good—but there was almost no economics, history, or philosophy. Rather, endless pages about the First and Fourteenth Amendments, gripes about the violation of due process, and proofs of the ambiguities of Clark Kerr, all relevant but not newsy.

I was wrong. Instead of depression, I found what I have called "calm excitement"—the phrase belongs to a youth in the establishment-oriented student government. (During the troubles, the Associated Students were rather unfriendly to the FSM, but part of the "calm excitement" is a *spreading* among the students of the insistence on freedom and meaning.) My error was that I did not realize that every step of the students' fight was desperately immediate, unchartered, and uncharted. But therefore the fruit of it was character-change, the first opening of new possibilities. Beautifully, a moral struggle has given the students a *habit* of good faith and commitment, and their solidarity has turned into community, like the auroral flush of a good society.

The existential language that I am beginning to slip into is entirely the students' own. It is the lingua franca of the revolutionary campus, and is used with simplicity and conviction. (When on another campus like Ann Arbor, I listen to even a fine group like the Students for a Democratic Society, their talk of "strategy" etc. is grating by comparison.) At Berkeley, there is a sprinkling of neo-Marxist lingo but it is noticeably heavy and dispiriting, except for an occasional Maoism, which is Chinese.

III. GOOD FAITH AND COMMITMENT

On February 10 occurred a curious dialogue between Jerry Byrne, the special counsel of a committee of the Regents of the University of California to investigate "the causes of student unrest," and a group of students from the government, newspapers, religious organizations, and leaders of the former FSM (now FU, movement for a Free University). Byrne is a frank and likeable guy, a lawyer, and I had previous evidence that he was earnest and somewhat unorthodox. He explained to the students his mandate and the questionnaire and interview methods that he intended to employ. He intended, he said, to be objective; he had chosen assistants from outside of Berkeley; he had no ax to grind; he meant business. He would present his recommendations to the Regents in three months. Were there any questions?

A slim dark-eyed youth spoke up: "Mr. Byrne, we have been through an existential moment. A composite picture of 'public' student opinion will not reveal our meaning." I take it that this meant that so-called objective methods would get him nowhere. "Yes," another student said, "Ideas don't pop out of data."

Byrne did not seem to grasp this epistemological subtlety; he assured the young man that he had "found students able to dissociate themselves from events last fall and simply work to future improvement." Later, however, the Counsel said to me privately,

"When that boy looked up at me, his eyes pierced to the bottom of my soul—there was no use in trying to lie to them. The discussion rose to another plane."

Another student (Mario Savio) asked a down-to-earth question: Was there any guarantee that the Regents would release the Byrne recommendations? No, said Jerry, they were the Regents' property. (But the Regents, gasped somebody else, were notorious for *falsifying* scholarly work, specifically a report on *braceros* made by the University.) Savio persisted: "How can the students cooperate with a report for the Regents, if the Board of Regents is itself a morally illegitimate body? how can *it* be the judge?" The bother was that the Regents consisted almost entirely of multimillionaires in aircraft, oil, banks, shipping, etc., with Max Rafferty representing Education!

The question now was whether they ought morally to be talking to Byrne at all, since his mandate was inauthentic. It was not that they questioned *his* integrity, a student assured him kindly. About this time, the Counsel's unfailing friendly smile began to tighten, so that it became increasingly impossible for him to get into contact with them, unless he wiped off the smile, which he couldn't do. Unluckily, none of the students knew enough psychosomatic medicine to point this out to him, and I kept my mouth shut. "Yes," said a student, "it's the genius of administration to turn a nice guy like you into a fink." "How do we know that the student opinion we give you won't be subpoenaed for the trial?" somebody asked ominously. Jerry firmly and believably declared that this would not happen.

A bright idea suggested itself. They could publish the interviews in progress, while they were still the students' property, so to speak: they could make tapes! Jerry vetoed this with alarm. "Then what *can* you suggest for us to do, what *action,* beginning *right now,* that will put pressure on the Regents and guarantee some results?"—a student asked this very earnestly.

"How was I supposed to answer that!" Jerry complained to me later. "In one corner was a reporter from the *Chronicle,* in another a reporter from the *Examiner,* and they ask me to suggest an action to coerce the Regents—" Some more *action* from the students of Berkeley was not, exactly, what the Regents were after!

"Oh, why didn't you just explain that to them, Jerry —with a smile? They're hip kids."

"Why," asked a young lady, "is Unrest something that must be 'remedied'?" "How far will the inquiry probe? Might the report suggest that government of the University should be given over to the students and faculty? Would the range of questions include whether U-CAL should accept war contracts?" "Why," asked a young fellow, "not let a Thousand Flowers Bloom?"—to my ear this question was entirely innocent, without desire to shock.

The Counsel fielded the questions well and generously. But he did not seem to satisfy. "Don't you see, Jerry," I said finally, "they want you to show a burning zeal to improve their school, and you're not showing it." "I don't feel any burning zeal," cried Jerry, "I just want to do a good honest job, and I intend to do it." "There you are," said Savio, "why don't you quit?"—But to my ear, this was said without hostility, even affectionately. It meant, quit them and join *us* and put your talents to an authentic use.

My total impression, indeed, was that the students, including the stars of the former FSM, intended to cooperate with the Counsel in his further study. They would follow the maxim of Gandhi: Always Cooperate. But they would be exquisitely simple in what they are doing and therefore far brighter than Jerry Byrne; and in the long run he would learn more from them than he, with his auspices, would be able to do for them.

IV. COMMUNITY

It is vividly clear on the Berkeley campus that there has been a breakthrough into communication, community. The causation seems to have been classical: justified protest, risky commitment, surprising solidarity and the development of mutual trust, shaking fear met with uncalculating courage, and then the breakthrough into the joyous feeling that "we have a say in the University," "it is our home," "we are free human beings."

They even speak of a founding Event, presumably the Faculty Senate vote that "justified" the students. (Correspondingly, Professor Wolin speaks of the "Faculty's finest hour," as if the

Faculty had been revived and "justified" by the students!) "There occurred on this campus the first human Event in 40,000 years," Michael Rossman assured me—I did not press him for the predecessor. Savio told me with scorn and amazement of a registrar who *after* the Event still tried to enforce a petty rule: "Don't you realize, I told her, that something *happened* yesterday?" The existential theory seems to be that by acting in freedom they made history, and conversely, the historical event made them free. (In a letter to the new Chancellor, Martin Meyerson, John Seeley of Brandeis speaks of the students' action as "the Boston Tea Party.")

An unknown professor came up to me and said, "Since those kids acted up, I feel twenty years younger."

So far as the essence of a community of scholars is the personal relation of students and teachers, Berkeley has already accomplished University Reform and Jerry Byrne's inquiry need go no further.[2] But in fact, in freedom, there is a buzz of activity toward legislating new institutions. Let me give a few examples.

The "Free University" is a para-university of voluntary study-groups off-campus, in which the collaboration of a teaching-assistant or assistant professor is invited. (Typical subjects, *Moral Responsibility and the Sciences, Marx and Freud, History of the Oppression of Women*). At a session I attended (*Anarchism*), a young lady complained rather tearfully that if they invited a professor to the next meeting just because he knew a lot about the subject, it would be just like the ordinary University; but the others, who were mostly graduates and undergraduates in History, assured her that the professor was very young. FU plans also "to launch projects for the general welfare of the larger community," e.g. a summer project to organize migrant farm labor; and not least, "to look into the nature of the University of California's financial connections, controls imposed on funds, indirect pressures on Professors."

---

[2] A former student of mine at Sarah Lawrence explained to me: "When Amy and I first came out, we didn't know anybody, so we invited our professor to tea. The other students thought that we were simply weird. But now it wouldn't be unusual."—This illustrates, by the way, that student-faculty estrangement is a two-way street. The paranoia of the students toward the grown-ups is probably stronger that the indifference of the professors toward the young.

To lighten the student load, I asked the new Chancellor—or Acting Chancellor, it is hard to know[3]—if academic credit couldn't be given for the para-courses, if they met certain standards. He could see no objection. A Regent, however, thought that the reactionaries in the Legislature might balk at some of the titles. . . .

Faculty proposals for University Reform—e.g. by Profs. Tussman and Trow—tend to small voluntary colleges within the University. In one model, 150 students and 10 professors will agree to study some Area or Issue that transcends departmental lines (as a gimmick to get around the entrenched Chairmen?). Professor Searle tells me that he had already tried such voluntary seminars last year, but the *students* didn't come—they needed the support of Credits and the Official Syllabus; but perhaps it would be better now.

I discussed these Faculty proposals with a Regent, who declared that they would cost too much. I think he is wrong. In my opinion, administrators misestimate by applying to a different, decentralized system, the costs that belong to the present over-centralized system. At present the Multiversity operates by tightly holding together essentially disparate parts; inevitably a tremendous amount of money is spent on administrative cement. This process, as I have shown elsewhere, usually leads to a mark-up of 3-400% over actual educational costs. Of course, from the Multiversity point of view, the inflation is more than paid for by the rich contracted research, no matter what, and government and foundation grants.

Professor Leggett, the sociologist, has already instituted (I think) an ingenious form of democracy for a lecture course. Each section elects two delegates who sit with him and the teaching-assistants at fortnightly meetings that criticize the course and chart its further progress. The little council is called a Soviet.

Chancellor Meyerson told me a good idea. He is after some Ford money for a community project in Oakland. This could be manned by students for academic credit as well as pay. In turn I proposed to him the following: Instead of discontinuing the

Since I wrote this, Kerr and Myerson "resigned" and were retained apparently as a bid for a vote of confidence against the reactionary wing of the Regents.

department of Journalism, as seems to be in the offing, rather make it for real by putting out a good daily newspaper which the Bay Area sorely needs. (It is interesting to speculate how Senator Knowland, who owns the Oakland paper, would take this competition, while CORE, recruited from the University, pickets his door for unfair labor practices!)

The Chancellor's best idea for University Reform, however, is a kind of tacit understanding between him and the students—at least so I have been told—that certain idiotic rules, which ought not to exist, need not necessarily be enforced in every jot and tittle.

I was crossing the campus with a Regent and he suddenly asked me, "Do you notice much change since you were here a couple of years ago?" "What are you driving at?" I asked. "Don't you think it's—more lively, more interesting?" "Oh Bill," I cried, "why can't you say that publicly? the kids would be so proud." "How can I say that in my position?" said the Regent. (His name is William Coblentz.) "Don't call them kids!" he said, "they're students."[4]

V. *"FAILURE OF COMMUNICATION"*

I have been describing a very simple situation, a kind of Fourth of August when the French barons gave up their feudal dues. (Alas! it probably won't last much longer than the Fourth of August, but let's not yet look into the future.) It is a situation where people talk to one another, mean what they say and intend to act on it, and therefore could conceivably improve their common lot. Is this extraordinary?

It is said that there was a "breakdown of communication" in Berkeley. There was, but why? The failure of communication is not an isolated cause but is endemic in the structure of American society and in the Multiversity as part of it. There is a limitless amount of information, polling, data-processing, and decision-

[4] Something like calling a Negro "boy." In many a Town-Gown fracas, the analogy of student and Negro is pretty obvious. At present in the town of Berkeley itself, there is an urban Renewal plan to clean up a street which, to me, seems very pleasant and lively, but it *is* occupied by students and their beatnik cronies.

making by objective computation; yet when the chips are down, it turns out that nobody has expressed himself or been understood. Given its exploiting motives, it is impossible for American education to take the young seriously, except as objects to manipulate.[5]

It seemed odd that Clark Kerr, who had made a reputation as a mediator in labor disputes, should have failed so badly precisely in communications. But indeed he acted impeccably as a professional mediator; he kept the parties apart in order to negotiate their demands. Unfortunately, good faith and commitment are in principle not negotiable; the students were not making "offers" with the intention of "settling" for something different. And in the context of a community of scholars, the technique suddenly appeared as obscene. When students and professors insisted that he, the mediator, was a party to the dispute and must confront them, Kerr's behavior was sociopathological. There were cases when he would not speak directly to the professors *by phone* but insisted on an intermediary. When the students were occupying Sproul Hall, he stayed at home and would not speak to them. Clinging to a petty ruling, he kept Regents and professors in separate rooms at the airport.

More seriously, there is evidence that men whom he involved as his intermediaries became utterly demoralized.

Inevitably, the militant students were caught in the toils and became administrative. Dealing with probably benevolent professors, they had to bring lawyers and speak through them, and they became acute experts in their rights under various Amendments to the Constitution of the United States. Yet what they ultimately wanted was just to be told the truth: E.g., if the tables were banned because of traffic congestion, why, when the aisles were kept clear, were the tables *still* banned? Instead they were told another lie.

Or so it seemed to them. But they were making a naive metaphysical error. They imagined that a mediator, one who avoids conflicts and negotiates, is a human being like you or me and makes propositions that are true or false. Thus they felt lied to and tricked and they got enraged. But they were really dealing with a

---

[5] This can be so hypocritical as to be nauseating. For instance, while I am writing this there is a to-do at Cornell about a marijuana "ring." This comes under the rubric of paternal concern, yet girls are dragged out of class and dormitories to be grilled by FBI-men without counsel.

juggling robot. Now, for a spell, disabused of their error, they can be serene—armed.

To be fair to Kerr, I doubt that it is possible, with honor, to avoid conflict among the forces working at the University of California: Birchite legislators, racist newspapers, Max Rafferty, the Atomic Energy Commission, Civil Rights, professors who might suddenly recall the Western tradition, students who might be naively moral. The only honorable alternatives are to quit, as Buell Gallagher did, or sometimes to take a stand and fight.

A Cuban student, not a Castroite, said to me, "Kerr made the same mistake as the U.S.A. with regard to Cuba. By refusing to talk, he left a vacuum. The extremists moved into it. Through the extremists, the mass discovered it had a community."

VI.

Besides the calm excitement and community, there is a third property of Berkeley in February that I, at least, found overwhelming: the fantastically expert organization of the students, as if for instant action *en masse.* Yet there does not seem to be top-down domination. The "leading figures" are rather easygoing, there is no jockeying for position, there is no party-line, and it looks as if new faces easily come to the fore. But as soon as there is an activity, the guerrillas are out in force. There is an evident discipline to attend meetings—naturally many students lost academic credit for the fall term. The Free University sponsored a speech of mine and 3500 students attended. When it was known I wanted to write this report, at once I received a list of key names and contacts all arranged: "he will phone you at 3:45"—one expected 15:45. They have put out phonograph records: Joan Baez songs, *FSM's Sounds and Songs of the Demonstration,* and a remarkable long-player of the Sproul Hall sit-in and the meeting of the Faculty Senate. The quantity of printed material is simply appalling. And a related aspect is the careful sociological research—one can learn immediately that 53% of students in FSM favored sit-ins before the movement started; there are precise political-science analyses of contending forces, legal briefs, property-holdings of each Regent. Never in history, I guess, has a spontaneous uprising been so meticulously polled. The students might object to the factory-University, but they have certainly mastered its arts and sciences.

It is a remarkable phenomenon, a kind of hyper-organized anarchy. Perhaps it is a way of creating a Free University in the conditions of high technology; if so—I am speaking seriously—it is a major social invention. Myself, I find it oppressive. My opinion is that when they begin to reach for positive cultural goods, rather than engaging in resistance and defense, they will have to become shaggier. But maybe I am prejudiced against social sciences—a writer—from the Twenties.

The proper function of such a disciplined student body, I think, is not to be the Free University, which must consist in piece-meal voluntary associations between teachers and students, but to be the Student Government, responsible for social and political rules; collective bargaining agent on food, housing, tuition and other finances; guardian of *Lernfreiheit* against administrative encroachments like grading, excessive courses, unreasonable policies of admission and transfer; mutual aid and self-protection against the local police.

VII.

Let us turn to a broader question: what is the relation of a liberated University to social change in the general community?

It was evident in the fall that the movement for the Negroes was a major background cause for the Free Speech Movement. It was part of the immediate bone of contention, the banning of recruiting; and more important, leaders who had taken their risks in Mississippi were not afraid to sit in against Clark Kerr.

Yet in February I did not hear a *single* spontaneous mention of this struggle. Testing, I raised the issue provocatively and was routinely put right and turned off. One of the leaders, Rossman, then explained to me that interest in Civil Rights was simply part of one's commitment, and it was exactly equivalent to the problem of making a classroom for real. (Rossman himself is a section-man in mathematics; he teaches "intuitive" mathematics—I did not have the chance to pursue whether this meant school of Brouwer or something else.) "Don't get me wrong," he said, "I picket *seriously*; just the same, it's a place to see the girls and sometimes we have a great time. It's our way of living."[6] He had a thing about Abstract Values being entirely dead for his generation, though they had had meaning for "my father and grandfather." I tried to show him that, for some of us, Social Justice with capital letters was not abstract but a concrete property of a tolerable environment, just like unpolluted rivers; and he was visibly impressed by the idea that a 3-year-old divides the candy-bar with another child for symmetry. (Maybe this was "intuitive" mathematics.)

In my opinion, the matrix of a community in which political action is a custom, is essential for the American future. And it is different, in both genesis and meaning, from the Solidarity engendered by fighting for political Causes. Those hostile to FSM have emphasized the number of off-campus participants, who are then called outside agitators, Maoists, Castroites, etc.; contrariwise, the champions of the students then prove that the outsiders are mostly alumni, wives, temporary dropouts. But historically, it is better to consider these university-centered politically active communities in terms of a "withdrawal" from the absurd System and its problems, and a return on more authentic premises.[7]

Consider the history of Beat youth as a type. The withdrawal into voluntary poverty, the community of the Illuminati, kicks On the Road, and finger-painting, did not provide much world. Yet almost from the beginning there were social needs that *were* taken for real, especially banning the Bomb, thwarting the Fuzz, and supporting Negroes and Spanish because they were friends and equally out-caste. In California specifically, it was hard not to join in the rage at HUAC; but even more important was the horror at the Chessman execution: here *was* the threatening Machine literally destroying human life, just as Camus had said.

[6] None of this was news to me. Several years ago I noted that students of Fair Play for Cuba had no "political" interest in Castro, but were enchanted by a young leader who spoke to everybody on the street and wrangled on national TV with conspirators against his life. To speak proleptically, he was not like—Clark Kerr.

[7] I suppose this is what these young people mean by their abuse of the word "Alienation." Certainly in Marxist or psychiatric terms they are less alienated than most other people. Hopefully, if they continue a path of commitment, they will discover they are "alienated" in Luther's meaning!

Inevitably, in this return to involvement, there was joining with proper politicals. But *the event has been not that the young exiles have been politicalized but that politics have been "existentialized" and brought into the community, even containing the dreadful sex and hasheesh.* And this is not because philosophy and pleasure have seduced people from the realities of life, but because *the thoughts and feelings of the young have been more relevant to the underlying realities of modern times,* the drive to rationalization, the abuse of high technology, and the hardware GNP, statism and the Bomb. These abuses occur in every modern country and ideology, whether U.S.A., U.S.S.R., China, or even the emergent African states; and Great Society, Neo-Marxism, and even moral Pacifism do not fundamentally address them.

Come now to the University. A basic trait of the young is that they don't know much, but also, beautifully, that they want to learn something and they hang around hopefully relevant teachers. The young Beats, of course, made a thing of voluntary ignorance like voluntary poverty; and the young Hippies boringly went in for tip-top expertise—they knew all about Black Boxes and Motivational Research—without knowing anything. But pretty soon young people were bound to gravitate, or gravitate back, to the University, as cronies of students, or as auditors, or as unmatriculated students, or as diffident and choosy students. To have a chance to learn something was a great advance for the dissident community; and it was certainly a vast advantage for the University to be infiltrated by a new breed of students who demanded authenticity and practical application. Yet, genetically and persistently, this fringe University community—with its own readings and music, political actions, free sexuality and hasheesh—is not identical with the *in loco parentis* and late-adolescent American college community. And administrators, incidentally, have heightened the tension by dissolving the fraternity system. Some of the young are then penned up in rule-ridden dormitories (built with Federal funds but rented at high rates); but the more spirited go off-campus and get lost in the fringe community.

The new community, returning to the University and magnetizing the collegians, is by its genesis and nature not simply economically exploitable, unlike the ordinary college community which is at the top of the 16- to 20-year ladder of school-processing. In principle, it has dropped out and returned. And it resists in the University the identical Organized System that it resists outside. It is suspicious of being "vocationally guided"— though unfortunately it does not yet have much sense of true Vocation. Correspondingly, it is resentful of the jet-set faculty busy with contracted research; and it correctly interprets the so-called "orientation to the discipline rather than to teaching" as nothing but careerism. Unfortunately, again, however, there is not yet any sense of what a real University of professionals would consist in. (I shall return to this.)

VIII. THE NEW UNIVERSITY CONSTITUTION

In the circumstances, there is an uncanny re-emergence of the primitive medieval University, with its fat-cat professors lecturing in the central halls, a ragged student community living in its own neighborhood, and, astoundingly, a new student leadership by the graduates and teaching-assistants, the very Masters of Arts who used to cause all the trouble in 1200! One would have expected, in the era of the Organization Man, that precisely the bright graduate-students, the junior-executives, would be the most conformist, to protect their status and advancement; yet we see at Berkeley that the teaching-assistants provided leaders and almost unanimously went on strike.

But as well as being a medieval fringe, the students *also* want "personal contact" with the dignitaries, as in a small American boarding-school. On the one hand they distrust everybody over 30; on the other, they want the professors to become part of the fringe community, to give it intellectual structure and self-assurance. And finally, as American citizens, they want self-rule, not only of their own social life like the medieval student-government, but also to have a say in the administrative and curricular doings: that is, the distant Regents are regarded as illegitimate. This novel amalgam, then, of a fringe community of the young and masters of arts; "personal relations" between the students and the professors; and student membership on the Board of Regents—this amalgam is the Free University.

On the campus, this ramshackle constitution proved to have

political power. The organized guerrillas sat in. Then, "when the teaching-assistants went out," said a professor, "it was all over, for we can't run the school without them, and if we fired them, we'd never get another good graduate in California." And then the Faculty, as Professor Wolin has put it, "stirred to ancestral memories of the ideal of a community of scholars bound together in the spirit of friendly persuasion and pledged to truth rather than abundance."—So the Governor had to send his troopers and for a couple of days Clark Kerr's Multiversity ceased to exist.

The question is: if such a Free University exists in the offing, to whom, to what government, will the Federal government, the foundations, and the corporations channel all that money that is the fuel of modern education? It's as bad as dealing with Saigon.

IX. UNIVERSITY TRUTH

The enigma remains the Faculty.

Let me recall a scrap of conversation with the new Chancellor. He was pointing out to me that the chief obstacle to University Reform was the teachers, inflexible, narrow, specialist, status-seeking. I cut him short impatiently: "Administrators have parroted this story to me verbatim at 50 colleges across the country. The fact is that for a hundred years you have cut their balls off and now you say they are impotent. Delegate power!" Meyerson reddened; he is himself a strong and broad mind, a professor, and, I suppose, an excellent teacher. A couple of days later he said to the counsel of Regents, "Goodman is right. Administration turns them into eunuchs and then complains that they are eunuchs."

The overwhelming Faculty vote for the students seems to have been a reaction of nausea at the Administration's lies, its subservience to outside pressure, its pathological avoidance of contact, and finally the presence of the cops. This is the kind of nausea that recalls decent but self-centered people to their plain duty. Professor Wolin says, the Faculty was "shocked out of its shameful neglect of teaching, its acquiescence in the bureaucratization of the University," and it recovered its "collective conscience." These explanations must be substantially accurate for they lead to the evident February situation of friendly contact with the students and cooperation in "University Reform" toward *Lernfreiheit,* student democracy, Faculty resumption of counselling, and so forth.

Nevertheless, although this breakthrough is splendid for the teachers as human beings—if professors don't like to associate with young people, why in the devil do they hang around schools?—in my opinion it does nothing for them as men. The revival of manhood can occur only if they come on again in the world as the University, as the protector of civilized standards, the professors of truth that makes a difference, and, in our country, the blasting critic of social baseness and lies. Every division and department is falling short. For instance, the University of California has "classified research," but this is entirely incompatible with the tradition of Western science and its theory as consensus. (Some great universities have refused such contracts.) There is, in the country, censorship and managed news in utter contradiction to the principle of the Humanities. The sex and narcotics laws of the community are grounded in superstitions that it is the business of the biological and social sciences publicly to expose, just as the Eastern professors exposed the hoax of the Shelter program. The engineers and architects do not speak as Faculties about the community-destroying Urban Renewal; and the education department does not speak as a Faculty about the compulsory mis-education, or at least Max Rafferty.

I don't think that the students can much help their professors to remember *these* ancient duties. The professors will have to come to their own resolve. But if they do, I think that the students of Berkeley will be proud of them, and I think the students will begin to understand what it is to have not only a free university but a University altogether.

I have tried to point out that the Regents and the new Chancellor could easily accept a more flexible, decentralized, and human "free university." (I don't mean that they *will,* for the Bourbons never learn and never forget.) But I don't think that University truth is acceptable in our society, any more than the democratic action of the Free Speech Movement is *finally* acceptable.

I mentioned these things to a couple of liberal Regents and

they turned pale. The new Chancellor didn't seem to relish them either—maybe I am wrong. And since the students asked me to address them, I talked about them at a mass meeting on campus. (It was an unnerving scene: the planes kept roaring over my head on their way across the Pacific to Vietnam.) To my judgment, the students did not dig what I was saying; they do not have much memory of the tradition of the West. They know what freedom is—yes, they do—but they don't really know what a University is. Kind of to encourage them, I told them of two ancient examples, where revolt in the University led to great social revolutions. First, the Averroists, the new science, the rediscovered Aristotle: this was squelched and "harmonized" after a fierce struggle at Paris, yet it persisted and brought on, at Padua, the heroic age of modern science; it took less than 400 years! And it took only 250 years for the University revolt of Wyclif and Hus to bring on the University-led Reformation.

The Berkeley students didn't much relish the thought of Hus at the stake, but they were crazy for the Wyclifites at Oxford standing on the ramparts and fighting off the King with bows and arrows.

February 1965

The Berkeley Free Speech Movement caught Goodman's imagination, and he was delighted when *Dissent* asked him to cover it on the spot. *Dissent* (Spring 1965).

A
Young
Pacifist

My son, Mathew Ready Goodman, was killed mountain-climbing on August 8, 1967, age 20. Burton Weiss, a close friend of his at Cornell, has sent me an account of Matty's political activities there—to which I will preface some memories of his similar activities before he went to college. Matty was essentially an unpolitical person; his absorbing intellectual interest was in sciences—in which he had gifts, and he wanted to live and let live in a community of friends—at which he remarkably succeeded. Nevertheless, he was continually engaged in political actions, against war and irrational authority. This pattern is common to many hundreds, and in increasing numbers, of brave and thoughtful young people these days; it is worthwhile to describe it in a typical example. In any case, the group at Cornell—Burt, Jerry Franz, Tom Bell, Bruce Dancis, and a few others whom I did not know personally—have managed to make that unlikely school one of the most radical in the country, with a strongly characteristic style: undoctrinaire yet activist, deeply communitarian and imbued with an extraordinary honesty and good faith. In this group, Matty was an important spirit.

145

Emotionally, from early childhood, Matty's pacifism was certainly related to his unusual protectiveness of his many animals. He identified with their lives. I remember him and his mother medicating and sometimes saving sick little turtles, tropical fish, white rats. Yet there was nothing squeamish or sentimental in his attitude. If he needed to feed his lizards, he calmly caught flies, tore their wings off and offered them; but otherwise he would not kill a fly but adroitly catch it and let it out the door. He gave up fishing around age 10 and began to rescue the fish and return them to the river. Mostly he liked just to watch the fish and pond life, for hours, in their natural habitat.

More intellectually, he was an ardent conservationist, indignant at the spoliation, opposed to insecticides. The focus of his scientific interests (in my opinion) was ecology, the community of living things in the appropriate environment. And in method he strongly favored—so far as the distinction can be made—naturalistic observation, letting things be, rather than experimenting and imposing programs. These were also his political biases.

My first political recollection of him is when, in junior high school, he called my attention to corporation advertising being used in his class. He collected the evidence and we succeeded, temporarily, in having it expelled. This involved his being called down and rebuked by the principal.

During his first year at Bronx Science High School he wrote a report on the life of Gandhi, who impressed him deeply. For a reason known only to himself, he took to fasting one day a week—and continued this sporadically later.

He was active in the antibomb protests in 1960-62. He used to take part in the "General Strike For Peace" thought up by Julian Beck. Since people were supposed to leave off work for a day and picket for peace, Matty took off from school and picketed the Board of Education on Livingston Street. Naturally he was captured as a truant and I had to go and rescue him. This was one of the few moments of pure delight I have ever had in the peace movement.

He was at the Times Square demonstration against the bomb-testing when the police rode their horses into the crowd. Matty was in the line of fire and came home shaken, saying, "This is serious."

As a junior in high school, he refused to take part in a shelter drill and he and three others who would not recant were suspended.

But there was considerable newspaper publicity and they were reinstated and allowed to stand aside during the drills, which were soon discontinued. His reasons for nonparticipation were (1) the shelters were unscientific, (2) the drill was an insult to intelligence in its form and (3) it predisposed to accepting nuclear war.

When reinstated, he was told he had a black mark on his record. I wrote to Admissions at Harvard asking if this was a disadvantage; when we received the expected reply that it would rather be judged as a sign of critical independence, Matty had the letter copied off and distributed around Bronx Science—which sorely needed the nudge.

By now he was a seasoned radical and when he was again threatened with punishment for pasting antiwar stickers in the school subway station, he faced down the administration by pointing out that the subway was not in its jurisdiction.

At age 15 he and other high-school students formed a city-wide association to protest against nuclear war. This came to nothing.

When he applied for admission to Cornell, Professor Milton Konvitz phoned me in alarm that he was likely to be rejected because he had sent a photo of himself with uncombed hair. Matty said, "If they don't want me as I really look, they can keep their lousy school." They admitted him anyway, but sometimes they may have regretted not following their routine impulse. Matty loved Cornell and therefore fought it tooth and nail.

At 18, he refused to register for the draft. I shall return to this later, but I recall that, the following summer, he distributed antiwar leaflets in front of the Army recruiting station in St. Johnsbury, Vermont, near where we have a summer home. This made me anxious, since of course he had no draft card. But he explained, "I can't live in fear every day. I must act as I ordinarily would." My guess is that he loved St. Johnsbury and wanted to redeem it for having a recruiting station.

II.

Burt Weiss writes as follows about Matty at Cornell (my own comments are in brackets):

"Students for Education, SFE, organized themselves in late February, 1965. Matty was in almost from the beginning. He was most active in the Grading Committee, whose only proposal he and I hammered out. The S-U option in it has since come to be offered in much weakened form by most of the Cornell colleges.

[In fact, insisting on another option in the proposal, Matty got his professors not to grade him at all, or to keep his grades secret from him. Later, to his annoyance, he found his name on the Dean's list, and crossed it out with a crayon and complained.]

"Astonishingly, Mathew attended all meetings and rallies of SFE and its steering committee. Such an attendance record was unique for him. He had little toleration for contentious political meetings, especially when the contention was made by those he loved. When he guessed that a meeting was likely to be angry and unfruitful, he usually stayed home. If he went despite his guess, or if the angry mood of a meeting took him by surprise, he left early. Several times, when he stuck it out, he was moved to the point of tears or actually cried. I loved him then very much, and respected his ability to mourn. He mourned that people were acting stupidly, timidly, or dishonestly. He mourned the sudden vanishing of community spirit.

"Later that spring, Matty took part in the 24-hour vigil in the Arts Quad and in the walkout while Rockefeller was speaking at the centennial celebration. Nobody got in trouble for either of these actions. But then came the Harriman lecture and the resulting fracas was widely reported in the press. Before Harriman spoke, he received the enclosed letter written by Matty and Jerry Franz. [The letter complains that official spokesmen evade real questions and warns that the students will insist on real answers. Harriman's behavior did turn out to be insulting to college-level intelligence and the students sat down around him.]

"In May came the sitdown—to block the ROTC review in Barton Hall. All (70) participants were prosecuted by the University, but Matty and Jerry walked out of the hearing before the Faculty Committee on Student Conduct. Here, according to the Cornell *Sun,* is what they said: 'The members of the group made a definite commitment to stand by each other if there was anything like differential punishment. Tonight they went back on their commitment. The group agreed that it was necessary to have a collective hearing so that past offenses could not be taken into account. Tonight the group agreed to let them take past offenses into account. Therefore we can no longer be associated.' They were summarily suspended, but reinstated when they appeared, just the two of them, at the next meeting of the Committee. They were placed on Disciplinary Probation.

"That was the exciting spring. We kept rushing about in no particular direction, although everything we did seemed to be of a piece. Most important things happened late at night, leaflet-writing, mimeographing, emergency meetings, passionate revelatory dialogue among friends.

"During our months in Europe—fall of '65—Matty had little to do with politics. One day in Paris—I think it was an International Day of Protest, Oct. 1965—he picketed the American Embassy. He had expected to meet others there. As it turned out, he was all alone, but picketed anyway. In Seville we went to see the American consul to register our protest against the Vietnam war. We did nothing to end the war, but did get a good idea of the sort of person who is appointed to American consulships.

"At Cornell in the spring of 1966, Matty and some friends founded the Young Anarchists. The group never did much, but it put out some neat broadsides. Nevertheless, as I later learned by accident, the very existence of a group of that name intimidated the administration and extensive files were kept, including glossy blown-up photos of every member.

[It is touching that I, a long-time anarchist, never heard of these Young Anarchists from my son.]

"In May a hundred students sat in at President Perkins' office to protest against Cornell's complicity with Selective Service. Matty was one of the first seven to get there and so was able to enter the presidential suite before the campus police locked the doors. The latecomers were kept in the corridor. Only the 'inner seven' were prosecuted by the University. The Undergraduate Judiciary Board, composed entirely of students, voted 'no action' and made us all proud. The Faculty Committee, however, changed this to 'reprimand.'

"The day after the sit-in, the University Faculty met in special session to discuss the relation between Cornell and Selective Service. As faculty members entered the meeting, they were handed 'A Plea Against Military Influence at Cornell,' written by Matty and Jerry.

"In the last year of his life, Matty was deeply involved with two groups, Young Friends and the Ithaca We Won't Go group. He was committed to the people in these groups and to the fraternal and community spirit among them. This was the only time since SFE that he was so committed.

"In the fall Matty helped organize the Five-Day Fast for Peace, explained in the enclosed leaflet that Matty helped to write. The fast was very successful in terms of the number who participated, the interest and sympathy roused on campus and in town, and the amount of money raised for medical aid [for North and South Vietnamese]. For some reason Matty gradually became the chief PR man for Young Friends. He was rather inept in that position.

[Again, I was surprised to learn of his Quaker connections. His mother and I had never been able to interest him in religion at all, even to read the Bible as literature.]

"Also that fall, Matty, Tom Bell, and I began talking about starting a local draft resistance group. The group grew slowly and beautifully, just as Tom Bell explained in *New Left Notes* last March. When Matty returned from inter-session in February, he was excited about the possibilities for mass draft-card destruction, and the desirability of starting on April 15 in New York. Everybody was interested, yet nobody seemed moved to action. Finally, Jan Flora and I were startled to realize how soon it would be April 15. We called Matty, rounded up a small meeting, and decided to go ahead. I was going to New York later that night and so I was asked to find out what people there thought. You were the first person I saw. The rest you know.

[I tried to rally help for them by a letter, to academics who had signed Vietnam ads in the *Times,* of which Matty distributed six thousand copies. On April 15, about 160 students burned their cards in the Sheep Meadow. Matty, who had no card, held up a sign—"20 Years Unregistered."

[And proud Matty would have been on October 16, that so

many who were leaders of the 1500 who turned in their cards had been his fellows in the Sheep Meadow on April 15.]

"For Matty, the most painful occurrence in connection with the draft-card destruction was the breakdown of community spirit that it, and the Easter Peace Bridge demonstration, occasioned in Young Friends. SDS was soliciting pledges in the student union. The Proctor was citing those responsible to appear before the Judiciary boards and suspending those who refused to give their names. Matty and others tried to get Young Friends to solicit the same pledges at their own table, in solidarity with fellow war-resisters. At first Young Friends went along, but then began to talk about backing out. At about the same time, Matty saw the official 'instructions' for the Easter demonstration at the Peace Bridge, in which Young Friends, including Epi and himself, had planned to participate. This document had nothing to do with love, fellowship, or respect for the individuality and holy spirit in every person, what Matty conceived to be the essence of Quakerism. There were strict rules governing both the demonstration itself and the personal behavior and attire of the participation. Worse, the document advised male participants to bring along their draft cards to show at the border. The whole thing made Matty sick. Yet his feelings seemed to be shared by only a minority of Young Friends. The group was falling apart in front of his eyes. . . .

"Matty had planned to go to Brazil this summer as part of a Cornell anthropological project. His main purpose, as he explained at the first meeting, would have been to work politically with Brazilian students and thereby help to foster an international community of radical students.

[This project was abandoned when, at the disclosure of C.I.A. tampering with American students, the Brazilian students had to dis-invite the Cornellians. Matty told me that previous South American trips had been exciting and useful. He had worked hard learning Portuguese.

[When Brazil was closed off, Matty at once proposed that the entire group should go to Cuba; this would be a reasonable and necessary retaliation to the C.I.A. system and was also worthwhile in itself. Dr. William Rogers, who was the director of the project, has written me as follows: "I won't detail the debate that followed

Matty's proposal. It was the age-old struggle of the soul between the single act of moral purity and courage, and the prudential and tactical considerations of effectiveness. We spoke of Jesus' parable of the Pearl of Great Price. Was this act the pearl for which a man will sell all that he has, in order to possess it? Matty, with an eschatological sense akin to the New Testament, seemed to think so. Considerations of the future did not weigh heavily with him. The important thing was to be moral, thoroughly moral, now. How much longer can we wait?'' Unfortunately, Matty did not persuade them.]

"Early in the spring Matty took part—as who did not?— in the riotous demonstration which defeated the DA when he came on campus to suppress the sale of the literary magazine. Matty's battle-cry was entirely his own: 'Fuck you, Thaler,' he said to that unfortunate man's face.

"Later in the spring he made it his business to operate the printing press in the We Won't Go office. He intended, next year, to spend considerable time there doing routine work."

On August 7, Matty and I drove down from Expo in Montreal, where we had attended the Hiroshima Day youth rally. In his sleeping bag Matty had hidden some contraband, a book of short stories bought at the Cuban pavilion as a gift for his teacher in a course on Mexican revolutionary novels. However, we decided to declare it, in order that the book might be seized and burned and we could complain to Robert Kennedy. The Customs offices obligingly acted up in the face of our high literary disdain, so we had fun planning our indignant letter. Next day Matty died on the mountain, but I have sent the letter.

III.

Matty refused to register for the draft on general pacifist grounds—the subsequent worsening of the Vietnam war merely confirmed what he already knew.

His method of refusal was not to recognize the draft system at all and to continue as usual, including, of course, his overt antiwar activity—now without a draft card. In fact, he stepped up this activity, but I think this was because of Vietnam rather than to force a showdown. I never saw any sign that he courted going to jail. He did not regard himself as a Witness in any way. On the other hand, he was entirely too open to live "underground." And the "tactical approach," of trying for C.O. or accepting II-S in order to carry on revolutionary activity, was also against his disposition: he could not live on an ambiguous basis. Besides, he believed it was bad politics; his enthusiasm for the mass draft-card burning meant that he believed in open massive noncooperation and active nonviolent resistance. His eyes twinkled at the idea of "nonviolent terrorism": if one is arrested, five others burn their cards on the courthouse steps.

The F.B.I. first got in touch with him in November 1966, purportedly about a classmate applying for C.O., for whom Matty had agreed to be a reference! (This was part of his "business as usual.") They visited him as a nonregistrant in March 1967 and set the wheels of prosecution going.

Matty's approach—to "do nothing"—is appropriate, in my opinion, only to young people who are sure of their own integrity and the human use of their own developing careers, who just need to be let be. Matty had this confidence. Besides, he was a balky animal: he would have found it impossibly humiliating, paralyzing, to try to move his feet toward anything he strongly disbelieved in, such as filling out a draft form. He was not, in my experience, "rebellious," defiant of authority as such. But he had learned that authority was very often irrational, petty, dishonest and sometimes not benevolent, so he was antiauthoritarian. (The school administrations he had dealt with were certainly not models of magnanimity, American democracy or even simple honor; and these are the only officials that a growing boy knows, unless he is a juvenile delinquent or on relief.) Matty was also unusually stubborn in general. He had to do things his own way, at his own pace, according to his own slowly developing concern or fantasy. This was often too slow for other people's wishes, including mine, but there was no hurrying him. Once he cared, he acted with energy and determination.

He refused to be a leader—at Cornell, as at Berkeley in its best days, leadership was regarded as a poor form of social organization. Yet it is clear in the above accounts that Matty often did lead. But this was because he acted according to his own inner belief, without ambition or ideology. He was frank, loyal and consistent, and his integrity was legendary. If, in an action, he was among the first, or seemed to be the most intransigeant and unwilling to compromise, it was not that he was brash or doctrinaire, but because of some elementary human principle. Naturally, then, others found security in him and went along. So far as I can discover, he had no enemies. Even administrators liked him personally and have sent me touching letters of condolence. His lust for community seems to have been equal to my own, but he had more luck with it.

After he became seriously illegal at 18 he, like others in a similar plight, showed signs of anxiety, a certain tightness, a certain hardness. This roused my indignation more than anything else, that the brute mechanical power of the State was distorting the lives of these excellent youth. For nothing. For far worse than nothing—abstract conformity, empty power, overseas murder. Nevertheless, in Matty's case at least, his formula of dismissing fear and acting as he ordinarily would, seemed to work spectacularly. Once he had made the hard choice, he threw himself into all his activities with increased enthusiasm; new energy was released and during this period—whatever the causal relationship—he embarked on an uninterrupted and pretty happy love affair with Epi Epton, who shared his convictions; this of course must have immensely increased his security, assertiveness and courage.

As I said at the outset, Matty was not essentially political; he was politically active only by duty, on principle. Rather he was a daring swimmer, a good handball player. He ground his own telescopes. He jeopardized his nonexistent II-S deferment and took off for Europe for a semester. He had found a method of meditation that suited him. Hungry for music, he sat for hours at the piano and was in charge of selecting the records in the library. He was an Honors student in anthropology and he was, I am told by Professor Joseph Calvo and Dr. Elizabeth Keller, beginning to do original work in genetics. But his political activity also blessed him with friends and community.

My own hope was that, after he was arrested, he would—having fought through to the end—skip bail and go to Canada, since jail did not seem to be the best environment for him. He said he would make up his mind when it was necessary. He had looked into it and made connections so that it would be possible for him to work politically in Canada.

Every pacifist career is individual, a unique balance of forces, including the shared hope that other human beings will become equally autonomous. Most people want peace and freedom, but there are no pacifist or anarchist masses.

As I tearfully review my son's brief pacifist career, the following seems to have been his philosophy: He had a will to protect life in all its forms and to conserve the conditions for it. With this, he had a kind of admiring trust in the providence of natural arrangements and liked to gaze at them. He felt that human beings too could form a natural and wise community and he was daringly loyal to this possibility. He was astonished to see people act with timidity, pettiness or violence. Yet he was not naive. He knew that people in power and people bureaucratized are untrustworthy and one has to be prepared for their stupidity and dishonesty and confront them. (I don't know if he thought that people as such could be malevolent.) As for himself, he felt that there was plenty of time to brood and mull and observe and wait for the spirit; it did not delay, and there was no need for pressuring or forcing votes. What he himself could do to help was to be open to the facts, honest in speech and as consistent as possible. When a practical idea occurred to him, it was never complicated or dilatory, but always a simplification and a way of immediately coming across.

It is a beautiful soul we have lost, who behaved well and had a good influence.

Perhaps the proudest moment in Goodman's life was on April 15, 1967, when his son Mathew joined about 160 other students who burned their draft cards in Central Park. Mathew, who had no draft card, held a big placard: "Twenty Years Unregistered." That summer Mathew was killed in a mountain-climbing accident in New Hampshire. Goodman never really recovered from the loss. His son's gravestone, surrounded by others decorated with American Legion flags, honoring those killed in Vietnam and our other wars, still bears Mathew's slogan: "20 Years Unregistered." From *Liberation* (September-October 1967).

A
Causerie
at
the
Military-Industrial

The National Security Industrial Association (NSIA) was founded in 1944 by James Forrestal, to maintain and enhance the beautiful wartime communication between the armament industries and the government. At present it comprises 400 members, including of course all the giant aircraft, electronics, motors, oil, and chemical corporations, but also many one would not expect: not only General Dynamics, General Motors, and General Telephone and Electronics, but General Foods and General Learning; not only Sperry Rand, RCA, and Lockheed, but Servco and Otis Elevators. It is a wealthy club. The military budget is $84 billion.

At the recent biennial symposium, held on October 18 and 19 in the State Department auditorium, the theme was "Research and Development in the 1970s." To my not unalloyed pleasure, I was invited to participate as one of the seventeen speakers and assigned the topic "Planning for the Socio-Economic Environment." Naturally I could make the usual speculations about why I was thus "co-opted." I doubt that they expected to pick my brains for any profitable ideas. But it is useful for feeders at the public trough to present an image of wide-ranging discussion. It is comfortable to be able to say, "You see? these far-outniks are impractical." And business meetings are dull and I am notoriously stimulating. But the letter of invitation from Henri Busignies of ITT, the chairman of the symposium committee, said only, "Your accomplishments throughout your distinguished career eminently qualify you to speak with authority on the subject."

What is an intellectual man to do in such a case? I agree with the Gandhian principle, always cooperate, within the limits of honor, truth, and justice. But how to cooperate with the military-industrial club! during the Vietnam war 1967! It was certainly not the time to reason about basic premises, as is my usual approach, so I decided simply to confront them and soberly tell them off.

Fortunately it was the week of the demonstration at the Pentagon, when there would be thousands of my friends in Washington. So I tipped them off and thirty students from Cornell and Harpur drove down early to picket the auditorium, with a good leaflet about the evil environment for youth produced by the military corporations. When they came, the white helmets sprang up, plus the cameras and reporters. In the face of this dangerous invasion, the State Department of the United States was put under security, the doors were bolted, and the industrialists [and I] were not allowed to exit—on the 23rd Street side. Inside, I spoke as follows:

R&D FOR THE SOCIO-ECONOMIC ENVIRONMENT OF THE 1970S

I am astonished that at a conference on planning for the future, you have not invited a single speaker under the age of thirty, the group that is going to live in that future. I am pleased that some of the young people have come to pound on the door anyway, but it is too bad that they aren't allowed to come in.

This is a bad forum for this topic. Your program mentions the "emerging national goals" of urban development, continuing education, and improving the quality of man's environment. I would add another essential goal, reviving American democracy; and at least two indispensable international goals, to rescue the majority of mankind from deepening poverty, and to insure the survival of mankind as a species. These goals indeed require research and experimentation of the highest sophistication, but not by you. You people are unfitted by your commitments, your experience, your customary methods, your recruitment, and your moral disposition. You are the military industrial of the United States, the most dangerous body of men at the present in the world, for you not only implement our disastrous policies but are an overwhelming lobby for them, and you expand and rigidify the wrong use of brains, resources, and labor so that change becomes difficult. Most likely the trends you represent will be interrupted by a shambles of riots, alienation, ecological catastrophes, wars, and revolutions, so that current long-range planning, including this conference, is irrelevant. But if we ask what *are* the technological needs and what ought to be researched in this coming period, in the six areas I have mentioned, the best service that you people could perform is rather rapidly to phase yourselves out, passing on your relevant knowledge to people better qualified, or reorganizing yourselves with entirely different sponsors and commitments, so that you learn to think and feel in a different way. Since you are most of the R & D that there is, we cannot do without you as people, but we cannot do with you as you are.

In aiding technically underdeveloped regions, the need in the foreseeable future is for an intermediate technology, scientifically sophisticated but tailored to their local skills, tribal or other local social organization, plentiful labor force, and available raw materials. The aim is to help them out of starvation, disease, and drudgery without involving them in an international cash nexus of an entirely different order of magnitude. Let them take off at their own pace and in their own style. For models of appropriate technical analyses, I recommend you to E.F. Schumacher, of the British Coal Board, and his associates. Instead, you people—and your counterparts in Europe and Russia—have been imposing your technology, seducing native elites mostly corrupted by Western education, arming them, indeed often using them as a dumping ground for obsolete weapons. As Dr. Busignies pointed out yesterday, your aim must be, while maintaining leadership, to allow very little technical gap, in order to do business. Thus, you have involved these people in a wildly inflationary economy, have driven them into instant urbanization, and increased the amount of disease and destitution. You have disrupted ancient social patterns, debauched their cultures, fomented tribal and other wars, and in Vietnam yourselves engaged in genocide. You have systematically entangled them in Great Power struggles. It is not in your interest, and you do not have the minds or the methods, to take these peoples seriously as people.

The survival of the human species, at least in a civilized state, demands radical disarmament, and there are several feasible political means to achieve this if we willed it. By the same token, we must drastically de-energize the archaic system of nation-states, e.g. by internationalizing space exploration, expanding operations like the international Geophysical Year, de-nationalizing Peace Corps and aid programs, opening scientific information and travel. Instead, you—and your counterparts in Europe, Russia, and China—have rigidified and aggrandized the states with a Maginot-line kind of policy called Deterrence, which has continually escalated rather than stabilized. As Jerome Wiesner has demonstrated, past a certain point your operations have increased insecurity rather than diminished it. But this has been to your interest. Even in the present condition of national rivalry, it has been estimated, by Marc Raskin who sat in on the National Security Council, that the real needs of our defense should cost less than a fourth of the budget you have pork-barreled. You tried, unsuccessfully, to saddle us with the scientifically ludicrous Civil Defense program. You have sabotaged the technology of inspection for disarmament. Now you are saddling us with the anti-missile missiles and the multi-warhead missiles (MIRV). You have corrupted the human adventure of space with programs for armed platforms in orbit. Although we are the most heavily armed and the most naturally protected of the Great Powers, you have seen to it that we spend a vastly greater amount and perhaps a higher' proportion of our wealth on armaments than any other nation.

This brings me to your effect on the climate of the economy. The wealth of a nation is to provide useful goods and services, with an emphasis first on necessities and broad-spread comforts, simply as a decent background for un-economic life and culture; an indefinitely expanding economy is a rat-race. There ought to be an even spread regionally, and no group must be allowed to fall outside of society. At present, thanks to the scientific ingenuity and hard work of previous generations, we could in America allow a modest livelihood to everyone as a constitutional right. And on the other hand, as the young have been saying by their style and actions, there is an imperative need to simplify the standard of living, since the affluent standard has become frivolous, tawdry, and distracting from life itself. But you people have distorted the structure of a rational economy. Since 1945, half of new investment has gone into your products, not subject to the market nor even to Congressional check. This year, 86 percent of money for research is for your arms and rockets. You push through the colossally useless Super-Sonic Transport. At least 20 percent of the economy is directly dependent on your enterprises. The profits and salaries of these enterprises are not normally distributed but go heavily to certain groups while others are excluded to the point of being out-caste. Your system is a major factor in producing the riots in Newark. [*At this remark there were indignant protests.*]

Some regions of the country are heavily favored—especially Pasadena and Dallas—and others disadvantaged. Public goods have been neglected. A disproportionate share of brains has been drained from more useful invention and development. And worst of all, you have enthusiastically supported an essentially mercantilist economics that measures economic health in terms of abstract Gross National Product and rate of growth, instead of concrete human well-being. Both domestically and internationally, you have been the bellwether of meaningless expansion, and this has sharpened poverty in our own slums and rural regions and for the majority of mankind. It has been argued that military expenditure, precisely because it is isolated and wasteful, is a stabilizer of an economy, providing employment and investment opportunities when necessary; but your unbridled expansion has been the chief factor of social instability.

Dramatically intervening in education, you have again disrupted the normal structure. Great universities have come to be financed largely for your programs. Faculties have become unbalanced; your kind of people do not fit into the community of scholars. The wandering dialogue of science with the unknown is straitjacketed for petty military projects. You speak increasingly of the need for personal creativity, but this is not to listen to the Creator Spirit for ideas, but to harness it to your ideas. This is blasphemous. There has been secrecy, which is intolerable to true academics and scientists. The political, and morally dubious co-opting of science, engineering, and social science has disgusted and alienated many of the best students. Further, you have warped the method of education, beginning with the primary grades. Your need for narrowly expert personnel has led to processing the young to be test-passers, with a gross exaggeration of credits and grading. You have used the wealth of the public and parents to train apprentices for yourselves. Your electronics companies have gone into the "education industries" and tried to palm off teaching machines, audio-visual aids, and programmed lessons in excess of the evidence for their utility. But the educational requirements of our society in the foreseeable future demand a very different spirit and method. Rather than processing the young, the problem is how to help the young grow up free and inventive in a highly scientific and socially complicated world. We do not need professional personnel so much as autonomous professionals who can criticize the programs handed to them and be ethically responsible. Do you encourage criticism of your programs by either the subsidized professors or the students? [*At this, Mr. Charles Herzfeld, the chairman of the meeting, shouted, "Yes!" and there was loud applause for the interruption, yet I doubt that there is much such encouragement.*] We need fewer lessons and tests, and there ought to be much less necessity and prestige attached to mandarin requirements.

Let us turn to urbanism. *Prima facie,* there are parts of urban planning—construction, depollution, the logistics of transportation—where your talents ought to be peculiarly useful. Unfortunately, it is your companies who have oversold the planes and the cars, polluted the air and water, and balked at even trivial remedies, so that I do not see how you can be morally trusted with the job. The chief present and future problems in this field, however, are of a different kind. They are two. The long-range problem is to diminish the urbanization and suburban sprawl altogether, for they are economically unviable and socially harmful. For this, the most direct means, and the one I favor, is to cut down rural emigration and encourage rural return, by means of rural reconstruction and regional cultural development. The aim should be a 20 percent rural ratio instead of the present 5 percent. This is an aspect of using high technology for simplification, increasing real goods but probably diminishing the Gross National Product measured in cash. Such a program is not for you. Your thinking is never to simplify and retrench, but always to devise new equipment to alleviate the mess that you have helped to make with your previous equipment.

Secondly, the immediately urgent urban problem is how to diminish powerlessness, anomie, alienation, and mental disease. For this the best strategy is to decentralize urban administration, in policing, schooling, social welfare, neighborhood renewal, and real-estate and business ownership. Such community development often requires heightening conflict and risking technical inefficiency for intangible gains of initiative and solidarity. This also is obviously not your style. You want to concentrate capital and power. Your systems analyses of social problems always tend toward standardization, centralization, and bureaucratic control, although these are not necessary in the method. You do not like to feed your computers indefinite factors and unknown parameters where spirit, spite, enthusiasm, revenge, invention, etc., will make the difference. To be frank, your programs are usually grounded in puerile theories of social psychology, political science, and moral philosophy. There is a great need for research and trying out in this field, but the likely cast of characters might be small farmers, Negro matriarchs, political activists, long-haired students, and assorted sages. Not you. Let's face it. You are essentially producers of exquisite hardware and good at the logistics of moving objects around, but mostly with the crude aim of destroying things rather than reconstructing or creating anything, which is a harder task. Yet you boldly enter into fields like penology, pedagogy, hospital management, domestic architecture, and planning the next decade—wherever there is a likely budget.

I will use the last heading, improving the quality of man's environment, as a catch-all for some general remarks. In a society that is cluttered, overcentralized, and overadministered, we should aim at simplification, decentralization, and decontrol. These require highly sophisticated research to determine where, how, and how much. Further, for the first time in history, the scale of the artificial and technological has dwarfed the natural landscape. In prudence, we must begin to think of a principled limitation on artifice and to cut back on some of our present gigantic impositions, if only to insure that we do not commit some terrible ecological blunder. But as Dr. Smelt of Lockheed explained to us yesterday, it is the genius of American technology to go very rapidly from R & D to application: in this context, he said, prudence is not a virtue. A particular case is automation: which human functions should be computerized or automated, which should not? This question—it is both an analytic and an empirical one—ought to be critical in the next decade, but I would not trust IBM salesmen to solve it. Another problem is how man can feel free and at home within the technological environment itself. For instance, comprehending a machine and being able to repair it is one thing; being a mere user and in bondage to service systems is another. Also, to feel free, a man must have a rather strong say in the close environment that he must deal with. But these requirements of a technology are not taken into account by you. Despite Dr. Smelt, technology *is* a branch of moral philosophy, subordinate to criteria like prudence, modesty, safety, amenity, flexibility, cheapness, easy comprehension, repairability, and so forth. If such moral criteria became paramount in the work of technologists, the quality of the environment would be more livable.

Still a further problem is how to raise the scientific and technical culture of the whole people, and here your imperialistic grab of the R & D money and of the system of education has done immeasurable damage. You have seen to it that the lion's share has gone to your few giant firms and a few giant universities, although in fact very many, perhaps more than half of, important innovations still come from independents and tiny firms. I was pleased that Dr. Dessauer of Xerox pointed this out this morning. If the money were distributed more widely, there would probably be more discovery and invention, and what is more important, there would be a larger pool of scientific and competent people. You make a fanfare about the spinoff of a few socially useful items, but your whole enterprise is notoriously wasteful—for instance, five billions go down the drain when after a couple of years you change the design of a submarine, sorry about that. When you talk about spinoff, you people remind me of the TV networks who, after twenty years of nothing, boast that they did broadcast the McCarthy hearings and the Kennedy funeral. [*This remark led to free and friendly laughter; I do not know whether at the other industry or at their own hoax.*] Finally, concentrating the grants, you narrow the field of discovery and innovation, creating an illusion of technological determinism, as if we *had* to develop in a certain style. But if we had put our brains and money into electric cars, we would now have electric cars; if we had concentrated on intensive agriculture, we would now find that this is the most efficient, and so forth. And in grabbing the funds, you are not even honest; 90 percent of the R & D money goes in fact to shaping up for production, which as entrepreneurs you should pay out of your own pockets.

No doubt some of these remarks have been unfair and ignorant. [*Frantic applause.*] By and large they are undeniable, and I have not been picking nits.

These remarks have certainly been harsh and moralistic. We are none of us saints, and ordinarily I would be ashamed to use such a tone. But you are the manufacturers of napalm, fragmentation bombs, the planes that destroy rice. Your weapons have killed hundreds of thousands in Vietnam and you will kill other hundreds of thousands in other Vietnams. I am sure that most of you would concede that much of what you do is ugly and harmful, at home and abroad. But you would say that it is necessary for the American way of life, at home and abroad, and therefore you cannot do otherwise. Since we believe, however, that that way of life itself is unnecessary, ugly, and un-American [*Shouts of "Who are we?"*]—we are I and those people outside—we cannot condone your present operations; they should be wiped off the slate.

Most of the 300 in the audience did not applaud these remarks, but there was quite strong applause from a couple of dozen. Afterward these sought me out singly and explained, "Thanks for having the courage" or more significantly, "Those kids outside are right. My son is doing the same thing in Boston—Ohio State—etc."

The chairman of the session, Charles Herzfeld of ITT, felt obliged to exclaim, "The remark about our committing genocide in Vietnam is obscene. He does not say what is really intolerable there, the Viet Cong single out college graduates for extermination."!!

More poignantly, the director of the symposium, a courteous and intelligent man, apologized to the gathering for having exposed them to me, which must have been a wrench for him to say. He had of course seen my text beforehand.

We went out by the exit onto the other avenue, and I was able to rejoin the more amiable company of the young people, who were now sitting with their backs pressed against the auditorium doors, still among the white helmets. I answered their questions about the proceedings and we dispersed.

This famous speech was delivered face-to-face with the top brass of America's war economy, assembled in Washington for their biennial meetings, the same week as the March on the Pentagon. First published in *The New York Review of Books* (November 23, 1967).

The
Duty
of
Professionals

I.

The idea of resistance is to make it impossible for society to continue a bad routine—and to awaken its better judgment. We assume that the Americans do not "really" will the Vietnam war but are morally asleep and brainwashed. If in fact they are so complacent, arrogant or callous that they do will it or don't care about it, we have to talk not about resistance but exile, going underground or civil war. But it seems to us, rather, that there has been usurpation by a hidden government which makes policy, and that an awakened populace can throw it off.

Violence and Resistance

The presence or absence of violence in such populist resistance is not of the essence, but the amount of violence is important and the purpose of the violence *is* of the essence. The body politic does not consist of clashing billiard balls; one cannot change minds and will by physical attack. Physically attacked, a policeman or soldier responds routinely with tear gas and bayonet, but the aim is to get him to respond as man and fellow citizen. Nevertheless, if resis-

166

tance is determined and especially if it is massive, there is bound to be a certain amount of violence. Let me spell this out.

(1) In the first place, confronted by people who say and act, "To the best of our ability we won't let you continue," a soldier or policeman, or the draft board or Dean who summons them, is bound at first to respond routinely as if attacked. The hope is that if we persist they cannot continue, because people do not really *mean* the whole package: so many jailed, hurt, gassed—police on the campus, martial law, the social atmosphere poisoned. They will have to think it over.

(2) But given the complacency, callousness and sheepishness of any people, and certainly of the Americans, there is unfortunately an advantage to a certain amount of violence; it wakes people up and makes them understand that the matter is serious. We see that the TV and press mainly want to notice incidents of violence. It seems that in nonviolent civil-rights protests it did not hurt to have some Black Panthers in the Wings.[1] Authorities will initiate the violence anyway if they feel threatened; the question is what is the right amount of provocation. If there is none, people are not really awakened and authorities sink back into another routine of carting off limp bodies. If there is too much, people do not think it over but promptly become routinely violent, which is second nature to them anyway. Certainly we do not *want* to frighten, panic or compel anybody.

(3) In a massive demonstration there is bound, mathematically, to be sporadic violence. In the heated atmosphere of crowds and troops of police and soldiers there is plenty of fear and panic on both sides. Almost invariably the police lose their cool first and one thing leads to another, but this is understandable, for they begin in a passive state, they are outnumbered, and they have no conviction or idea about what they are for. Having set up merely formal boundaries that are spontaneously disregarded by excited people, policemen panic and become brutal. Morally, in my opinion, this sporadic violence is neither right nor wrong, though sad. The

[1] Probably, in the South, threatened black violence is even a stabilizing factor, securing the rules of fair play. But this is in counties where black and white are approximately equal in numbers, and in the framework of federal intervention if there is massive violent repression. There is nothing comparable in the peace movement.

co-presence of a mass of aroused citizens and numerous representatives of authority is an exalted experience, but it entails broken heads and ugly scenes. It would be better if smart-aleck police technicians did not also invent booby-traps and if young hot-heads did not act their age; but these things are inevitable.

(4) There are also Nazi, Birchite, Teamster counterdemonstrators, and resentful sailors spoiling for a fight. So far, at least, the evidence is that the police put these down. The TV, however, plays them up tremendously as if they were equal adversaries, though the ratio is a thousand to one.

(5) I must now turn to the violent on "our" side who are wrong in principle. First, there are those who want disorder for its own sake as part of a theory of general (world) breakdown and insurrection. These are Maoists, Trotskyists, etc., who hold that there can be no decent society except by world upheaval. They do not want the Vietnam war itself to stop—they do not believe it can stop; they prefer to aggravate it for a greater future good. This is a respectable theory; there is, unhappily, evidence for it. I profoundly disagree with it—mankind has gone this route for thousands of years—but the problem is how to cope with its presence in our demonstrations, since, as a populist, I also profoundly support the principle of excluding nobody. I don't know.

(6) And there is the violence caused by young people, Oakland style, who want to stop the Vietnam war by tiny minority putsches, "taking over" or burning down draft boards, blocking traffic, derailing troop trains, numerically draining the recruitment of soldiers sufficiently to make an appreciable difference. Some of this is a misreading of Ernesto Guevara's guerrilla tactics devised for hill country among friendly peasants. It is not, however, mere fantasy, if the guerrillas are relevant to the conditions: in a complex technology, a small group of alienated Ph.D.'s and daring helpers *can* produce a shambles. There are plenty of mad scientists and high young computers around, not all in government employment, though most. But a shambles is not "creative disorder."

But I must not lose my perspective about these activists, although they bug me. The Oakland young are not thinking about poisoning the water of American cities and causing major power failures; it is stupid to argue them to their "logical conclusions." To be a Provo pain in the neck to both the police *and* the peace movement is not a mortal sin; and perhaps such people do more good than harm by adding hugely to the accumulation of troubles to society caused by the Vietnam war. Despite the alarming editorials in the *Times,* I doubt that the Americans are outraged by them.

Nonviolent Terrorism

More attractive and potentially more effective is the opposite alternative of the young: nonviolent terrorism—for example, when a draft-card burner is arraigned, five others burn their cards in the courtroom. Such a program draws on the strongest single energy of young people today, their fantastic peer-group solidarity against irrational authority. It can be effective if the government is finally forced to meet the challenge and make widespread prosecutions; that moment, I think, is at hand.

We cannot hold back acts of indignation and outrage; they justify themselves as part of the elementary stuff of humanity. And as the last years have shown, it is hard to restrain the impatience of people who feel themselves powerless while horrors continue. Yet in general, we must use those tactics of opposition that in themselves do not prevent the reconstruction of a better society. In the end, all will have to live in community again. For this, a confronting conflict, mainly nonviolent, is better than either false peace or violence. Further, the challenge to authority is itself a creative political act in modern societies which have been vastly over-centralized and brainwashed. Best of all is to fight in groups and with methods of organization that we want to live with if we win, and to pinpoint for attack those evils that we really want to get rid of permanently.

II.

These have been commonplace topics which I repeat in order to make clear (also to myself) where I stand. Let me go on to matters closer to my own concern.

We can distinguish three kinds of necessary resistance: popular or mass resistance; citizenly or legal resistance; professional or institutional resistance. So far our movement has rapidly developed popular and legal resistance, but it has been badly lagging in professional resistance.

Big Demonstrations

October 16-21 again proved, in the cities, on the campuses and at the Pentagon, the human value of big demonstrations: the courage given by the company of like-minded thousands; the ability spontaneously to over-ride official rules and permits; above all, the heady sense of being the sovereign people, the body politic. All this is politically transistory and it often involves moral ambiguities, but it is a unique human experience and energizes all other resistance. It is *not* ineffective or "merely symbolic" (whatever that means). It is the exercise of the right of petition guaranteed by the Bill of Rights[2] and it is contagious to others as well as cementing solidarity among ourselves. Even among the

[2] Like all hoary antiquities of direct democracy, it puts the government on the spot. The government cannot suppress the right without social shock; it cannot permit it without the situation getting out of hand. This dilemma becomes the origin of new controversy—"comfort to Hanoi,", "what about our boys?" etc. The fashionable expedient is to make Byzantine rules, lie about the numbers, and assert via Hubert Humphrey that it all means nothing at all. Which opinion is then echoed by Students for a Democratic Society. But in fact what it means is what it generates, as Rosa Luxemburg knew.

The distinction between what is "symbolic" and what is "real" is a spurious one; the correct distinction is between what leads further and what does not (and to what it does lead). Consider a few years back, the mass advertisements signed by hundreds and then thousands of teachers, professionals, etc. At present at meetings these ads are referred to as the height of futility; but this betrays a short memory. When they appeared, they in fact produced a shock of excitement at how numerous we were. When the government dramatically escalated the war in the face of these "humble petitions," there was a deeper shock, the awareness of powerlessness; but this awareness was a new fact. Rhetoric changed rapidly to impatience and anger, and there is no question that this in turn both enormously increased the size of the public demonstrations—for people said, "We have to do *something*"—and led to the invention of new tactics—for people said, "We have to *do* something." Do the young militants imagine that their own involvement was not profoundly influenced and strongly encouraged by these ads? And incidentally, the professors were not simply unrealistic. Their ads had had a practical effect in stopping the bomb testing and the shelter program, for these were scientific issues in which academics wielded public authority. Now the most recent ad has been from Veterans of the Vietnam War. Almost surely this too leads somewhere, in the armed forces and in the public concern for "our boys."

police and soldiers there were cases of coming over, in Oakland and Washington. When students sat down in front of the State Department auditorium when I was telling off the gentlemen of the National Security Industrial Association (see *The New York Review of Books,* November 23, 1967), a dozen even of these representatives of the military-industrial came to me privately and said, "Those youngsters are right; my own son and daughter are doing the same." Naturally the problem is to get them to speak publicly and quit.

In my opinion, if such demonstrations continue to grow, with increasing willingness to risk jail and injury and with the self-feeding conviction of sovereignty, the usurping government in fact cannot continue its course; and its jittery alarm and excessive mobilization of troops show that it knows it. Will it then order a massacre? Or will it cede? We shall see.

The twelve hundred draft cards turned in on October 16, plus the thousands of statements of complicity and the pledges of war-tax refusal, are citizenly resistance. It goes without saying that they are statements of moral conscience, but their deliberate purpose and obvious effect is to challenge the legal structure—the system of trust, contract and compliance—that makes government possible. It is not necessary (or possible) physically to deplete the armed forces or bankrupt the Treasury. We who resist in this way are usually asserting by our challenge that we are legitimate and the government is illegitimate. And we have—though fearfully, for the penalties are severe—welcomed a test in the courts, hoping that when everything is duly and publicly aired, we shall be vindicated. The always-emerging meaning of the law will support us, just as the civil-rights trespassers became legal. Naturally the government has been loath to pick up the challenge and has tried to pick off individuals as convenient, in order to deter. From the mass draft-card burning of April 15, there has still been only one arrest (Gary Rader); and on October 16 the marshals and the Attorney General tried to refuse the turned-in cards. But here again it is clear that the climate has changed and we are getting across. Since late October there has been a flurry of subpoenas to the Grand Jury. Will the government finally order a mass trial of the draft refusers, *and include the older people who egged them on and are largely responsible anyway?* We shall see.

But occupational, professional, institutional resistance has so far been feeble. I mean action springing from what a man works at and the function he performs in the fabric of society. For many people, if not most, their vocations are what they are most deeply, what they know most about, care most about, and where they have most influence. And inevitably, in an interlocked and centralized society like ours, it is impossible to practice most vocations without connecting with the war system. Yet workers and professionals, who may resist in demonstrations and take part in civil disobedience, go on with their jobs as ordinary.

I will merely mention as the most obvious and probably most important group the unionized workmen in war industries and the scientists and engineers; these may be opposed to the war and yet they do not quit. I cannot dig this.

Faculty Resistance

Resisting academics have done better, in using faculty power against the draft tests and class listings, backing up resisting students and refusing to discipline them, and opposing war contracts. But they have not yet, to my knowledge, begun the long-overdue campaign to free the major universities from the incubus of military-industrial financing. Since the present university expansion is largely founded on this, such a campaign would be a showdown. An important case in point is the usual faculty mishandling of student protests against the Dow Chemical recruiters. Faculty members may abhor the manufacturer of napalm and the defoliants, but they hesitate to exonerate the students from discipline because of the need to preserve "free speech" or because, if the Peace Corps and Macy's and S.N.C.C. are allowed to recruit, so must Dow be allowed. But these other organizations are not an overwhelming threat to the essence of the University; the military-industrial corporations are such a threat and must be purged—just as the McCarthy witch hunt was such a threat and Harvard finally simply barred the door against it. This year eighty-six percent of the money for Research and Development is for military purposes!

The doctors who came to Dr. Levy's defense, refusing to

practice phony political medicine, did well. In general, it is a touchy question how physicians can resist: if they become politically involved, they lose the immunity which entitles them to the impartial compassion necessary for the practice of medicine altogether. Yet there must be some way for them to try to prevent the ghastly situation where useless and immoral horrors are committed and they then feebly do the best they can.

Consider, again, a typical group of professionals strongly and actively opposed to the war, the Institute for Policy Studies in Washington, of which I am an associate. Some of us, by our expertise and connections, are continually and even intimately in contact with government-policy makers. In these professional contacts, were there not opportunities for confrontation and resistance during October 16-21? One of us spoke at the Lincoln Memorial, others were in the crowd; but, in my opinion, it would have been better for a few of us to have been making it a little more lively in McNamara's or William Bundy's office, with whatever supporting voices one could muster in. Naturally such behavior might have had unpleasant professional consequences.

Professional Dissidents

My point is not that professionals should be "radicalized," but that they should come on as authentic professionals, autonomous and ethically responsible. (This is, of course, what Ralph Nader, Rachel Carson, Lewis Mumford, my brother and others have been saying.) In my opinion, it is unacceptable for a professional to deviate a jot from professional obligations and standards for even the best of causes. But since it is the genius of our society to co-opt the professions to subserve money and authority, for a professional to be authentic means to be in conflict. And since the system of institutions is interlocked and centralized, it is impossible to be in conflict without being gradually involved with general reform and even revolution. This approach to becoming revolutionary has one great advantage over "radicalization": The dissident professional has a more concrete and knowledgeable program of what needs to be done to reconstruct a decent society.

The professional dissident in his own terms is likely to be less passionately committed than the "radicalized" professional, the one who devotes himself directly to hot causes like community development, peace action, etc. But I think he tends to be more enduringly committed, and he has more far-reaching and daring ideas. If activism has no room for authentic and absorbed professionals and does not use them on their own terms, it is a loss all around.

Professionals and the Movement

Let me say a word also about professional students. The New Left has been urging students to leave school and get into the world of real conflict. This certainly makes sense for many students who are wasting their time in universities and should never have been there. But for those who are potentially authentic professionals— who are good at something and want to build livable neighborhoods, improve health, report the news, teach children, explore the unknown, find the right use of new technology—the best advice is still Prince Kropotkin's:

Think about the kind of world you want to live and work in. What do you need to know to help build that world? Demand that your teachers teach you that.

Then, in their own professional terms, most such students will also soon resist the Vietnam war and enter other areas of conflict, and may carry some of their teachers along.

First published in *Liberation* (November 1967).

How well they flew together side by side
the Stars and Stripes my red and white and blue
and my Black Flag the sovereignty of no
man or law! They were the flags of pride
and nature and advanced with equal stride
across the age when Jefferson long ago
saluted both and said, "Let Shays' men go.
If you discourage mutiny and riot
what check is there on government?"

Today

the gaudy flag is very grand on earth
and they have sewed on it a golden border,
but I will not salute it. At our rally
I see a small black rag of little worth
and touch it wistfully. Chaos is Order.

IV

THE
BLACK
FLAG
OF
ANARCHISM

Reflections
on
the
Anarchist
Principle

Anarchism is grounded in a rather definite proposition: that valuable behavior occurs only by the free and direct response of individuals or voluntary groups to the conditions presented by the historical environment. It claims that in most human affairs, whether political, economic, military, religious, moral, pedagogic, or cultural, more harm than good results from coercion, top-down direction, central authority, bureaucracy, jails, conscription, states, pre-ordained standardization, excessive planning, etc. Anarchists want to increase intrinsic functioning and diminish extrinsic power. This is a social-psychological hypothesis with obvious political implications.

Depending on varying historical conditions that present various threats to the anarchist principle, anarchists have laid their emphasis in varying places: sometimes agrarian, sometimes free-city and guild-oriented; sometimes technological, sometimes anti-technological; sometimes Communist, sometimes affirming property; sometimes individualist, sometimes collective; sometimes speaking of Liberty as almost an absolute good, sometimes relying on custom and "nature." Nevertheless, despite these differences, anarchists seldom fail to recognize one another, and they do not consider the differences to be incompatibilities. Consider a crucial modern problem, violence. Guerilla fighting has been a classical anarchist technique; yet where, especially in modern conditions, *any* violent means tends to reinforce centralism and authoritarianism, anarchists have tended to see the beauty of non-violence.

Now the anarchist principle is by and large true.[1] And far from being "utopian" or a "glorious failure," it has proved itself and won out in many spectacular historical crises. In the period of mercantilism and patents royal, free enterprise by joint stock companies was anarchist. The Jeffersonian bill of rights and independent judiciary were anarchist. Congregational churches were anarchist. Progressive education was anarchist. The free cities and corporate law in the feudal system were anarchist. At present, the civil rights movement in the United States has been almost classically decentralist and anarchist. And so forth, down to details like free access in public libraries. Of course, to later historians these things do not seem to be anarchist, but in their own time they were all regarded as such and often literally called such, with the usual dire threats of chaos. But this relativity of the anarchist principle to the actual situation is of the essence of anarchism. There *cannot* be a history of anarchism in the sense of establishing a permanent state of things called "anarchist." It is always a continual coping with the next situation, and a vigilance to make sure that past freedoms are not lost and do not turn into the opposite, as free enterprise turned into wage-slavery and monopoly capitalism, or the independent judiciary turned into a monopoly of courts, cops, and lawyers, or free education turned into School Systems.

[1] I, and other anarchists, would except certain states of temporary emergency, if we can be confident that the emergency is *temporary*. We might except certain simple logistic arrangements, like ticketing or metric standards or tax-collection, if we can be confident that the administration, the "secretariat," will not begin to run the show. And we might except certain "natural monopolies," like epidemic-control, water-supply, etc.

First published in *Anarchy 62* (April 1966).

The
Forms
and
Content
of
Democracy

I.

When the revolution of 1776-83 re-
moved the top structure of British authority from the American
colonies, this country was fundamentally organized as a network of
highly structured face-to-face communities, each fairly autonomous: town-meetings, congregational parishes, gentry families and
yeoman families. These had hierarchical structures: master and ap-
prentice, indentured servants, family slaves, professionals and their
clients, pastors and parishes; but each person was in frequent contact with those who initiated and decided.

For the first twenty-five years of the republic, in important
respects there was virtually a community anarchy with regard to the
central or state governments. The franchise was heavily restricted
by requirements of property, sex, education, religion, *etc.*; but very
few of those enfranchised bothered to vote anyway—often only
one or two per cent of the population.

For immigrants and for the poor who felt too disadvantaged in
the existing structured communities, the frontier was an open area
for independence.

Yet the "anarchist" communities were by no means non-
political. Rather, the independent elite regarded one another as a
band of citizen-friends. The Declaration of Independence was an

act of such self-assumed society makers (with a decent respect for the opinion of mankind). When it seemed that the presidency would take on a superior aura, especially under John Adams, Jefferson deliberately tried to brush it away. His first Inaugural has the character of the offhand remarks of a former professor who has been elected temporary Dean by his own faculty. Madison defined the advantage of decentralism as a policy: it is a system for social experiment; if the experiment fails, only a small community is hurt (and the others can help out); if the experiment succeeds, it will be imitated and the advantage will spread.

The rhetorical and intellectual style fitted such a system of citizen-friends. There was an easy sharing of assumptions in moral philosophy and on the nature of Man. There was an easy acceptance of diversity but a (misplaced) confidence that there need be no party divisions, though of course, there would be factions. There was felt to be no conflict between reason and feeling, objectivity and engagement; but on the contrary, existing conditions were thought to be plastic and amenable to improvement by practical proposals that would be put into effect by the meeting of minds. Past "history," correspondingly, was assiduously studied (and made the chief subject of compulsory primary education) as a source of examples for present action and to teach the moral lesson of the excellence of freedom.

For specific purposes of necessary centralization, the constitutional style was to set up a polarity between the structured smaller communities and the general Sovereign. The calling of a constitutional convention implied that others could and would be called (perhaps "every twenty years"). The preferred form of coordination was federation. The Sovereign had limited powers, and even these were subject to checks and balances. The disruptive Shays' rebellion was repressed but then condoned.

II.

During the Jacksonian period we find a pronounced homogenization of the structured groups. Master-apprentice and indenture relations give way to paternal capitalism and then proletarianization (the two phases can be seen in the first twenty years of Lowell and the subsequent decades). Family slavery gives way to field slavery and there is an increase of cash-cropping on a big scale. Absentee ownership and abstract money (banking) increases.

It is felt that there are irreconcilable clashes of sectional and "impersonal" interests, and with this there is the formation of mass Parties, with the aim of seeking an advantage in the conflict of things as they are: history is no longer plastic to practice. The presidency regains its aura, with the president a victorious party leader, and to the victor belong the spoils. Instead of accepted diversity, there tends to be a tyranny of the majority. Policy is a compromise in the struggle, rather than a reasoned solution. The voters vote on issues and platforms, rather than for trusted persons to meet with one another.

"History" (*e.g.,* as described in Jackson's Bank Message) is the tendency of "objective" conditions, which a party may influence in one or another direction. (The texture of argument is more statistical.) The moral philosophy (*e.g.,* in Calhoun) is more argumentative and postulates types of men and irreconcilable interests. The patriotism of the whole is expressed in a much more symbolic and emotional rhetoric, full of "heritage" and geographical metaphor. There began to be a pedantry of the text of the constitution; it is no longer a man-made document that may be remade. The populace falls into sectional, ethnic, and religious blocs; and the universal ideal of education lapses into sectarian and elite schooling.

In this situation, the idea of the Frontier begins to mean Individual Anarchy as against coercive and corrupt "civilization," and, as in Thoreau, there is a glorification of the individual against the consensus. The Sovereign is no longer the agreement of the society makers, but is an impersonal arbiter among the conflicting mass groups.

III.

The populist era, of 1870-1900, coinciding with the confused beginnings of the labor movement, is the critical period for the centralization and interlocking system of top-down powers of modern times. The alliance of government and monopolists, the manipulation of credit, the growth of the trusts, the squeezing of the farmers by railroads, packers and manufacturers, the centralization and alienation of the political parties, the cheap labor of mass immigration, the rapidly increasing urbanization: these in fact contributed a closing trap, to which the Populists responded with a mixture of heroic self-reliance and tragic paranoia.

"History" was now out of control, an apocalyptic period: "confronted by conditions for which there is no precedent in the history of the world" (according to the Populist platform of 1892). There is passionate "total dissent" from the existing system, to be met by "the avenging wrath of an indignant people" (William Jennings Bryan). There is a call for a Messianic democracy, "one united brotherhood of free men"; the early attitude of the labor movement is also one of fervent brotherhood: "May its spirit enter all hearts for the salvation of the Republic and the uplifting of mankind." But fundamentally, this is a quasi-religious movement rather than a politics. The rallying cry is now the *Preamble* to the Constitution, the American Way (*e.g.,* the Grange Manifesto of 1874).

With this goes a paranoic and know-nothing suspicion of all strangers, who belong to the diabolic enclosing forces: the absentee owners are Jews, the poor immigrants are allied with them. At first the Negroes are equally oppressed brothers; but then they are diabolically strange. The East consists of Cities of Sin; it poisons the food with preservatives and makes shoddy and obsolescent manufactures to bilk the honest. There is a plan for a north-south waterway—Great Lakes, Mississippi River, the Gulf of Mexico—which will exclude the East from the national economy altogether. The differences in situation finally make real cooperation between Populism and the labor movement impossible: the proletarianized workers living in cities and dependent on jobs, the farmers wanting cheap goods—so that they cannot see through to their common good. Government is distrusted as part of the oppressive cabal; "politics" is dirty, and both Populism and the labor movement are unpolitical; the religious ideology is apocalyptic, but there is no revolutionary politics. Again, however, nothing is consistently thought through: there is a clamor for nationalization of the railroads, utilities, and some industries; for strengthening of the civil service; for the establishment of federal regulatory agencies. These become the platform of the lapse of Populism into Progressivism and modern Liberalism.

Nevertheless, despite the paranoia and confusion, there are rational and constructive attempts to recreate an initiating citizenry in the mass-democracy and centralized economy. Cooperative merchandising and some manufacture; remarkable, though quixotic, attempts to create from the grass roots cooperative railroads and telephone systems. The pushing of initiative, referendum, and recall as political means. Emphasis on universal education of practical value: good vocational high schools, the development of the land grant colleges, adult education on the Chautauqua model. The pragmatism, functionalism and progressive education of Dewey, Veblen, Louis Sullivan are best understood as the good flowers of Populism and the labor movement, aiming at humanizing the new industrialism and re-establishing democratic community.

During this period, politically, free enterprise and initiative recur only in the uncitizenly, anti-communal theory of Social Darwinism.

IV.

With the lapse of Populism into Progressivism and Liberalism, centralization and bureaucratization of the labor movement, and the fixing of the warring trusts into the system of semi-monopolies, we come to our present organization of society. The country is now the chief imperialist world power, with a vast permanent military and overcapitalized industries to support it. (In 1916, Wilson hesitated to enter the war since it would be necessary to subsidize industries to produce the armaments, and he foresaw that they would never be cut back.) There has been galloping urbanization and suburbanization, with the Federal government as the chief promoter of real estate. In the present generation the whole system has been further frozen by the atomic Cold War.

Such a thing as an initiating and deciding citizenry is no longer thought of. In 1928, Franklin Roosevelt (then Governor) declared that the day of the "politician" was past and "the day of the Enlightened Administrator has come." In 1932, he said, "The greatest duty of a statesman is to educate." (To Madison it was the duty of democracy itself to educate.) The implication is paternalistic: there is a mass of clients who do not know how to fend for themselves—especially the "underprivileged"—rather than prudent or angry citizens.

Scientists, inventors, sociologists, *etc.,* are organized into the government or big corporations, often operating secretly and under patent control, determined by top-down programs.

The constitution is, in fact, democracy by consent. The present spirit is post-political unanimity, with no issues between the "parties"; the solution of all social problems is sought by giving them over to proliferating Alphabetical Agencies and by organizing school-monks. Instead of candidates, the public is presented with personalities and finally with TV images.

The ideal of progressive education first lapses into "adjustment" and now all education is geared to apprentice-training of the organized professionals and attempted regimentation of the rest.

Actual policy and "power" belong to para-political government: the Central Intelligence Agency, the Federal Bureau of Investigation, the Pentagon, the entrenched Civil Service, the scientific foundations, and so forth, not subject to political decision. Congress exercises at most a veto power, expressed mainly by stalling.

But in such a closed system, there is little possibility of thought or activity at all, for everything is interlocked and the structure is too immense. "Pragmatic" comes to mean that the structure works without information or goal outside itself. In both domestic and foreign policy, history consists of coping with unanticipated *faits accomplis,* almost on a day to day basis. Typically, an accurate prediction by a subordinate will be filed away because it is not "pragmatic" for the day's news: when the predicted event comes to pass, it is too late to make a prudent choice.

There is widespread urban *anomie* and the withdrawal of the middle class into suburban privacy without civic responsibility. The central city is left to segregation and blight. The authority of law degenerates to mere force.

Correspondingly, what citizenly initiative there is begins to express itself almost entirely in para-political forms: spontaneous picketing, obstruction, and protest—but inevitably the economic and political demands are vague. There is sporadic but intense "reform" politics on a minutely local level, usually to prevent some new encroachment of the Establishment, *e.g.,* "urban renewal."

At the same time there is a flood of powerful "social criticism" proving that every part of the system is not working and cannot work; yet few attempts are made to present comprehensive alternatives that could rally new politics. The established system, however, makes no effort to justify itself morally: the prevailing tone is rather resignation than cynicism. There is therefore a problem of disaffected youth. But the disaffected themselves tend either to withdraw, *e.g.,* into hallucinogens, or to engage in "existentialist" extreme-situation history, no different from the official policy of coping with the *fait accompli.*

This early draft from chapter 2 of *People or Personnel* was first published in *Liberation* (June-July 1964).

Notes
on
Decentralization

I. WHAT IS MEANT
BY DECENTRALIZATION
AND WHAT IS NOT MEANT

*D*ecentralizing is increasing the number of centers of decision-making and the number of initiators of policy; increasing the awareness by individuals of the whole function in which they are involved; and establishing as much face-to-face association with decision-makers as possible. People are directly engaged in the function.

Conversely, centralization is organization with top-down decision-making (on the basis of "upward communication"), departmentalization of the function, chain-of-command or bureaucracy, and maximum standardization of performance and procedure. People are personnel of the organization that performs the function.

Decentralization is not lack of order or organization but a different kind of coordination. Western science from 1500-1900 was entirely decentrally coordinated. In its high early period, the free enterprise system of joint-stock companies was decentrally

185

coordinated. The American political system of limited powers and checks and balances is decentralist in principle.

Many functions must be centralized by their nature: Where there are no natural limits, or the function extends over the whole system, or the logistics is more important than the particulars—e.g., epidemic-control, setting of standards, certain kinds of production and distribution, unification and scheduling of transportation. Also, in situations where force must be collected and directed to an emergency. At present, we ought to centralize further in some functions: e.g., we ought to have modular standards and standard parts in building and in machinery. "Natural monopolies" like telephone-telegraph or railroads. And, internationally, where vast capital is required, like the moon shot.

At present, there is a strong trend to spontaneous decentral political action—in the direct-action movements, and also some trend in cultural fields, like off-Broadway or Summerhill. But to decentralize, to delegate autonomy to many centers, can also be a political decision of a central power, usually compelled by the fact that the centralization is not working. For example, the New York City Board of Education is experimenting with decentralizing.

In the present period, decentralized centers need not be narrow, isolated, or "provincial." We exist in a post-urban, post-mass communication, post-centralist period. The decentralist kib-butzim might, by some, be considered as fanatical, but hardly provincial.

The fact of great populations does not prevent decentralization. Decentralizing is primarily a question of sociological organ-ization rather than geographical dispersal, though that is some-times involved. In a big city, the organization of arrondisements with neighborhood city-halls can importantly decentralize. A big university should be run by its many faculties.

Decentralizing is largely an empirical question and requires research and experiment (which it is not getting). The maxim of decentralization is to decentralize where, how much, and how it is expedient. For example, a gang or collective contract is used in important assembly-line manufacture in Coventry, whereby the gang determines its own working schedule, persons, and opera-tions. In what industries in the U.S. is this feasible? How should it be tailored?

II. PRESENT EXCESSIVE
CENTRALIZATION

In some aspects of social organization, there is historically a discernible cyclical swing between excessive centralization and excessive decentralization. Within the nation states at present there is, in most major functions, excessive centralization or centralism on wrong principles (just as internationally there is decentralization on wrong principles). Our emphasis ought to begin to be the other way.

Our present over-developed centralism goes back to a bureaucratic style perfected in the 18th century for taxation and policing; a military style developed with the emergence of the nation-states for logistics and to wage war; an economic style dominated by abstract money-profits rather than specific uses and work-processes; and—to a lesser degree—a style of industry determined by large concentrations of machinery around steam prime-movers, cash-cropping, and enclosures.

These have produced over-capitalized and often inappropriate technology, an inflexible and insecure tightly interlocking economy, ignorant mass-consumption with a complicated standard of living of inferior quality, the development of sprawling urban areas rather than towns and cities, brain-washing mass-communications, mass-democracy without real content, and mass-education that is both wasteful and regimenting.

With these, there is a prevalent superstition that no other method of organization could be more efficient or is even possible, and that in all functions the reasonable mode of operation is by "rationalization" (subdivision, standardization, cash-accounting). Because of the superstition and the inflexible organization, these beliefs are self-proving. No other kind of operation or administration is paid attention or subsidized; no research is done into possibilities of decentralizing. Breakdowns in the centralizing system are handled not by examining the system but by patchwork or imposing new levels of control according to the same administrative style. Meantime the hidden costs involved in centralization are omitted from the cash-accounting.

This superstition confounds the real confusion accompanying unique conditions of modern life, new technology, urbanization, and one-world. For instance, automation, a centralized mode of production, is applied both where it is appropriate and where it is inappropriate, but little attempt is made to analyze these differences.

My bias is that automation should be applied to the maximum in the production of hardware and perhaps subsistence goods, in clerical work, etc.; but automation, computing, and standardizing methods in general, should be severely restricted in all human services, education, restaurants, social work, hospitals; e.g., there should be a standard high-grade TV machine made by the millions and at minimum price—even though this would lose certain excellences of highest quality, styling, workmanship—but the larger part of programming should be decentralized and for specific audiences.

In all forecasts of the fairly immediate future, it is said that employment in commodity-production will be sharply diminished. But for useful leisure, the development of community culture, human services, and education, the rationalizing and cash-accounting style is inappropriate, whereas the decentralist style is enriching.

The grave threat in modern urbanization is *anomie,* the rootlessness and helplessness of individuals, the loss of citizenry. When it tries at all to cope with this, centralized administration tries to encourage "participation," but participation is empty unless it involves the possibility of initiating and deciding, that is decentralized administration. It is interesting to contrast the dull formality of a PTA meeting at which nothing important can be decided, with the liveliness of the public meeting of a local school board to which important authority has been delegated.

"Association" and "participation" are not mere interpersonal relations; they are sharing an objective enterprise.

III. PREVALENT OR INEVITABLE DEFECTS OF CENTRALIZATION

However competent, the few at the top who decide in large centralized enterprises are not enough minds to do an adequate job. Top-managers—and independent professionals—are the most overworked members of society.

In "upwards communication" of information, at each level there is processing and abstraction from the concrete; and with each abstraction there is the accumulation of mere approximation and of actual misfitting. Much is left out altogether.

To cope with the multifarious details and persons of large enterprises, recourse is had to standardization. This leads to inevitable misfitting and loss of peculiar appropriateness and quality. It is rare that the standard procedure is the best in any particular case.

The subordinates, meanwhile, necessarily become stupider, since they cannot learn by initiation and responsibility. In a departmental system, much of each man's capacity is unused. Each man knows only part of the process and so cannot really understand what he is doing. There is increased reliance on extrinsic motivations of salary, security, and perquisites, because subordinates cannot take satisfaction in completing the function. Finally, activity becomes time-serving and maintaining status, regardless of the function.

In established organizations, those who rise to the top also tend to be chosen by systematic rather than functional criteria. They are safe men. The image of performance is more important than the actuality. Since those who could criticize, colleagues, consumers, electorate, become stupider, the top men also become stupider.

The inflexible departments do not always dovetail; communication breaks down since few men have a sense of the whole. The resulting difficulties are solved by adding higher levels of control, more administrators.

Finally, the systems tend to run for their own sake. Since so much capital and so many persons are tightly interlocked in them, they cannot afford to risk any change; and any novelty or experiment involves dislocations and is "not worth the trouble." A system running for its own sake loses touch with its ostensible function and becomes isolated from the environment; its chief function is to protect, reward, and incestuously recruit its own personnel; its chief business is paper-work, public relations, and the maintenance of a routine production.

Unfortunately, when such systems are very large, they preempt the social means and space for carrying on their functions at all. There is no way to be effective outside the system and no way in the system, so people with inventive ideas and initiative become discouraged and either drop out or resign themselves to token performance. Worst of all, in many functions of society, simple direct action becomes quite impossible, even though it is common-sense and would meet with general approval. Eagerness and earnestness are stymied by licenses, merely formal standards, due process, confronting stuffed shirts, and the need for amounts of capital entirely disproportionate to the enterprise.

By and large, our country at present is constituted of a rather small number of great commercial baronies, organized as described, which are private powers; these are checked by the great public Power of governments; and there are also great entrenched organizations like the Pentagon, the FBI, the major Universities and school systems, the labor unions, and a few others.

The baronies compete semi-monopolistically, fix prices, and generally maintain the structure; and their relations with the labor unions are analogous. When Private Power confronts Public Power, e.g., in the regulatory agencies, the result is often a stalemate, so that there is no social motion. Often, however, there are alliances, as in the military-industrial, scientific agencies-universities, Urban Renewal-real estate promoters, etc., and these alliances lead to further aggrandizement of the same overgrown organizations and the products are not distinguished by ingenuity, beauty, thrift, or precise utility.

Despite the good intentions of many individuals in the system, this vast machinery of social power is almost powerless in most simple practical matters. Everyone in society, from lowly citizens to topmost leaders, shares the sneaking suspicion that "Nothing Can Be Done."

IV. EXAMPLES OF OVERGROWN SYSTEMS

New York School System: A Classical Bureaucracy

(Let me say that I have affection for the earnestness of the

N.Y.C. school system, its attentiveness to the children as the main object, its sincere equalitarianism, its concern for all types and conditions; its dreamy desire to experiment. But its structure is a disaster.)

The structure has been aggrandized from an ancient plan with little change. E.g., in 1900, 6% of 17-year-olds graduated from high school; now more than 60%. The system now serves 1,000,000 children, there are 750 schools rather rigidly controlled by one headquarters; the annual budget exceeds $700 millions—excluding capital improvements.

The following are expected, and actual, situations: to remove rats from a school, the principal cannot call an exterminator but must appeal to headquarters and go, in principle, to the Board of Estimate. To remove a door-catch ("city property") requires years of appeal.

An architect is told that he is not allowed to consult the teachers of a school he is to replace; he must simply adapt standards plans that are a generation out of date, and were not good to begin with. Because of specific pedagogic conditions, a principal asks for sound-proofing, but no money can be allotted for that, although there is provision for much less urgent needs. A very old-fashioned type of door-hardware is specified, which is kept in production, for reasons of nepotism, only for the N.Y. school system.

Despite this bureaucratic pedantry, there are public scandals because janitors have been taking home $50,000 a year, or a roof costs $750,000 to fix, and still leaks. On the other hand, there are scandals because of trivialities: a high-school student has done carpentry on a boat for a school official.

When local school-boards (with rather unspecified powers) were re-established in 1962, at the end of a year of operation it was said that their main achievement so far was to make it possible for the field superintendents to communicate with headquarters (through the free-wheeling of the local boards), something which had not occurred in two generations. For instance, a rubber-stamp from the superintendent in charge of building was required to make alterations to a wall to install a valuable new press given to the School of Printing; all this would cost the city nothing, yet the rubber-stamp was delayed for nearly two years and a mountain of correspondence, till a local board complained loudly and got the stamp.

In recruiting teachers for such a vast system, processing takes nearly a year. Naturally, many of the bright new graduates go elsewhere, to the suburban communities. (Yet the civil service type of procedure is necessary to avoid nepotism and political pressure.) Entirely irrelevant qualifications, and the tie-in with the graduate schools that license teachers, keep many fine teachers out. It takes many years to change an outmoded rule; for instance, the rule that a teacher must have no trace of a foreign accent, that made sense during the height of the immigration three generations ago, was a disaster when some districts had 35% Puerto Rican children who could not speak English, yet one could not recruit bi-lingual teachers; yet the rule has only now been modified.

The administrators, superintendents and secretaries, principals, assistants, clerks, guidance, attendance-officers, etc., proliferate; yet the fundamental educational fact, the number of children per teacher, cannot be altered because of the expense; but the large classes do positive damage to both children and teachers, so that the whole system perhaps does more harm than good. Correspondingly, each school is too large. Where intelligent principals ask for 400, there are schools of 1800 and the official limit has finally been reduced to 1200. The requirements of educational community are necessarily sacrificed to administrative convenience and ignorant public pressure.

Timidity, administrative unwieldiness, the need for standardization put insuperable obstacles in the path of experiment. When an experiment—e.g., the tailor-made Higher Horizons—succeeds on a small scale, it is diluted by being standardized.

(A considerable useful leeway *is* given to the principals—both in staffing and methods—so that the schools differ a good deal depending on the principal; but the teachers and staff-meeting have far too little leeway.)

Finally, this vast system is made increasingly inflexible by its interlocking with the other aggrandizing systems of society, to form one nationwide educational monolith. E.g., the textbook manufacturers, the graduate schools of education, the National Science Foundation, the proliferating national testing services, the corporations, the church, the Pentagon.

Monolithic Mass-Communications:
A Constitutional Danger

The interlocking systems of mass-communications with a few decision-makers at the top of each system produce inevitable brainwashing and makes democracy impossible.

Some kinds of news and events do warrant standard national researching and broadcast. Only great news services and networks can perform such services. Therefore we need a mixed system.

Fewer than 60 towns have competing newspapers (in 1900 there were 600). These are served by, now, only 3 international news services. With the best will in the world, these few persons cannot know what is all the real news. Three big broadcasting networks get most of their news from the same source.

The standard of living (how to be decent) and what is correct and tolerable in expression and entertainment is determined by these networks, the movies, and a few national magazines; but the sustaining advertisers are the same and the ownership elaborately interlocks.

This system requires creating a pervasive mass-audience and attitude. Anything that might offend a large segment (a few hundred thousand) must be excluded; the vast capitalization demands a vast coverage to pay for itself. There is thus an inevitable restriction to the sensational and the bland. (The Storm of Angry Letters that the sponsors fear may finally be as few as 20.)

Since there must be limited broadcasting channels, if the networks control most of them, there is an implicit censorship. And this becomes explicit when tapes are wiped out and certain speakers are officially or unofficially blacklisted. The FCC has proved powerless to compel reasonable coverage of everything worthwhile. The licenses once given are apparently in perpetuity.

The networks once established can wield enormous political pressure. (In one case of being threatened, a network was promptly able to produce 10,000 telegrams sent by children.) The equal-time provision has been abrogated for national elections—the networks are trying to extend the revocation to State elections. If they also control most of the local stations, this makes it impossible for new political thought to enter into discourse.

The expensive network time makes for minute and second

scheduling, and thus a format that prevents freedom of thought or art. Also the discouragement of using especially TV to cover actualities—since these might always prove either boring or untoward.

In publishing of books, there is similar concentration of capitalization (huge presses and teams of salesmen and promotion), and this increasingly determines the content and format of books, in order to make it possible to set such big capital in motion. And there is interlocking with magazines for serialization, with book clubs, with Hollywood.

The weight of publication, broadcasting, and journalism in the style, format, and acceptable content of the mass-media, decided by the few who rise to the top in such vast semi-monopolies, finally simply swamps independent and dissenting thought and style and constitutes a virtual censorship-in-depth. Overexposed to one fairly homogeneous kind of interpretation, and under-exposed to any rival interpretations (and in some localities and on the TV medium not so exposed at all), people begin to take the interpretation of the interlocking mass-media for the reality; that is, they are brainwashed. This is a constitutional crisis for democracy.

Cars and Roads: Hypertrophy of a System Beyond Function

During the 20's, automobiles began to be sold for style and status rather than more serious function and convenience; this removed natural limitations on the proliferation of such formidable and expensive objects. Meantime, the middle-class suburbanites pressured the building of parkways. There is now a car for every 2.7 Americans, considerably more than one to a family.

The cars exist as the crucial element in a vast complex—of fuel, servicing, and highways—that entirely transforms the environment. Highways are built at a cost varying from a half million to three million a mile. After armaments, highway construction is the big item in Federal budgets, and it looms immensely in State budgets.

By 1970 the cost, with accrued interest, of roads for a single car-trip five miles to the center of Washington will come to two and a half dollars (per car trip) each way. 50% of central Los Angeles has been given over to the roadways.

General Motors alone employs 600,000 people; its annual turnover is $14 billions. The automotive complex (including oil and roads) has become indispensable to keep the economy going, so that a falling off of car sales can precipitate a serious recession. "What is good for General Motors is good for the country."

Three or four car manufacturers control the market, competing semimonopolistically with fixed prices and improvements spooned out slowly. Progress in design has been determined entirely by profits; the increase in power has been largely for sales and is unfunctional for most situations. Even safety features are neglected. (Forty thousand are killed annually in automobile accidents.) Only the competition of European small cars made, for a time, a radical change. No effort has been made, e.g., to develop an efficient small slower-moving electric for urban use (taxis). Also, expensive as they are, cars are built not to last, and the companies push for laws to exempt them from supplying repair-parts for longer than five years.

Because of direct and indirect subsidy, cars and trucks have pushed other kinds of transportation out of the picture, especially for commuting. There is little effort to achieve a balanced transit pattern, using all means for the general convenience. In most large cities, traffic congestion and parking are almost intolerably inconvenient; the fleets of cars on the suburban parkways make no economic or psychological sense.

The cars and highways have imposed an entirely new and disruptive community plan. The tremendous suburbanization has become their creature. Villages and city neighborhoods are disrupted by highway shopping centers. Families are dispersed and the lives of children depend on automobility. Centralized plants, including central schools, claim per product efficiency, but the hidden costs of the highways and transportation are not counted.

Of course, most of this imposition of a new pattern would have been impossible if there had not been advantages and conveniences in the cars; but by hypertrophy the system has itself become the dominant cause. The highway planning now occurs independently and determines the location of communities and the manner of life in them.

In the mess we are in, however, the only conceivable remedy is public centralized regulation and planning. The automotive complex must now be treated as a "natural monopoly" and regulated.

Supermarkets: Logistic Planning That Proves to Be Inefficient

The effect of the hyper-organization of food-production, processing, distant transportation, and supermarket retailing has been that the farmer's share of the take has persistently diminished (e.g., 44% in 1953, 38% in 1963), whereas the profits of the chains themselves have *not* risen, and food prices to the consumer have risen slightly. This is an application of Borsodi's Law: as the cost of production per unit diminishes because of centralized operation, the cost of processing and distribution increases disproportionately. This law is relevant especially for bulky and perishable commodities like food-stuffs, and where the fixed capital investment *can* be relatively low in proportion to the product (as in natural farming).

At present, $1 out of every $2 spent for food goes to 100 corporate or (not Rochdale) cooperative chains. 70% of all food sales is through the central systems. The 10 largest chains sell 30% of all food.

In this system, both farmers and retailers fall under the control and decision-making of the chains. Farmers contract long beforehand, regardless of weather or the ability to take advantage of sudden opportunities. The emphasis is entirely on large-scale cash-cropping. Farmer's markets in the towns and cities are closed. Inevitably, marginal farms must discontinue, and this is an important cause of the present excessive urbanization. (Farm families now make up less than 8% of the population.)

It is clear that in many thousands of cases, people would choose the farm way of life, if there were any possibilities of getting any cash at all; e.g., in some states a small rise in the farmer's price for milk results in many marginal farms resuming operation. But at present, farm subsidies overwhelmingly favor the big operators.

With the concentration of growing in huge plantations in Texas, Florida, California, etc., breeding and hybridization are determined by terms of canning, ability to preserve and ship, and appearance for mass-sale, rather than freshness, flavor, or nutrition. Very little is naturally nurtured or naturally ripened. There is excessive use of pesticides.

In the retailing, there is a profound change in consumer habits. Packaging assumes great importance, no matter what is in the packages. Consumers pay several cents more for a brand-name product (e.g., Clorox, although a locally bottled bleach is identical in every respect). Independent grocers are forced out, adding to the anonymity and anomie of urban neighborhoods.

Nevertheless, despite these disruptive changes in the way of life of farm and city, brought on by rationalization of food-production and distribution, there is little increase of actual efficiency.

V. COSTS IN SERVICE ENTERPRISES WITH DIFFERENT ORGANIZATION AND MOTIVATION

Consider a range of services where staff and overhead are the chief costs. With extrinsic motivation and organization not growing from the function, the cost may rise by a factor of 5, 10, or more. E.g. the following somewhat comparable enterprises:

On Broadway, a modest play (without music) requires upward of $100,000 to rehearse and mount and $20,000 a week to run. The standard estimate for an off-Broadway production, e.g., at the Living Theatre, is $20,000 to mount and $2,000 a week to run. Professionally, these productions will be comparable in every way—we are not here considering the esthetic or community value. Contrast with both these types, an *ad hoc* production by artists, e.g., a play in the loft of the Judson Church: this might cost $50 to $500 to mount and nothing at all to run, since the script, acting, staging and space are all gratis.

In TV, NBC sponsored time costs $143,000 an hour for 220 stations, $650 per outlet for the network, or $2,000 for one station. This does not include the cost of the program: a very modest half-hour program costs $10,000 to produce. Now compare two non-profit (educational TV) stations: WNDT in New York costs $650 an hour to run, not much cheaper than commercial television (but this figure includes the cost of programming). On the other hand, KQED in San Francsico runs for $225 an hour. The difference is that the top salary at WNDT is $45,000, the staff about 150, etc., whereas at KQED the top salary is $15,000, the staff about 50, etc. Professionally the two stations are equivalent, but KQED is much more daring and lively. (Characteristically, the staff-turnover at KQED is almost nil—we are obviously relying on artistic and technical motivation—whereas WNDT is a way-station for persons moving toward higher salaries elsewhere.)

In radio, WMCA charges $700 an hour for air-time, excluding the cost of the program. But WBAI, a listener-supported station of comparable power, costs $38 an hour to run, including programming (provided gratis by artists, academics, or the politically minded). WBAI is one of the 3 stations of the Pacifica Federation, which exchange tapes but are entirely independent.

A good non-residential private school in New York, class size 20, costs about $850 per pupil per year, not counting plant and some endowment. An elementary pupil in the New York Public School system costs $650, also excluding capital costs for plant and replacement; the class size is officially 29, but in fact most classes are 32-35. Thus public and private costs are similar. By contrast, a Summerhill school in Stony Point charges $450 per child, provides, for 50 children, 3 full-time paid instructors and the equivalent of about 5 more voluntary teachers from among parents who are artists or professionals and teach part-time. (The Public system, by and large, discourages the entry of unlicensed teachers into the classroom.)

College tuition at Columbia or Cornell is $1700, which' is estimated to be a little more than 50% of the actual cost per student for "education and educational administration." The mark-up over actual classroom costs is 400%. (At smaller liberal arts colleges, e.g., Wesleyan in Connecticut, the mark-up is 300%.) Especially in the freshman and sophomore classes, the professors lecture to very large classes and the smaller groups are taught by ill-paid section-men. In the small colleges proposed in *The Com-*

munity of Scholars, the tuition is estimated at $650, with 10 professors for 150 students.

The Peace Corps is a model of efficient and dedicated bureaucracy. Yet it costs more than $14,000 to select, train, and maintain a volunteer for one year. ($9,000 for the volunteer, $5,000 for central administration, liaison with host countries, etc.) The Friends Service VISA program, which is comparable in essential respects, provides the same service for $3,500 a volunteer. For another comparison, Operation Crossroads, pro-rated for the same period, costs $5,000. Important causes of expense in the Peace Corps are the very rigid selection to protect the Image abroad (only 1 of 8 original applicants are finally sent), training in the setting of an American university, and propaganda and promotion. The Friends spend nothing at all on administration (the program is taken care of as an extra duty by their regular offices), prefer to train in the field where conditions are known, and their candidates have a service philosophy to begin with.

Official Urban Renewal planned for the West Village in New York City was to cost $30 million (including a $7 million subsidy), to provide net 300 units after demolition and relocation. A counter plan proposed by a neighborhood group would cost $8½ million, without subsidy for net 475 units, without neighborhood disruption and relocation. The savings in this case come from tailoring to the actual needs by real architects rather than bureaucrats and promoters. The neighborhood plan comes to $18,000 a unit. Incidentally, in a similar neighborhood, with the unpaid labor of friends, I remodelled a commercial loft to a comparable standard for $500, and the rental at ordinary market value and amortization came to considerably less. That is: the professional neighborhood housing is cheaper than official housing, but artists' lofts are cheaper still.

There is no mystery what swells costs in commercial, official, and Establishment enterprises, where the organization, motivation, and procedure are not designed directly to fulfill the function. It is profits, patents, and rents; semi-monopolistic fixed prices; need for union-protection of workmen hired for somebody else's enterprise, union scales and featherbedding; salaries determined by considerations of status because the personnel is not intrinsically motivated to the task; expense accounts; proliferation of administrators, paper work, business machines; the waste of skill by departmentalizing task-roles and standardizing procedure inflexibly; high cost of contingencies because of tight scheduling; public relations and promotion to shore up the Image.

On the other hand, when enterprises are run autonomously by professionals and artists intrinsically committed to the task, people make do on means and procedure; they become inventive by making decisions flexibly as opportunity presents; they keep their eye on the essence rather than the convention; they put in as many hours as are necessary without watching the clock; they use all available skills wherever available; they eschew status and sometimes live on a subsistence wage; and administration and overhead are tailored to what is indispensable for the concrete function.

VI. TYPOLOGY OF ENTERPRISES IN TERMS OF ENGAGEMENT

Enterprises Extrinsically Motivated as part of the Organized System:

1. Commercial enterprises, run for Profit as well as Status, etc. (E.g., NBC or the Broadway theatre.)
2. Official or Establishment Non-profit enterprises (E.g., Columbia University, WNDT.)

Enterprises Determined by the Function or Concrete Task:

3. Professional (E.g., KQED, Living Theatre, Friends Service, West Village Neighborhood.)
4. Artistic or Community (E.g., Judson players, WBAI, the Barker School, artists' lofts.)

Profit-motivated enterprises may or may not be more efficient than Establishment non-profit enterprises. Since performance in the non-profit field is largely symbolic, there is no attempt to cut costs. But the cutting of costs in profit enterprises is largely offset by the grasping, padding, and status-seeking of the personnel. An extremely extravagant model is the *combination* of centralized commercial and official, as in cost-plus contracts. This is the opposite of the TVA idea, where the official was to serve as a yardstick.

Intrinsic professional performance necessarily costs more than Artistic and community performance (which really costs nothing beyond materials and subsistence) because the persons are members of a licensed or peer-group guild; they are institutions, and this is usually necessary for continuous operation over a range of occasions. Artistic performances, on the contrary, are *ad hoc*. (For a continuously productive artist, each work is *ad hoc*.)

Add to these 4 Types, 2 other extreme types of production and service. On the one hand there are family, amateur, and folk enterprises, which do not enter the cash nexus at all, but are very important for the economic and social well-being. For instance, one nation might have a per capita "income" several times more than another, and yet the actual standard of living be very little different, since the "poorer" nation is more skilled and self-reliant.

On the other hand, there are the great background enterprises that fill universal needs, necessary for a modern society to function: municipal services, natural monopolies, literacy, subsistence, etc. It is probably most convenient and efficient to run all of these by free appropriation. The standards and motives of personnel should be strictly professional. (This is Marx's "administration" that is supposed to supersede the "withering away of the State," but, in my opinion, he extends the range of these functions too far and would make the whole society lifeless. These functions are best regarded as merely supportive and background.)

VII. IDEA OF A MIXED SYSTEM

The above 6 types of enterprise are, in one form or another, operative in any modern society. But the proportions are, of course, very various—so the United States, Russia, Sweden, Nigeria, etc. have different real constitutions.

The idea of a Mixed System is a proportioning among types of enterprise so that they in fact influence one another pluralistically and if necessary can check one another.

A mixed system would try to keep the proportion of the types roughly within limits of maximum cost efficiency. (I doubt that the American proportion is at all within these limits. E.G., it takes $30,000 in new investment to re-employ 1 workman.) This might involve *lowering* the GNP: e.g., cooperative enterprises often avoid cash transactions; a quality standard of living is less cultured and often costs less; skilled and engaged people do more directly for themselves and one another, e.g., repairs; a better rural-urban ratio, say 20% instead of 8%, would be more efficient, as well as more socially and culturally satisfactory.

A mixed system would allow various types of motivation and organization to do what they can do most appropriately and cheapest.

A mixed system would re-open opportunities for people to choose the way of working and living that most suits them, and would thus re-create the possibility of engagement.

These were notes Goodman made for the writing of *People or Personnel,* first published in *Dissent* (Autumn 1964).

The
Black
Flag
of
Anarchism

*T*he wave of student protest in the advanced countries overrides national boundaries, racial differences, the ideological distinctions of fascism, corporate liberalism and communism. Needless to say, officials of the capitalist countries say that the agitators are Communists, and Communists say they are bourgeois revisionists. In my opinion, there is a totally different political philosophy underlying—it is Anarchism.

The actual "issues" are local and often seem trivial. The troubles are usually spontaneous, though there is sometimes a group bent on picking a fight in the brooding unrest. A play is banned, a teacher is fired, a student publication is censored, university courses are not practical or facilities are inadequate, the administration is too rigid, there are restrictions on economic mobility or there is technocratic mandarinism, the poor are treated arrogantly, students are drafted for an unjust war—any of these, anywhere in the world, may set off a major explosion, ending with police and broken heads. The spontaneity, the concreteness of the issues, and the tactics of direct action are themselves characteristic of Anarchism.

Historically, Anarchism has been the revolutionary politics of skilled artisans and farmers who do not need a boss; of workmen in dangerous occupations, e.g., miners and lumbermen, who learn to trust one another, and of aristocrats who can economically afford to be idealistic. It springs up when the system of society is not moral, free or fraternal enough. Students are likely to be Anarchists but, in the immense expansion of schooling everywhere, they are new as a mass and they are confused about their position.

Political Anarchism is rarely mentioned and never spelled out in the press and TV. West and East, journalists speak of "anarchy" to mean chaotic riot and aimless defiance of authority; or they lump together "communists and anarchists" and "bourgeois revisionists, infantile leftists and anarchists." Reporting the troubles in France, they have had to distinguish Communists and Anarchists because the Communist labor unions promptly disowned the Anarchist students, but no proposition of the Anarchists has been mentioned except for Daniel Cohn-Bendit's vaunting statement, "I scoff at all national flags!"

(The possibility of an Anarchist revolution—decentralist, anti-police, anti-party, anti-bureaucratic, organized by voluntary association, and putting a premium on grassroots spontaneity—has always been anathema to Marxist Communists and has been ruthlessly suppressed. Marx expelled the Anarchist unions from the International Workingmen's' Association; Lenin and Trotsky slaughtered the Anarchists in the Ukraine and at Kronstadt; Stalin murdered them during the Spanish Civil War; Castro has jailed them in Cuba, and Gomulka in Poland. Nor is Anarchism necessarily socialist, in the sense of espousing common ownership. That would depend. Corporate capitalism, state capitalism and state communism are all unacceptable, because they trap people, exploit them and push them around. Pure communism, meaning voluntary labor and free appropriation, is congenial to Anarchists. But Adam Smith's economics, in its pure form, is also Anarchist, and was so called in his time; and there is an Anarchist ring to Jefferson's agrarian notion that a man needs enough control of his subsistence to be free of irresistible pressure. Underlying all Anarchist thought is a hankering for peasant independence, craft guild self-management and the democracy of medieval Free Cities. Naturally it is a question how all can be achieved in modern technical and urban conditions. In my opinion, we could go a lot further than we think if we set our sights on decency and freedom rather than delusory "greatness" and suburban "affluence.")

In this country, where we have no continuing Anarchist tradition, the young hardly know their tendency at all. I have seen the black flag of Anarchy at only a single demonstration, when 165 students burned their draft cards on the Sheep Meadow in New York, in April, 1967—naturally, the press noticed only the pretentiously displayed Vietcong flags that had no connection with the draft-card burners. [1] Recently at Columbia, it was the red flag that waved from the roof. The American young are usually ignorant of political history. The generation gap, their alienation from tradition, is so profound that they cannot remember the correct name for what they in fact do.

This ignorance has unfortunate consequences for their movement and lands them in wild contradictions. In the United States, the New Left has agreed to regard itself as Marxist and speaks of "seizing power" and "building socialism," although it is strongly opposed to centralized power and it has no economic theory whatever for a society and technology like ours. It is painful to hear students who bitterly protest being treated like IBM cards, nevertheless defending Chairman Mao's little red book; and Carl Davidson, editor of *New Left Notes,* has gone so far as to speak of "bourgeois civil liberties." In the Communist bloc, unlike the Latin countries, the tradition is also wiped out. For instance, in Czechoslovakia, Poland and Yugoslavia, students who want civil liberties and more economic freedom are called bourgeois, although in fact they are disgusted by the materialism of their own regimes and they aspire to workers' management, rural reconstruction, the withering away of the state, the very Anarchism that Marx promised as pie in the sky.

Worst of all, not recognizing what they are, the students do not find one another as an international movement, though they have a common style, tactics and culture. Yet there are vital goals which, in my opinion, can be achieved only by the immense potential power of youth acting internationally. Certainly, as a first

---

[1] A black flag was also raised along with a red flag at the national convention of Students for a Democratic Society in East Lansing last month.

order of business, they ought to be acting in concert to ban the nuclear bombs of France, China, Russia and the United States; otherwise they will not live out their lives.

The protesting students are Anarchist because they are in a historical situation to which Anarchism is their only possible response. During all their lifetime the Great Powers have been in the deadlock of the Cold War, stockpiling nuclear weapons. Vast military-industrial complexes have developed, technology has been abused, science and the universities have been corrupted. Education has turned into processing, for longer years and at a faster pace. Centralized social engineering is creating the world forecast in Orwell's *1984*. Manipulated for national goals they cannot believe in, the young are alienated. On every continent there is excessive urbanization and the world is heading for ecological disaster.

Under these conditions, the young reject authority, for it is not only immoral but functionally incompetent, which is unforgivable. They think they can do better themselves. They want to abolish national frontiers. They do not believe in Great Power. Since they are willing to let the Systems fall apart, they are not moved by appeals to law and order. They believe in local power, community development, rural reconstruction, decentralist organization, so they can have a say. They prefer a simpler standard of living. Though their protests generate violence, they themselves tend to nonviolence and are internationally pacifist. But they do not trust the due process of administrators and are quick to resort to direct action and civil disobedience. All this adds up to the community Anarchism of Kropotkin, the resistance Anarchism of Malatesta, the agitational Anarchism of Bakunin, the Guild Socialism of William Morris, the personalist politics of Thoreau.

The confused tangle of Anarchist and authoritarian ideas was well illustrated by the actions of Students for a Democratic Society in leading the protest at Columbia.

The two original issues, to purge the university of the military and to give local power to the Harlem community, were Anarchist in spirit—though, of course, they could be supported by liberals and Marxists as well. The direct action, of nonviolently occupying the buildings, was classically Anarchist.

The issues were not strictly bona fide, however, for the SDS chapter was carrying out a national plan to embarrass many schools during the spring, using any convenient pretexts, in order to attack the System. In itself, this was not unjustifiable, since the big universities, including Columbia, are certainly an important part of our military operations, which ought to be stopped. But the SDS formulation was not acceptable: "Since we cannot yet take over the whole society, let us begin by taking Columbia." I doubt that most of the students who participated wanted to "take over" anything, and I am sure they would have been as restive if ruled by the SDS leadership as by the president and trustees of Columbia.

When the faculty came to life and the students' justified demands began to be taken seriously—in the normal course of events, as has happened on several other campuses, the students would have gone unpunished or been suspended for 45 minutes—SDS suddenly revealed a deeper purpose, to "politicize" the students and "radicalize" professors by forcing a "confrontation" with the police: if the police had to be called, people would see the System naked. Therefore the leadership raised the ante and made negotiation impossible. The administration was not big-souled enough to take it whence it came, nor patient enough to sit it out; it called the police and there was a shambles.

To have a shambles is not necessarily unjustifiable, on the hypothesis that total disruption is the only way to change a totally corrupt society. But the concept of "radicalizing" is a rather presumptuous manipulation of people for their own good. It is Anarchist for people to act on principle and learn, the hard way, that the powers that be are brutal and unjust, but it is authoritarian for people to be expended for the cause on somebody's strategy. (In my experience, a professional really becomes radical when he tries to pursue his profession with integrity and courage; this is what he knows and cares about, and he soon finds that many things must be changed. In student disturbances, professors have not been "radicalized" to the jejune program of *New Left Notes,* but they *have* recalled to mind what it means to be a professor at all.)

Ultimately, when four leaders were suspended and students again occupied a building in their support, the SDS tendency toward authority became frankly dictatorial. A majority of the students voted to leave on their own steam before the police came, since there was no sense in being beaten up and arrested again; but the leadership brushed aside the vote because it did not represent the correct position, and the others—I suppose out of animal loyalty—stayed and were again busted.

Nevertheless, the Columbia action was also a model of Anarchism, and the same SDS leaders deserve much of the credit. In the first place, it seems to have halted the university's displacement of poor people, whereas for years citizenly protests (including mine) had accomplished nothing. When, because of police brutality, there was a successful strike and sessions of the college and some of the graduate schools were terminated for the semester, the students rapidly and efficiently made new arrangements with favorable professors for work to go on. They organized a "free university" and brought a host of distinguished outsiders to the campus. A group, Students for a Restructured University, amicably split from SDS to devote itself to the arts of peace and work out livable relations with the administration. For a while, until the police came back, the atmosphere on the campus was pastoral. Faculty and students talked to one another. Like Berkeley after its troubles, Columbia was a much better place.

In Anarchist theory, "revolution" means the moment when the structure of authority is loosed, so that free functioning can occur. The aim is to open areas of freedom and defend them. In complicated modern societies it is probably safest to work at this piecemeal, avoiding chaos which tends to produce dictatorship.

To Marxists, on the other hand, "revolution" means the moment in which a new state apparatus takes power and runs things its own way. From the Anarchist point of view, this is "counterrevolution," since there is a new authority to oppose. But Marxists insist that piecemeal change is mere reformism, and one has to seize power and have a strong administration in order to prevent reaction.

At Columbia the administration and the authoritarians in SDS seem to have engaged in an almost deliberate conspiracy to escalate their conflict and make the Marxist theory true. The administration was deaf to just grievances, it did not have to call the police when it did, and it did not have to suspend the students. It has been pigheaded and vindictive. Worse, it has been petty. For instance, during the strike the sprinklers were ordered to be kept going all day, ruining the grass, in order to prevent the students from holding "free university" sessions on the lawn. When a speaker addressed a rally, a sweeper had been instructed to move a noisy vacuum cleaner to the spot to drown him out. William J. Whiteside the director of buildings and grounds, explained to a Times reporter that "these bullhorn congregations lead to an awful lot of litter, so we have to get out there and clean it up." This from a university founded in 1754.

Consider two key terms in New Left rhetoric, "participatory democracy" and "cadres." I think these concepts are incompatible, yet both are continually used by the same youth.

Participatory democracy was the chief idea in the Port Huron Statement, the founding charter of Students for a Democratic Society. It is a cry for a say in the decisions that shape our lives, as against top-down direction, social engineering, corporate and political centralization, absentee owners, brainwashing by mass media. In its connotations, it encompasses no taxation without representation, grass-roots populism, the town meeting, congregationalism, federalism, Student Power, Black Power, workers' management, soldiers' democracy, guerrilla organization. It is, of course, the essence of Anarchist social order, the voluntary federation of self-managed enterprises.

Participatory democracy is grounded in the following social-psychological hypotheses: People who actually perform a function usually best know how it should be done. By and large, their free decision will be efficient, inventive, graceful, and forceful. Being active and self-confident, they will cooperate with other groups with a minimum of envy, anxiety, irrational violence or the need to dominate.

And, as Jefferson pointed out, only such an organization of society is self-improving; we learn by doing, and the only way to educate cooperative citizens is to give power to people as they are. Except in unusual circumstances, there is not much need for dictators, deans, police, pre-arranged curricula, imposed schedules, conscription, coercive laws. Free people easily agree among themselves on plausible working rules; they listen to expert direction when necessary; they wisely choose pro tem leaders. Remove authority, and there will be self-regulation, not chaos.

And radical student activity has in fact followed this line. Opposing the bureaucratic system of welfare, students have devoted themselves to community development, serving not as leaders or experts but as catalysts to bring poor people together, so they can become aware of and solve their own problems. In politics, the radical students usually do not consider it worth the trouble and expense to try to elect distant representatives; it is better to organize local groups to fight for their own interests.

In the students' own protest actions, like the Free Speech Movement in Berkeley, there were no "leaders"—except in the TV coverage—or rather there were dozens of pro tem leaders; yet FSM and other such actions have moved with considerable efficiency. Even in immense rallies, with tens of thousands gathering from a thousand miles, as in New York in April, 1967, or at the Pentagon in October, 1967, the unvarying rule has been to exclude no groups on "principle," no matter how incompatible their tendencies; despite dire warnings, each group has done its own thing and the whole has been well enough. When it has been necessary to make immediate arrangements, as in organizing the occupied buildings at Columbia or devising new relations with the professors, spontaneous democracy has worked beautifully. In the civil rights movement in the South, Martin Luther King used to point out, each locality planned and carried out its own campaign and the national leadership just gave what financial or legal help it could.

Turn now to "cadres." In the past few years, this term from the vocabulary of military regimentation has become overwhelmingly prevalent in New Left rhetoric, as it was among the various Communist sects in the thirties. (My hunch is that it was the Trotskyists who gave it political currency. Trotsky had been the commander of the Red Army.) A cadre or squad is the primary administrative or tactical unit by which small groups of human beings are transformed into sociological entities, to execute the unitary will of the organization, whether army, political party, work force, labor union, agitation or propaganda machine. In Marxian terms, it is the unit of alienation from human nature, and young Marx would certainly have disapproved.

"Cadre" connotes the breaking down of ordinary human relations and transcending personal motives, in order to channel energy for the cause. For purposes of agitation, it is the Jesuit idea of indoctrinating and training a small band who then go forth and multiply themselves. The officers, discipline and tactics of military cadres are determined in headquarters; this is the opposite of guerrilla organization, for guerrillas are self-reliant, devise their own tactics, and are bound by personal or feudal loyalty, so that it is puzzling to hear the admirers of Che Guevara use the word "cadres." As a revolutionary political method, cadre-formation connotes the development of a tightly knit conspiratorial party which will eventually seize the system of institutions and exercise a dictatorship until it transforms the majority to its own doctrine and behavior. Etymologically, "cadre" and "squad" come from (Latin) *quadrus*, a square, with the sense of fitting people into a framework.

Obviously, these connotations are entirely repugnant to the actual motives and spirit of the young at present, everywhere in the world. In my opinion, the leaders who use this language are suffering from a romantic delusion. The young are not conspiratorial but devastatingly open. For instance, when youth of the draft resistance movement are summoned to a grand jury, it is very difficult for their Civil Liberties lawyers to get them to plead the Fifth Amendment. They will sacrifice themselves and get their heads broken, but it has to be according to their personal judgment. They insist on wearing their own garb even if it is bad for Public Relations. Their ethics are even embarrassingly Kantian, so that ordinary prudence and reasonable casuistry are called finking.

And I do not think they want "power" but just to be taken into account, to be able to do their thing, and to be let alone. They indeed want a revolutionary change, but not by this route. Except for a while, on particular occasions, they simply cannot be manipulated to be the shock troops of a Leninist coup. (I have never found that I could teach them anything else either.) If the young go along with actions organized by the Trotskyists or the Progressive Labor Party or some of the delusions of SDS, it is because, in their judgment, the resulting disruption does more good than harm. Compared with the arrogance, cold violence and inhumanity of our established institutions, the arrogance, hot-headedness and all-too-human folly of the young are venial.

The trouble with the neo-Leninist wing of the New Left is a different one. It is that the abortive manipulation of lively energy and moral fervor for a political revolution that will not be, and ought not to be, confuses the piecemeal social revolution that is brightly possible. This puts me off—but of course they have to do it their own way. It is inauthentic to do community development in order to "politicize" people, or to use a good do-it-yourself project as a means of "Bringing people into the Movement." Everything should be done for its own sake. The amazing courage of sticking to one's convictions in the face of the police is insulted when it is manipulated as a means of "radicalizing." The loyalty and trust in one another of youth is extraordinary, but it can turn to dis-illusionment if they perceive that they are being had. Many of the best of the young went through this in the thirties. But at least there is no Moscow gold around, though there seems to be plenty of CIA money both at home and abroad.

Finally, in this account of confused Anarchism, we must mention the conflict between the activists and the hippies.

The activists complain that the dropouts are not political and will not change anything. Instead, they are seducers who drastically interfere with the formation of cadres. (We are back to "Religion is the opium of the people" or perhaps "LSD is the opium of the people.") Of course, there is something in this, but in my opinion the bitterness of the New Left polemic against the hippies can only be explained by saying that the activists are defensive against their own repressed impulses.

In fact, the dropouts are not unpolitical. When there is an important demonstration, they are out in force and get beaten up with the rest—though they are not "radicalized." With their flowers and their slogan "Make Love Not War," they provide all of the color and much of the deep meaning. One hippie group, the Diggers, has a full-blown economics, has set up free stores and has tried to farm, in order to be independent of the System, while it engages in community development.

The Yippies, the Youth International Party (would that it

were!), devote themselves to undermining the System; they are the ones who showered dollar bills on the floor of the Stock Exchange, tied up Grand Central Station and tried to exorcise the Pentagon with incantations. And the Dutch Provos, the "provotariat," who are less drug-befuddled than the Yippies, improvise ingenious improvements to make society better as a means of tearing it down; they even won an election in Amsterdam.

On their side, the hippies claim that the New Left has gotten neatly caught in the bag of the System. To make a frontal attack is to play according to the enemy's rules, where one doesn't have a chance; and victory would be a drag anyway. The thing is to use jujitsu, ridicule, Schweikism, nonviolent resistance, by-passing, infuriating, tripping up, seducing by offering happy alternatives. A complex society is hopelessly vulnerable, and the 14-year-olds run away and join the gypsies.

This criticism of the New Left is sound. A new politics demands a new style, a new personality and a new way of life. To form cadres and try to take power is the same old runaround. The Anarchism of the dropouts is often quite self-conscious. It is remarkable, for instance, to hear Emmet Grogan, the spokesman of the Diggers, make up the theories of Prince Kropotkin right out of his own experiences in Haight-Ashbury, the Lower East Side and riot-torn Newark.

But I think the dropouts are unrealistic in their own terms. Living among the poor, they up the rents. Trying to live freely, they offend the people they want to help. Sometimes blacks and Spanish-Americans have turned on them savagely. In my observation, the "communication" that they get with drugs is illusory, and to rely on chemicals in our technological age is certainly to be in a bag. Because the standard of living is corrupt, they opt for voluntary poverty, but there are also many useful goods that they have a right to, and needlessly forgo. And they are often plain silly.

The more sophisticated Provos have fallen for a disastrous vision of the future, New Babylon, a society in which all will sing and make love and do their own thing, while the world's work is done by automatic machines. They do not realize that in such a society power will be wielded by the technocrats, and they themselves will be colonized like Indians on a reservation.

In general, I doubt that it is possible to be free, to have a say, and to live a coherent life, without doing worthwhile work, pursuing the arts and sciences, practicing the professions, bringing up children, engaging in politics. Play and personal relations are a necessary background; they are not what men live for. But maybe I am old-fashioned, Calvinistic.

Perhaps Goodman's most widely reprinted argument for decentralist principles, this essay was first published in *The New York Times Magazine* (July 14, 1968).

Anarchism and Revolution

*I*n anarchist theory, the word *revolution* means the process by which the grip of authority is loosed, so that the functions of life can regulate themselves, without top-down direction or external hindrance. The idea is that, except for emergencies and a few special cases, free functioning will find its own right structures and coordination.

An anarchist description of a revolutionary period thus consists of many accounts of how localities, factories, tradesmen, schools, professional groups, and communes go about managing their own affairs, defending themselves against the central "system," and making whatever federal arrangements among themselves that are necessary to weave the fabric of society. An anarchist history of the French Revolution is not much concerned about Paris and the stormy assembly but concentrates on what went on in Lyons—how the bakers carried on the production and distribution of bread though everything seemed to be in chaos, how legal documents were burned up, and how a hastily assembled militia fought off an invader. And of course general history is concerned, not with kings, statesmen, warriors, and politics, but with molecular social conditions, cultural and technical innovation, and the long-range development of religious attitudes and social "movements."

From this point of view, Western history has had some pretty good anarchist successes; anarchy is not merely utopian dreams and a few bloody failures. Winning civil liberties, from Runnymede to the Jeffersonian Bill of Rights; the escape of the townsmen from feudal lords, establishing guild democracy; the liberation of conscience and congregations since the Reformation; the abolition of serfdom, chattel slavery, and some bonds of wage slavery; the freeing of trade and enterprise from mercantilism; the freedom of nations from dynasties and of some nations from imperialists; the development of progressive education and the freeing of sexuality—these bread-and-butter topics of European history are never called "anarchist," but they are. The anarchist victory was won by human suffering and often at the cost of blood; it has somewhat persisted; and it must be vigilantly defended and extended. Any new political revolution, even if it calls itself liberation, cannot be relied on to care for these ancient things. In fact, we see that some liberators impatiently brush them aside—civil liberties go overboard, labor unions are castrated, schooling becomes regimentation, and so forth. But even this is not so annoying as to hear defenders of the present status quo with its freedoms call those who want to extend freedom aimless anarchists.

With regard to freedoms, even "eternal vigilance" is not enough. Unless freedoms are extended, they are whittled away, for those in power always have the advantage of organization and state resources, while ordinary people become tired of battle and fragmented. We may vigilantly defend constitutional limitations and privileges that we have won, but new conditions arise that circumvent them. For instance, new technology like wiretapping and new organizations like computerized Interpol must be offset by new immunities, public defenders, etc.; otherwise the adversary system of Runnymede is nullified. Labor leaders become bureaucrats and are co-opted, and union members do not attend meetings, unless new demands revitalize the labor movements—in my opinion, the labor movement can at present only be revitalized by turning to the idea of workers' management. Triumphant science, having won the battles of Galileo and Darwin, has become the new orthodoxy. We see that ecological threats have created a brand new freedom to fight for—the right to have an environment.

On the positive side, the spirit of freedom is indivisible and quick to revive. A good fight on one issue has a tonic effect on all society. In totalitarian countries it is very difficult to control a "thaw," and we have seen how contagious populist protest has been in recent years in the United States. In Czechoslovakia an entire generation was apparently totally controlled since 1948, but—whether because of native human wildness or the spirit of Hus, Comenius and Masaryk—the youth acted in 1968 as if there were no such thing. And in the United States, twenty-five years of affluent consumerism and Organization mentality have not seemed to dampen the youth of the present decade.

Anarchists rely on the inventiveness, courage, and drive to freedom of human nature, as opposed to the proletarian industrialized mentality of Scientific Socialism, which takes it for granted that people are essentially and totally socialized by their historical conditions. But anarchist philosophers disagree sharply on the conditions that encourage freedom. (Characteristically, disagreements among anarchists are taken by them as "aspects" of some common position, rather than as "factions" in a power struggle, leading to internecine strife.) Bakunin, for instance, relies on the unemployed, the alienated, the outcasts, the criminal, the uprooted intelligentsia—those who have nothing to lose, not even their chains. But Kropotkin, by contrast, relies on the competent and independent, the highly skilled—small farmers with their peasant community traditions, miners, artists, explorers, architects, educators. Student anarchism at present tends to be Bakuninist because, in my opinion, the students are inauthentically students; they are exploited and *lumpen* in principle—kept on ice. "Students are niggers." But hopefully the Movement is now beginning to have a more Kropotkinian tendency—authentic young professionals in law, medicine, and ecology. The March 4 (1969) movement of the young scientists at M.I.T. is significant of the new trend.

REVOLUTION
AND COUNTER-REVOLUTION

In ordinary usage, of course, including both liberal and Marxist usage, the word *revolution* has meant, not that controls cease to operate and hinder function, but that a new regime establishes itself and reorganizes the institutions according to its own ideas and interests. (To anarchists this is precisely the counter-revolution, because there is again a centralizing authority to oppose. The counterrevolution occurred with Robespierre, not during Thermidor or with Napoleon.) Liberal historians describe the abuses of the tyrant that made the old regime illegitimate and unviable, and they show how the new regime instituted necessary reforms. Marxists show how in changed technological and social conditions, the class conflict between the dominant and exploited classes erupts: the old dominant group is no longer competent to maintain its power and ideology, the system of belief that gave it legitimacy. Then the new regime establishes institutions to cope with the new conditions, and from these develop a "superstructure" of belief that provides stability and legitimacy. Agitational Marxism, Leninism, works to *make* the old regime unable to cope, to make it illegitimate and to hasten its fall; it is then likely to take power as a minority vanguard party which must educate the masses to their own interests. In this stringent activity, any efforts at piece-meal improvement or protecting traditional freedoms are regarded as mere reformism or tinkering, and they are called "objectively counterrevolutionary." After the takeover by the new regime, there must be a strong and repressive administration to prevent reaction; during this period (indefinitely prolonged) anarchists fare badly.

Of the political thought of the past century, only Anarchism or, better, anarcho-pacifism—the philosophy of institutions without the State and centrally organized violence—has consistently foreseen the gross dangers of present advanced societies, their police, bureaucracy, excessive centralization of decision making, social engineering, processing, schooling, and inevitable militarization—"War is the health of the State," as Randolph Bourne put it. The bourgeois State of the early nineteenth century may well have been merely the instrument of the dominant economic class, as Marx said, but in its further development its gigantic statism has become more important than its exploitation for profit. It and the socialist alternatives have not developed very differently. All have tended toward fascism—statism pure and simple. In the corporate liberal societies, the Bismarckian welfare state, immensely extended, does less and less well by its poor and outcast. In socialist societies, free communism does not come to be, labor is regimented, surplus value is mulcted and reinvested, and there is also a Power Elite. In both types, the alarming consequences of big-scale technology and massive urbanization, directed by the State or by baronial corporations, make it doubtful that central authority is a workable structure.

It could be said that most of the national states, once they had organized the excessive fragmentation of the later Middle Ages, outlived their usefulness by the seventeenth century. Their subsequent career has been largely their own aggrandizement. They have impeded rather than helped the advancing functions of civilization. And evidently in our times they cannot be allowed to go on. Perhaps we could be saved by the organization of a still more powerful supranation; but the present powers being what they are, this would require the very war that would do us in. And since present central powers are dangerous and dehumanizing, why trust superpower and a central international organization? The anarchist alternative is more logical—to try to decentralize and weaken top-down authority in the nation states, and to come to international organization by piecemeal functional and regional arrangements from below, in trade, travel, development, science, communications, health, etc.

Thus, for objective reasons, it is now quite respectable to argue for anarchy, pacifism, or both, whereas even a generation ago such ideas were considered odd, absurd, utopian, or wicked. I do not mean that anarchy answers all questions. Rather, we have the dilemma; it seems that modern economies, technologies, urbanism, communications, and diplomacy demand ever tighter centralized control; yet this method of organization patently does not work. Or even worse: to cope with increasingly recurrent emergencies, we need unified information, central power, massive resources, repression, crash programs, hot lines; but just these things produce and heighten the emergencies. There is real confusion here, shared by myself.

ANARCHISM AND THE YOUNG

In any case, now hundreds of thousands of young people, perhaps millions, call themselves anarchists—more so in Europe, of course, where there has been a continuing trádition of anarchist thought. It is hard to know how to assay this. There are isolated phrases with an anarchist resonance: "Do your thing!" "Participatory democracy," "I scoff at all national flags" (Daniel Cohn-Bendit). These do not get us far, but certain attitudes and actions are more significant. The young are severely uninterested in Great Power politics and deterrence "strategy." They disregard passport regulations and obviously want to do without frontiers. Since they are willing to let the Systems fall apart, they are not moved by appeals to Law and Order. They believe in local power, community development, rural reconstruction, decentralist organization, town-meeting decision making. They prefer a simpler standard of living and try to free themselves from the complex network of present economic relations. They balk at IBM cards in the school system. Though their protests generate violence, most tend to non-violence. But they do not trust the due processes of administrators, either, and are quick to resort to direct action and civil disobedience. All this adds up to the community anarchism of Kropotkin, the resistance anarchism of Malatesta, the agitational anarchism of Bakunin, the anarchist progressive education of France, the guild socialism of William Morris, the personalist politics of Thoreau. Yet in the United States at least, except for Thoreau (required reading in Freshman English), these thinkers are virtually unknown.

The problematic character of youthful anarchism at present comes from the fact that the young are alienated, have no world for them. Among revolutionary political philosophies, anarchism and pacifism alone do not thrive on alienation—unlike, e.g., Leninism or fascism. They require a nature of things to give order, and a trust in other people not to be excessively violent; they cannot rely on imposed discipline to give the movement strength, nor on organized power to avert technological and social chaos. Thus, historically, anarchism has been the revolutionary politics of skilled artisans (watchmakers or printers) and of farmers—workers who do not need a boss; of workmen in dangerous occupations (miners and lumbermen) who learn to trust one another; of aristocrats who know the inside story and can economically afford to be idealistic; of artists and explorers who venture into the unknown and are self-reliant; among professionals, progressive educators and architects have been anarchist.

We would expect many students to be anarchist, because of their lack of ties, their commitment to the Republic of Letters and Science, and their camaraderie; and so it was, among many European students of the classical type—just as others were drawn to elitist fascism. But contemporary students, under the conditions of mass education, are in their schedule very like factory proletariat, and they are not authentically involved in their studies. Yet their camaraderie is strong, and in some respects they are like aristocrats *en masse*. The effects are contradictory. They are daring in direct action, and they resist party discipline; they form communities; but they are mesmerized by the charisma of administration and Power, and since they only know going to school, they are not ready to manage much.

In both Europe and America, the confusion of alienated youth shows up in their self-contradictory amalgam of anarchist and Leninist thoughts and tactics, often within the same group and in the same action. In my biased opinion, their frank and clear insight and their spontaneous gut feeling are anarchist. They do not lose the woods for the trees, they feel where the shoe pinches, they have a quick and naive indignation and nausea, and they want freedom. What they really hate is not their countries, neither repressive communism nor piggish capitalism, but how Modern Times have gone awry, the ubiquitous abuse of technology and administration, and the hypocritical distortion of great ideals. But their alienation is Leninist, bent on seizing Power. Having little world for themselves, they have no patience for growth; inevitably frustrated, they get quickly angry; they want their turn on top in the Power structure, which is all they know; they think of using their youthful solidarity and fun-and-games ingenuity to make a *putsch*.

As anarchists, they should be internationalist (and regionalist) and create an international youth movement; but in the United States, at least, their alienation betrays them into the stupidity of simply fighting the Cold War in reverse, "smashing capitalism" and "building socialism." Of course, this does not ally them with the Soviet Union, which in obvious ways looks uncomfortably like their own country and worse; about Russia, they tend to say nothing at all. They say they are allied with the underdeveloped socialist countries—China, Cuba, North Korea, North Vietnam—and all anticolonial liberation movements. This is a generous impulse, and it provides them a relevant activity that they can work at, trying to thwart American imperialist intervention. But it is irrelevant to providing models or theory for their own problems in the United States. I am afraid that an advantage of the "Third World" is that it is exotic, as well as starving; one does not need to know the inner workings. Certainly their (verbal) alliance with it has given the Leninist militants some dubious bedfellows—Nkrumah, Nasser, Kim Il Sung, Sukarno, Che Guevara in Bolivia, etc. In the more actual situation of the Vietnam war protest, where young militants might have had some influence on American public opinion, I have always found it impossible to have a serious discussion with them whether it was to the advantage of the South Vietnamese farmers to have a collective Communist regime or just to get rid of the Americans and aim at a system of small landowners and cooperatives, as the radical Buddhists seemed to favor. To the Leninists it was more satisfactory to chant "Ho Ho Ho Chi Minh, the NLF is going to win"; but anarchists might prefer the Buddhist solution, since, as Marxists scornfully point out, "Anarchism is a peasant ideology," and pacifists cannot help but see the usual consequences of war, the same old story for ten thousand years.

Historically, the possibility of an anarchist revolution—decentralist, antipolice, antiparty, antibureaucracy, organized by voluntary association, and putting a premium on grass-roots spontaneity—has always been anathema to Marxist Communists and has been ruthlessly suppressed. Marx expelled the anarchist unions from the International Workingmen's Association. Having used them to consolidate their own minority power, Lenin and Trotsky slaughtered the anarchists in the Ukraine and at Kronstadt. Stalin murdered them in Catalonia during the Spanish Civil War. Castro has jailed them in Cuba, and Gomulka in Poland. In the Western press, *anarchy* is the term for chaotic riot and aimless defiance of authority; in official Marxist statements, it appears in the stereotype "bourgeois revisionists, infantile leftists, and anarchists." They are bourgeois revisionists because they want civil liberties, a less restricted economy, and a better break for farmers. They are infantile leftists because they want workers' management, less bureaucracy, and less class distinction.

YOUTH AND POWER

The American young are not really interested in political economy. Their "socialism" is a symbolic slogan, authentic in expressing disgust at the affluent standard of living and indignation at the existence of so many poor people. Historically, anarchists have been noncommittal or various about socialism, in the sense of collective ownership and management. Corporate capitalism, State capitalism, and State communism have all been unacceptable to anarchists, because they trap people and push them around; and there can easily be too much central planning. But pure communism, the pie-in-the-sky future of Marxists, connoting voluntary labor and free appropriation operating by community spirit, is an anarchist ideal. Yet Adam Smith's free enterprise, in its pure form of companies of active owner-managers competing in a free market, without monopoly, is also congenial to anarchists and was called anarchic in Smith's own time. There is an anarchist ring to Jefferson's agrarian notion that a man needs enough control of his subsistence, or tenure in his work, to be free of irresistible political pressure. Small community control—kibbutzim, workers' management in factories, producers' and consumers' cooperatives—is congenial to anarchism. Underlying all anarchist thought is a hankering for peasant independence, craft guild self-management, and the democracy of the village meeting or of medieval Free Cities. It is a question how all this can be achieved in modern technical and urban conditions, but in my opinion we could go a lot farther than we think if we set our sights on decency and freedom rather than on delusory greatness and suburban affluence.

If young Americans really consulted their economic interests, instead of their power propaganda or their generous sentiments, I think they would opt for the so-called Scandinavian or mixed economy, of big and small capitalism, producers' and consumers' cooperatives, independent farming, and State and municipal socialism, each with a strong influence. To this I would add a sector of pure communism, free appropriation adequate for decent poverty for those who do not want to make money or are too busy with nonpaying pursuits to make money (until society gets around to overwhelming them with the coin of the realm). Such a sector of pure communism would cost about 1 percent of our Gross National Product and would make our world both more livable and more productive. The advantage of a mixed system of this kind for the young is that it increases the opportunities for each one to find the milieu and style that suits him, whereas both the present American cash nexus and socialism necessarily process them and channel them. (Cf. *People or Personnel,* Vintage edition, 1968, pp. 114-22.)

Despite their slogans of "Student Power" and "Power to the People," I do not think that the young want "power," but just to be taken into account and to be able to do their thing—just as, despite the bloodthirsty rhetoric, the most militant seem to be pacifist: with meticulous planning, they blow up a huge Selective Service headquarters and meticulously see to it that nobody is injured. (The slogan "Black Power" has more substance, since it means getting absentee landlords and foreign social workers, cops, and schoolteachers off the backs of the black communities; but here again, despite the bloodthirsty rhetoric, there has been little personal violence, except that instigated by the police.)

The young indeed want a revolutionary change, but not by the route of "taking over." So except for a while, on particular occasions, they simply cannot be manipulated to be the shock troops of a Leninist coup. If a large number of young people go along with actions organized by Trotskyites or the Progressive Labor party or with some of the delusions of the various splinters of Students for a Democratic Society, it is because, in their judgment, the resulting disruption does more good than harm. And let me say that, compared with the arrogance, cold violence, and occasional insanity of our established institutions, the arrogance, hot-headedness, and all too human folly of the young are venial sins.

My real bother with the neo-Leninist wing of the New Left is that its abortive manipulation of lively energy and moral fervor for a political revolution that will not be, and ought not to be, confuses the piecemeal social and cultural change that is brightly possible.

This puts me off—but of course it is their problem, and they have to do it in their own way. In my opinion, it is inauthentic to do community development in order to "politicize" people, or to use a good do-it-yourself project as a means of "bringing people into the Movement." Good things should be done for their own sake and will then generate their own appropriate momentum. The amazing courage of sticking to one's convictions in the face of the police is insulted when it is manipulated as a means of "radicalizing." The loyalty of youth to one another is extraordinary, but it can turn to disillusionment if they perceive that they are being had. Many of the best of the young went through this in the thirties, and it was a bad scene.

In an important sense, the present bandying about of the word *revolution,* in its usual connotations, as in the present symposium, is counterrevolutionary. It is too political. It seems to assume that there could be such a thing as a Good Society or Body Politic, whereas, in my judgment, the best that is to be hoped for is a tolerable society that allows the important activities of life to proceed—friends, sex, arts and sciences, faith, the growing up of children with bright eyes, and the air and water clean.

I myself have a conservative, maybe timid, disposition; yet I trust that the present regime in America will get a lot more roughing up than it has: from the young who resent being processed; from the blacks who have been left out; from housewives and others who buy real goods with hard money at inflationary prices, hiked by expense accounts and government subsidies; from professionals demanding the right to practise their professions rather than be treated as personnel of the front office; not to speak of every live person in jeopardy because of the bombs and chemical-biological warfare. Our system can stand, and profit by, plenty of interruption of business as usual. It is not such a delicate Swiss watch as all that. The danger is not in the loosening of the machine but in its tightening up by panic repression.

It is true that because of massive urbanization and interlocking technologies, advanced countries are vulnerable to catastrophic disruption, and this creates intense anxiety. But there is far more likelihood of breakdown from the respectable ambitions of Eastern Air Lines and Consolidated Edison than from the sabotage of revolutionaries or the moral collapse of hippies.

In a modern massive complex society, it is said, any rapid global "revolutionary" or "utopian" change can be incalculably destructive. I agree. But I wish people would remember that we have continually introduced big rapid changes that have in fact produced incalculable shock. Consider, in the past generation, the TV, mass higher schooling, the complex of cars, roads, and suburbanization, mass air travel, the complex of plantations, government subsidies to big planters, chain grocers, and forced urbanization, not to speak of the meteoric rise of the military industries. In all these there has been a big factor of willful decision; these have not been natural processes or inevitable catastrophes. And we have not yet begun to compound with the problems caused by these utopian changes. Rather, in what seems an amazingly brief time, we have come to a political, cultural, and religious crisis, and talk of "revolution." All because of a few willful fools.

A decade ago it was claimed that there was an end to ideology, for the problems of modern society have to be coped with pragmatically, functionally, piecemeal. This seems to have been a poor prediction, considering the deafening revival of Marxist-Leninist rhetoric and Law and Order rhetoric. Yet it was true, though not in the sense in which it was offered. The ideological rhetoric is pretty irrelevant; but the pragmatic, functional, and piecemeal approach has not, as was expected, consigned our problems to the expertise of administrators and engineers but has thrown them to the dissenters. Relevant new thought has not been administrative and technological, but existentialist, ethical, and tactical. Pragmatism has come to be interpreted to include the character of the agents as part of the problem to be solved; it is psychoanalytic; there is stress on engagement. (Incidentally, it is good Jamesian pragmatism.) Functionalism has come to mean criticizing the program and the function itself, asking who wants to do it and why, and is it humanly worth doing, is it ecologically sound. Piecemeal issues have gotten entangled with the political action of people affected by them. Instead of becoming more administrative as expected, every problem becomes political. The premises of expert planning are called into question. The credentials of the board of trustees are scrutinized. *Professional* and *discipline* have become dirty words. Terms like *commitment, dialogue, confrontation, community, do your thing* are indeed anti-ideological—and sometimes they do not connote much other thought either—but they are surely not what *The End of Ideology* had in mind.

THE CRISIS OF AUTHORITY

Our revolutionary situation is not a political one, and yet there *is* a crisis of authority. This is peculiar.

There is a System and a Power Elite. But Americans do not identify with the ruling oligarchy, which is foreign to our tradition. A major part of it—the military-industrial and the CIA, and FBI—even constitute a "hidden government" that does not thrive on public exposure. The daily scandals in the press seem to indicate that the hidden government is coming apart at the seams. Politicians carefully cajole the people's sensibilities and respect their freedom, so long as these remain private. And we have hit upon the following accommodation: in high matters of State, War, and Empire, the oligarchy presents *faits accomplis;* in more local matters, people resent being pushed around. Until 1969, budgets in the billions were not debated, but small sums are debated. From a small center of decision, it has been possible to spend a trillion dollars for arms, employ scores of millions of people, transform the universities, distort the future of science without public murmur; but where a regional plan might be useful—e.g., for depollution or better distribution of population—it fails because of a maze of jurisdictions and private complaints.

In such a case, what is the real constitution? The social compact becomes acquiescence to the social machine, and citizenship consists in playing appropriate roles as producers, functionaries, and consumers. The machine is productive; the roles, to such as have them, are rewarding. In the galloping economy, the annual tax bite, which ordinarily strikes home to citizens everywhere, has been tolerable. (Only the draft of the young hits home, but this was noticed by few until the young themselves led the protest.) Then, human nature being what it is, the Americans have accepted the void of authentic sovereignty by developing a new kind of allegiance to the rich and high-technological style itself, which provides the norm of correct behavior for workmen, inspires the supermarkets, and is used to recruit soldiers.

A typical and very important class is the new professionals. Being essential to tend the engine and steer it, they are high-salaried and prestigious. An expensive system of schooling has been devised to prepare the young for these roles. At the same time, these professionals are mere personnel. There is no place for the autonomy, ethics and guild liberty that used to characterize professionals as persons and citizens. *Mutatis mutandis,* the same can be said of the working class. It reminds one of the development of the Roman Empire, when personal rights were extended under the *jus gentium,* but the whole world became one prison.

On the other hand, large groups of the population are allowed to drop out as socially useless—farmers, racial minorities, the incompetent and deviant, the old, many of the young. When these are not altogether neglected, they are treated as objects of social engineering and are also lost as citizens. This too is like Rome.

In an unpolitical situation like this, it is hard for good observers to distinguish between riot and riotous protest, between a juvenile delinquent, a rebel without a cause, an inarticulate guerrilla, a protestant for legitimacy. Student protest may be adolescent identity crisis, alienation, or politics. On a poll, to say "I don't know" might mean one is judicious, a moron, or a cynic about the questions or the options. Conversely, good behavior may be rational assent, apathy, obsessional neurosis, or a dangerous prepsychosis about to murder father, mother, and four siblings.

With this background, we can understand the rash of "civil disobedience," "lawlessness," and the general crisis of authority. What happens politically in a country like the United States when the government steers a disastrous course? There is free speech and assembly and a strong tradition of democracy; it is false that these do not exist, and—with some grim exceptions—they have been pretty well protected. But the traditional structures of remedy have fallen into desuetude or become phony, or are terribly rusty. Critical professionals, bourgeois reformers, organizations of farmers and industrial workers, political machines of the urban poor have been largely co-opted. Then, inevitably, protest appears at a more primitive or inchoate level.

"Civil disobedients" are nostalgic patriots without available political means. The new "lawless" are the oppressed without political means. Instead of having a program or party, protesters have to try, as Mario Savio said, to "throw themselves on the gears and levers to stop the machine." Scholars think up ways to stop traffic. Professionals form groups to nullify a law. Middle-class women go by trainloads to Washington to badger senators and are hauled off to jail for disorderly conduct. The physically oppressed burn down their own neighborhoods.

The promising aspect of it is the revival of populism—sovereignty reverting to the people. One can sense it infallibly during the big rallies, the March on Washington in '63 or the peace rallies in New York and at the Pentagon in '67 and in Washington in '69. Except among a few Leninists, the mood is euphoric, the heady feeling of the sovereign people invincible—for a couple of hours. The draft-card burners are proud. The children of Birmingham attacked by dogs look just like Christians. Physicians who support Dr. Levy feel Hippocratic, and professors who protest classified research feel academic right back to Abelard. On the other hand, the government with the mightiest military power in the history of the world does not hasten to alter its course because of so much sweet determination. The police of the cities have prepared arsenals of antiriot weapons. Organized workmen beat up peace demonstrators. Judge Hoffman does not allow relevant evidence to be heard in court. Tear gas is dropped on the Berkeley campus because some people have planted trees.

I do not think this conflict is much the result of evil motives, though there are some mighty stupid people around. There are few "pigs" as well as few "subversives" and plenty of patriots on both sides. And I have not heard of any institutional changes that would indeed solve the inherent dilemmas of Modern Times. The crisis of legitimacy is a historical one. Perhaps "social contract," "sovereignty," and "law" in any American sense are outmoded concepts.

THE CRISIS OF BELIEF

Among the young especially, the crisis is a religious one,

deeper than politics. The young have ceased to "believe" in something, and the disbelief occurs at progressively earlier years. What is at stake is not the legitimacy of American authority but of any authority. The professions, the disciplines, reasoning about the nature of things—and even if there is a nature of things—these are all distrusted.

Thus, for instance, the dissenting scientists and professors of MIT and Harvard, who want to change the direction of research and alter the priorities of technology, do not seem to me to understand the profound change in popular feeling. (They often seem just to be griping that the budget for Basic Research has been reduced.) Put it this way: Modern societies have been operating as if religion were a minor and moribund part of the scheme of things. But this is unlikely. Men do not do without a system of meanings that everybody puts his hope in even if, or especially if, he doesn't know anything about it—what Freud called a "shared psychosis," meaningful simply because shared, and with the power that resides in dream. In advanced countries it is science and technology themselves that have gradually and finally triumphantly become the system of mass faith, not disputed by various political ideologies and nationalisms that have also been religious. Marxism called itself "scientific socialism," as against moral and utopian socialisms, and this has helped it succeed.

For three hundred years, science and scientific technology had an unblemished and justified reputation as a wonderful adventure, pouring out practical benefits and liberating the spirit from the errors of superstition and traditional faith. During the twentieth century, science and technology have been the only generally credited system of explanation and problem-solving. Yet in our generation they have come to seem to many, and to very many of the best of the young, as essentially inhuman, abstract, regimenting, hand in glove with Power, and even diabolical. Young people say that science is antilife, it is a Calvinist obsession, it has been a weapon of white Europe to subjugate colored races, and manifestly—in view of recent scientific technology—people who think scientifically become insane.

The immediate reasons for this shattering reversal of values are fairly obvious—Hitler's ovens and his other experiments in eugenics, the first atom bombs and their frenzied subsequent developments, the deterioration of the physical environment and the destruction of the biosphere, the catastrophes impending over the cities because of technological failures and psychological stress, the prospect of a brainwashed and drugged 1984. Innovations yield diminishing returns in enhancing life. And instead of rejoicing, there is now widespread conviction that beautiful advances in genetics, surgery, computers, rocketry, or atomic energy will surely only increase human woe.

In such a crisis it is not sufficient to ban the military from the universities, and it will not even be sufficient, as liberal statesmen and many of the big corporations envisage, to beat the swords into plowshares and turn to solving problems of transportation, desalinization, urban renewal, garbage disposal, cleaning up the air and water, and perfecting a contraceptive. If the present difficulty is religious and historical, it will be necessary to alter the entire relationship of science, technology, and human needs, both in fact and in men's minds.

I do not myself think that we will turn away from science. In spite of the fantasies of hippies, we are going to continue to live in a technological world; the question is, is that viable?

The closest analogy I can think of is the Protestant Reformation, a change of moral allegiance: not giving up the faith, but liberation from the Whore of Babylon and a return to the faith purified.

Science, the chief orthodoxy of modern times, has certainly been badly corrupted, but the deepest flaw of the affluent societies that has alienated the young is not, finally, imperialism, economic injustice, or racism, bad as these are, but the nauseating phoniness, triviality, and wastefulness, the cultural and moral scandal that Luther found when he went to Rome in 1510. And precisely science, which should have been the wind of truth to clear the air, has polluted the air, helped to brainwash, and provided weapons for war. I doubt that most young people today have even heard of the ideal of the dedicated researcher, truculent and incorruptible, and not getting any grants—the "German scientist" that Sinclair Lewis described in *Arrowsmith*. Such a figure is no longer believable. I don't mean, of course, that he doesn't exist; there must be thousands of him, just as there were good priests in 1510.

The analogy to the Reformation is even more exact if we consider the school system, from educational toys and Head Start up through the universities. This system is manned by the biggest horde of monks since the time of Henry VIII. It is the biggest industry in the country. It is mostly hocus-pocus. And the abbots of this system are the chiefs of Science—e.g., the National Science Foundation—who talk about reform but work to expand the school budgets, step up the curriculum, inspire the endless catechism of tests, and increase the requirements for mandarin credentials.

These abuses are international, as the faith is. For instance, there is no essential difference between the military-industrial systems, or the school systems, of the Soviet Union and the United States. There are important differences in way of life and standard of living, but the abuses of technology are very similar—pollution, excessive urbanization, destruction of the biosphere, weaponry, disastrous foreign aid. Our protesters naturally single out our own country, and the United States is the most powerful country, but the corruption we are speaking of is not specifically American nor capitalist; it is a disease of modern times.

But the analogy is to the Reformation; it is not to primitive Christianity or some other primitivism, the abandonment of technological civilization. There is indeed much talk about the doom of Western civilization, young people cast horoscopes, and a few Adamites actually do retire into the hills. But for the great mass of mankind, that's not where it's at. Despite all the movements for National Liberation, there is not the slightest interruption to the universalizing of Western civilization, including most of its delusions, into the so-called Third World.

Needless to say, the prospect of a new Reformation is a terrifying one. Given the intransigeance and duplicity of established Power on the one hand, and the fanaticism of the protesters on the other, we may be headed for a Thirty Years' War.

When Goodman wrote this for *Encyclopedia Britannica* he was glad to be in the tradition of his hero Prince Peter Kropotkin, who had written the article on anarchism for the famous 11th edition of the *Britannica*. *The Great Ideas Today*, ed. Robert Hutchins and Mortimer Adler, Chicago: Encyclopedia Britannica, 1970.

Confusion
and
Disorder

I.

*I*n the old anthropology there was an important proposition about how a tribe took on culture from its neighbors: If the cultural trait had to do with a new utility or technique, e.g. better seeds, a new plough, or making vessels out of clay, it was picked up readily and it diffused rapidly; but if the trait was moral, psychological, or religious, e.g. a change in tabu, kinship, child-rearing, or music, then its adoption was resisted and it diffused slowly. People want what is useful and lightens labor, but they refuse what makes them anxious and seems to threaten their moral integrity. Sometimes there may be an odd compromise: basket-weavers will pick up fired pottery, but they paint the old basket design on the new pots, for people are conservative about esthetics.

Our supermarkets readily sell Danish ham and cheese, but we are much slower in buying the equally salubrious Danish ideas about pornography. The Japanese enthusiastically adopted Western technology but, at least up to World War II, they clung with remarkable tenacity to their ancient ideology, emperor-worship, and suicide.

The case is quite different when the new cultural trait is not picked up *by* the tribe but is imposed *on* the tribe, for instance by conquest, or by overwhelming technical and economic superiority of an advanced nation that cannot be resisted. Then the moral integrity of the tribe *is* shattered, it is "colonized." People are disoriented; they can no longer pick and choose what suits them and what they can assimilate at their own pace. Obviously there are then problems of de-colonization: the former colonized people have to find *themselves* again. (According to Fanon, in this process they have to become irrational and violent, so the forgotten can return from the unconscious.)

There is cultural imperialism as well as military imperialism. Even without military conquest, a technical culture appearing on the border may be so foreign that it totally distrupts tribal morale and way of life. Consider a people for whom the sentence "I'll come in due time" means "I'll come when the corn is yea high, if the moon is not in the third quarter which is bad luck in my clan." And suppose they take on an interlocked high technology where "in due time" means "8:30 a.m. by the clock," for in the division of labor and the interlocking of machinery everybody and everything has to mesh and start off together. Then the entire way of life, family pattern, eating habits, sexuality, and community will be disrupted. The technology cannot work without a drastic change in social organization, and the technology disrupts the existing pattern in order to create the necessary social organization. The people become "alienated." Some may die of depression.

II.

I suggest that for a couple of hundred years, and suddenly at an accelerating rate, modern societies have colonized and disoriented themselves, imposing on themselves a technology, urbanization, and centralized social organization that they cannot morally and psychologically cope with.

The usual way of saying this is that our physical sciences and technology, have made giant strides but our social sciences, politics, and ethics have not kept pace. This is true but it is a misleading formulation. It implies that using the same attitude and methods but being busier about moral matters, we can catch up and restore the balance. But if advanced peoples have indeed been colonized by their own advances, they are confused and have lost their capacity to pick and choose what they can assimilate. We certainly manifest a remarkable rigidity in our social institutions, an inability to make inventive pragmatic adjustments. And perhaps worse, the sociology and politics that we do think up have the same technological, centralizing, and urban style that is causing our derangement. The remedies make things worse.

I need not spell out, in *Earth* magazine, the evidence that people are confused. Here are four analogous items from one day's *N.Y. Times*. There is an epidemic increase in gonorrhea because a new strain has developed that is immune to antibiotics; but relying on that treatment, young people have not kept up the cautious habits of previous times. A new hybrid of corn is so efficient to breed that it has been universally adopted and no supply of other seeds was stored; but now the new strain proves to be liable to a disastrous and rapidly spreading blight. (These cases are identical with the Europeans wiping out the Aztecs and Polynesians by infecting them with diseases to which they were not immune; except that we are both the carriers and the victims.) In the general haste to introduce methadone in New York to get addicts off heroin, it is distributed without safeguards, and there are now a couple of thousand methadone addicts who never were heroin addicts. Lastly, a statistical study at Princeton Theological Seminary shows that seminarians will stop to succor a (planted) "man in need" if they are not late for an examination, but they will pass him by if they are late; so the Good Samaritan, who was lower class and no doubt did not have important engagements, had time for the man in needs, but the Priest and the Levite, who had important engagements, were in the high-hurry category.

Our lovely impulses have ugly results. I like to live in Hawaii because it's beautiful. But with the new franchises for the jets, 3 to 5 million others a year are going to come for the same reason I do; the native population is 800,000 and there's not much room. Similarly, it's a grand thing for kids to go on the road and see the world, and also for them to gang together in their tribes, making human togetherness their chief sacrament. But the mathematical result is that they turn Telegraph Avenue and Harvard Square into slums and they are a threat to the Yosemite Valley. It's not *necessarily* because adults are uptight that they don't want the ravening horde to descend. I don't know the answer to these problems. One can limit tourism by imposing a whopping airport and hotel tax, but that would exclude the lower middle class, who are poignantly appreciative tourists, to the advantage of the upper middle class who are so so. Or are we supposed to give people at birth a limited number of tickets to the beauties of the world that they can visit?

Luckily, our confusion is such that evil predictions are also unreliable. For instance, from Huxley's *Brave New World* through Orwell's *1984* to Marcuse's *One-Dimensional Man,* it looked certain that we were headed for universal regimentation, drugged conformity, and brainwashing. But the present does not look that way; there are drugs, but the style is ragged and disorderly and likely to become more so. There are unruly crowds in almost every country. In America at least, the new generation is far less consumerist than the old, in spite of the TV ads—maybe because of the TV ads. Consider how in Czechoslovakia since 1947 the regime used every means of thought-control, the press, TV, schools, labor-unions, dragnet trials of dissenters; yet in 1968, Czech youth, brought up entirely in these circumstances, rose almost unanimously against the regime; they were—no doubt are—just biding their time.

My own view is that people cannot be "dehumanized"; they can just be made unhappy. Their apparent docility and conformity simply mean that, for the time being, they have no available alternative. Real brainwashing, internalizing Big Brother's voice, requires actual physical fright, not advertisements or propaganda. Unless a man's marrow freezes, he doesn't replace his own mind with somebody else's.

Our confusion is world-wide, and it is not interesting to assign blame for it. No doubt, centuries of bad policy, profits, power, Statism, racism, and wars have exacerbated the abuse of science, immodest technology, enclosure of the countryside and herding into cities, growth of bureaucracy, and wildly distorted social priorties. Nevertheless, there is no present evidence that any political regime or ideology is exempt from the plight of modern times.

With few exceptions, the rates of excessive urbanization and the decay of rural life are higher in the "Third World" countries of Asia, Latin America, and Africa than in North America and Europe—and of course the technologically underdeveloped countries can afford it less. Shanghai, even without automobiles, is said to have as much smog as New York, and Mexico City, with scads of automobiles and dirty gasoline, is worse than either. The Hudson, the Rhine, and the Danube are polluted. Lake Superior and Lake Baikal are threatened. To make a vast sugar plantation of Cuba for the Russian market, it is necessary to DDT whole provinces, just as Americans use insecticides to make vast plantations for chain-grocers. The delusion of compulsory schooling for extended years crosses every ideology. Episodes of youth dissent turn up in Spain, China, France, Egypt, the United States, Mexico, Czechoslovakia, Ceylon, you name it. In the past decade, the Americans have shared the honor of using advanced weapons to mow down hundreds of thousands with Indonesia, Nigeria, and now perhaps Pakistan. Even when "aid" has not been weapons, the United States, European nations, and Russia have all given aid to underdeveloped countries that has done more harm than good. Bureaucracy, Statism, and social-engineering are universal. Every nation belongs to one power-bloc or another, although this decreases everybody's security.

It is a sad picture. Yet the plausible—and charitable—and distressing explanation is not that modern people are wicked or perverse or stupid, any more than mankind has usually been, but that they are unusually confused. On the one hand, many of our problems are unprecedented; and on the other hand, disoriented people lose their pragmatic inventiveness and often even their common sense. There are new problems that would be deeply puzzling in the best of circumstances: How to maintain any stability and rootedness with the possibility of speedy travel that we have? How to go about one's business when there is so much instant world-wide communication? What to do with One World that has suddenly emerged? Since general war has finally gotten to be out of the question—it never did make sense—how to organize peace? What *is* the political constitution that, under modern conditions, can further individuality and community and collective justice? What is the right blend of centralization and decentralization? What to automate and what not to automate? Is there really over-population and if so, what then? If the nuclear family doesn't work under modern conditions, what then? What the devil to do with organ transplants and genetic transformation? Is there really a substitute for the Calvinist Ethic? (In my opinion, the mass of mankind has always succeeded in integrating life only by *some* kind of productive activity in the environment, though not, of course, activity tied to making money or making a living.)

Problems of this philosophical depth could perhaps be faced and solved by a mankind that was in possession of its wits. They are honorable and interesting problems—not something to be indignant about. They are not problems like unjust war, social injustice, pollution, piling up armaments, mis-education and mandarinism, where indignation is in order; these are outrages and the answer to them is clear-cut: stop doing it, period. But the right solution of the new honorable problems of civilization would make an amazingly different civilization. Even seriously working at such problems, experimentally and thoughtfully, would make a worthwhile and interesting civilization.

Unfortunately, just this mess of brand new problems and age-old outrages is faced by mankind not in possession of its wits but self-colonized and confused, because we have taken on but been unable to assimilate the quantum jumps of science, technology, urbanization, and complex social organization. And the matter is not helped by the prevalent sentiment among the young that "there is no time." Then confusion becomes quiet panic. In my opinion, the sentiment of immediate crisis has some justification but not as much as young people think. It is partly a rationalization for their own inability to bear frustration, unwillingness to learn anything, and the plain spite of the powerless. To be sure, *these* hang-ups, psychological hang-ups, are inevitable: the young have no world, and *that* is not their fault.

Let me repeat and make clear what I don't mean and what I do mean by this diagnosis. I do *not* mean that we can temporize about outrages like imperialist war, social injustice, pollution, and endless schooling. But I do mean that the most fundamental problems are due to modern times and are world-wide. I have not heard any traditional political or ideological answer to them. It confuses matters worse to single out the Americans as special devils. Nor are older people especially finks, hypocrites, plastic, and uptight, while the young are innocent, natural, frank, and morally courageous.

It is no doubt hard to engage vigorously in politics, to stop outrages, and especially activist politics, without having slogans to shout and clear-cut enemies to hate and abuse, and without taking sides in the Cold War. It is hard for a militant in the Movement to point out with the disapproval it deserves that the Panthers feed small children propaganda with free breakfast, or that China or North Korea have a Statist idolatry that turns your stomach, or that Cuba jails its anarchists, dissident poets, and queers (I happen to be all three). Yet it is necessary to be clear about such things and not tell half-truths, especially to oneself, or one becomes stupider oneself; and other people aren't fools and won't buy the rhetoric anyway.

III.

This is the problem as I see it, but I don't know the answer, being confused myself, and worse as I get older and in poorer health—I am 60. Since I am asked, however, I can safely give the old prescription of Hippocrates: With a systemic disorder like confusion, the thing is to slow down, take it easy, let things fall apart and hopefully fall into place, until you catch up with yourself. Plain food, breathing exercises, afternoon siesta. Change of scene, preferably in the country. No new commitments, but don't increase guilt by neglecting what is necessary. Don't look for a miracle cure but gradually diminish tension and build up resistance all along the line. *Natura sanat non medicus:* nature heals, not the doctor.

In fact, the drift of my programmatic ideas, of which I have been so prolific, has always been toward withdrawal and simplification. In *Communitas,* my brother and I called it "neo-functionalism," the first principle of design is to ask if it is worthwhile to have the thing at all! Let me repeat half a dozen examples.

At present the right maxim of technology is to innovate

nothing, unless it is an innovation that simplifies the technical system. If there is a choice of a solution, choose the alternative that cuts back; e.g. to diminish smog, it is better to ban private cars from the cities rather than to clean the engines. Design machines that are repairable by the user, to diminish dependency on middlemen. Prefer the technological style that avoids interlocking, so that a system can break down without wide catastrophe, e.g. the Dutch or Danish style of intensive agriculture. (Incidentally, it is absurd for people who want to do organic farming just for themselves and their families to import potato-beetles and praying-mantises so as not to use chemicals. This is ideology. Grow something else instead. If a raccoon eats 10% of my corn, I don't build a fence but plant another row.) Technology is not autonomous, though science is; it is a branch of moral philosophy, with the criteria of prudence, safety, modesty, common sense.

The first question about transportation is not private cars and highways versus public transportation, but why the trip altogether. I have not heard this question asked either in Congress or in City Hall. Why must the workman live so far from the job? Could that be remedied? Why do I travel 2,000 miles to give a lecture for an hour? But let me say that I am grateful to the thousands of taxi-drivers, bus-drivers, pilots, and railroad engineeers who have so far brought me home safe and rarely ever late.

Social organization is now usually over-centralized. People in an enterprise cannot know the process, initiate, make decisions, communicate face to face. The maxim is to decentralize wherever it can be done without too great loss of efficiency. Urban mini-schools and the rural little red schoolhouse instead of central schools, not to speak of educational parks. Indeed, as I showed in *People or Personnel,* in enterprises where the chief cost is people rather than fixed capital and raw materials, the small scale will always show savings of 300% or more; so-called economies of scale are eaten up by overhead and administration to glue the people together and hamstring their efforts. Keep in mind Borsodi's law that, even in manufacturing and processing, as the unit cost of production decreases, the cost of distribution rises, and at some point it catches up. Similarly, the "external" costs of a big concentrated plant should be assigned to the manufacturing cost;

e.g., the hours of commuting of workers, the roads they commute on, the housing problems and increase in rent that occur. The human advantages of decentralization, in initiative and face-to-face communication, often pay off in inventions and improvements.

In the United States, we can realistically aim at a rural ratio of 20% like Canada's rather than the present 5%. I distrust the concept of New Towns as a way of thinning out the cities; they are fantastically expensive and repeat the urban style. It is better to build up the countryside and revive the old towns as regional centers. City and country thrive best in symbiosis, by their *difference*. I agree that for the foreseeable future small farmers in America cannot make a living by cash-farming; but it is possible to get money back to small farms, and encourage new subsistence farms, by using the country to do for the cities many things that the cities do very badly for themselves. Many families on city welfare would prefer to live on the land, if they could get the same check. Many city parents would send their children to country schools for a year or two—city school costs run nearly twice country costs, and the money could be divided between the country school and the farmers who room-and-board the children. Many in old people's homes would certainly prefer to live on the farm or in the village. 90% locked in insane asylums are harmless to themselves and others but cannot cope in the city; many of these would do well in freedom in the country. Vast sums spent for urban renewal and rehousing, with little or no improvement of life, would provide drastic improvement of life for very many more if spent in the country. If more of us had country cousins, we could have better and cheaper vacations than we get at city-owned resorts.

With automobiles, power tools, and TV, rural life is at least as desirable as middle class city life. Nevertheless, from age 15 to 30 it is boring to live in a rural area; I would try to get to the city where the action is. After 30 it is another story.

Note that I am proposing a rural ratio of 20%, not 98%. In general in these proposals for decentralization and dispersal, I am thinking not of global solutions but of 2% of this, 3% of that, 7% of the other. Perhaps 10% of children might opt to go to country schools for one year; 5% of old people; 2% of the insane; 20% of urban renewal money. The aim is not to find a "solution" but to de-tensify, erode, cut down to size the problems that have quite suddenly gotten out of hand. It is only a few percent difference that has caused power shortages, water shortages, traffic congestion, overcrowded clinics, overcrowded buses, garbage that cannot be hauled away, not enough housing vacancies so that people cannot move when it is convenient (this is a major reason for commuting to the job). Below a certain tipping point, city services can be performed and the city is livable; above that point, nothing works, costs rapidly mount, enlargement or replacement is ruinously expensive and disruptive, the city becomes unlivable, people who can afford it move to the suburbs, the tax base diminishes, the services become still worse. But if we can de-tensify by 2% of this and 3% of that, it might add up to 20% and we have an alternative option.

My brother says it is not necessary to go to the Columbia School of Architecture to remodel a farmhouse.

Schools are an intermediary between the young growing up and the world of activity that is for real. It is a poor society where the young cannot enter the active world directly and learn something; but they are denied access—really they are useless and being kept on ice, just as the old are pensioned off as soon as possible. Schools are now the chief public expense, more than $80 billion annually; even the Pentagon, paying for past, present, and future wars, spends only $65 billion. It is better to spend a lot of the school money to provide direct access into the world for the young. (There are dozens of ways of doing this, like apprenticeships, travel, community work, conservation jobs, hiring them in laboratories, design offices, theaters and TV studios, etc.) The high schools are especially worthless; the money should be put directly in the pockets of adolescents if they are doing anything useful for themselves or society—it costs $1,600 a year to keep a youth in a New York high school. The evidence is that there is no correlation between years of schooling and actual competence on most jobs; the schooling is a dispiriting waste, but necessary in order to get a paper credential. There should be access to the professions *before* going on to higher education rather than after; then a young person can case the situation, find out if it suits and what one needs to learn academically—often there is nothing—and then take the necessary courses with one's own motivation. The present mandarin obstacles to access are especially disastrous for poor youth, who can't afford to waste their time and don't have the school style, though they perform well enough on jobs that are for real. What poor people should be demanding for their children is not "quality education" and open enrollment, but a change in the licensing and hiring practices. Naturally, if I say this in a black neighborhood, I am called an elitist honky, but I am right nevertheless. I agree that poor people must have an equal right and opportunity to act as stupidly as everybody else; but I will not agree to hush up that it is stupid.

In giving technological aid to "underdeveloped" regions, what must be avoided is destroying the way of life and the community, creating inflation and instant urbanization, causing farms to be abandoned, piling up machinery that cannot be used because there are no skills and replacement parts, making the region dependent on imports priced on the world market. The answer is Intermediate Technology: the use of high science and modern analysis to devise techniques that use only native social organization, local raw materials, skills that exist or can be easily learned. The aim is to help people out of disease, starvation, and drudgery, but nothing more. They must then accumulate capital and take off at their own pace in their own style; there is no other way to avoid being culturally colonized. To be sure, this kind of foreign aid cannot serve to dump the donor's surplus or outmoded equipment; what is useful may be *too* old-fashioned. Nor is Intermediate Technology highly palatable to the receiving countries that have "rising aspirations." Simple folk want shiny goods; and their sophisticated political leaders, trained in Princeton, Cambridge, or Moscow, hanker after the whole Western package, including a 12-lane boulevard from the port to the capital, a steel mill, a high school system that consumes a third of the national product, and a retinue at the United Nations that eats up the rest.

I have mentioned Fanon's thesis that the colonized must become narrow and violent, to cast off their self-hatred and affirm themselves. In our advanced self-colonized societies, we have seen a certain amount of this among the young, projecting onto their parents, and onto the System, the hated traits they feel in themselves. But of course this projection cannot succeed, the hatred cannot stick, because the parents are *not* different enough; they are equally confused, as well as being mostly decent human beings and usually dear. Instead, we have hit on a quite different way to eradicate the internalized enemy, namely disorder. Since Modern Times, the Establishment, etc. are keeping things in control, for the time being liberation means letting the cat out of the bag.

IV.

I am sure that the reader has by now gotten my idea, such as it is. So let me close with another kind of thought.

In the coming decade, our society must learn to tolerate disorder, and profit from it. Disorder will increase, not necessarily explosively but in the more interesting forms of erosion, raggedness, disobedience, institutions falling apart. Many more 12-year-olds will be truant. Some of the expanded neo-Glassic community colleges and State universities will become ghost towns. The cities will decay right on. The invisible people and pariahs will continue to come out of the walls, blacks, redskins, adolescents, women, gays, jailees. At long last we may give up trying to legislate morals, gambling, sex, drugs. We may even learn—but I doubt it, it seems to be against "human nature"—to stop putting undesirables in jail because there is no percentage in it, the process always creates more crime than it prevents. It may become difficult neatly to distinguish the employed and the unemployed—hopefully we will adopt the guaranteed income instead of welfare. The country will teem with communes and life-styles. And more and more pilgrims to rock festivals and Ivan Illich in Cuernavaca. Populist protests, crowds suddenly gathering on every kind of issue, will be an accepted method of politics. There will also be more crime-in-the-streets—and we had better remember that the kind of civil peace we have had for a few generations has been unique in history; at all other times and places people used to carry swords and lock themselves in at night.

I suspect that our trillion-dollar economy won't flourish as well when the system is not so highly tuned. But if the falling off is gradual, this could be a good thing. (Except for folk who simply didn't have enough to eat, the Great Depression was not a bad time to be young in—I was class of '31.)

To me as an anarchist and psychologist, it is promising when things fall apart. They have been meshed together too tightly and artificially. Maybe some things will fall into their natural parts and recombine into more natural wholes. "Chaos is order" is an old anarchist epigram. Anyway, as Freud pointed out, once contents have come out of repression, it is impossible to cram them back; any attempt to do so produces distortion and violence; you must let them run their course and find their own integration. Disorder as such is not dangerous—though it *can* be a nuisance if one is busy. When people are really vitally threatened, they respond with authentic anxiety and tone the noise down.

The real dangers are otherwise. On the one hand, there are those who want to re-establish Law and Order. On the other hand, there are crazies who foment disorder artificially, with some fantasy that they can direct it. Between them, these two groups are likely to cause a lot of unnecessary suffering.

From *Earth* (August 1971).

Hallowe'en 1969

O goblin with your yellow fiery eyes
and jagged mouth that frightened me to carve,
glaring out of our window at the street,
protect us from the candidates for mayor.

V

TALKING
SENSE:
THREE
IMPROMPTU
OCCASIONS

"Our
Standard
of
Living"

The issue raised in the following interview seems to me important—perhaps embarrassingly important—in the present discussion of poverty. Certainly people who are at present deprived in society must have as much right and opportunity as anybody else to get useless goods, better bad education, and so forth. Nevertheless I, at least, cannot enthusiastically support legitimate (and politically and psychologically necessary) demands which I deeply feel to be foolish. It has often been wisely said that the poor in this country cannot settle for merely rising into the middle class; but not much has been said about what is meant by this proposition. Unfortunately, the following sensible and rather obvious remarks have no political appeal whatever. People who have lived in misery cannot be expected to opt for decent poverty; that is a luxury of those who are not in despair. P.G.

Roger Ebert: You spoke last night about the problems which our standard of living throws up against people who are trying to discover themselves. What do you think about the structure of our standard of living?

Goodman: It seems to me that the idea of a standard of living is quality of life, and that means what people have in terms of happiness, intellectual growth, spiritual growth, and so forth. I really got on this problem for myself, vividly, a couple of years ago up in New Hampshire where I live; my wife was shopping and I was out in the car and there was a gang of kids, ten to thirteen years old, across the street in the playground, playing softball not very well. When I went past that same place again four hours later, the same kids were still playing.

And then I thought. Supposing people actually did the things which really absorbed them, which they felt they were getting something out of and which they kept doing therefore for long hours. Now what would those things be? Well, playing games. Then, for instance, there's gambling. I like to play poker for, oh stakes of five or ten cents. And you can play five, six hours once a week, my wife and friends...and it might cost us, loss or gains, four or five dollars by the end of the night if you have very bad or very good luck. Then, most people, and I, myself, have a very absorbed time looking for love—it's not exactly sex; a mixture of love, friendship, sex. And if one has luck, then, also enjoying that. These are the really absorbing things which you can do.

An activity that a lot of people like—like, or have to do, or feel very much involved in—is "real" politics, as opposed to the kind of politics of electing people for office (unless they're reform candidates). Active politics, you know, such as civil defense protesting or pacifist demonstrations, carrying signs, preparing leaflets, et cetera. And Lord knows how many days of my life I've spent, very absorbedly, not very pleasantly, but absorbedly, engaged in that.

Then there are at least a large number of people who really like to read, and you can devote hours to that. So between the arts and the sciences, reading and nature, you spend a lot of time. There are some people who are religiously inclined. I myself tend rather to go into psychotherapy sessions, which are really Quaker meetings, so that's a kind of religious occupation.

So, one thing or another, if you put together all of these things which people really *would* do, and are absorbed in doing, you'll find that they have practically no market value. You require no equipment to play...the kind of handball we play outdoors in New York; we use a little rubber ball and we don't use any gloves or stuff. For sex, all you require is health and affection. If sex requires money, there's something wrong with it. Reading requires books, but that's not a very great expense. Political activity of the kind I'm describing, real political activity, costs nothing at all; you just scrawl out signs, and, you know, get together with your neighbors and call a meeting in somebody's home or in a church or someplace.

Now if the great mass of the people, I feel, were allowed to spend their time in the way that really gave them the most satisfaction, I'm afraid the gross national product might be cut as much as fifty percent. It's a fantastic thing. Well then what does this mean for our society? It seems to me that, by and large, a chief purpose of our economy must be to prevent people from having the real satisfactions of life—the satisfactions which would enable them to grow, and be happy, and so. That's a rather ghastly thought, isn't it?

Ebert: In other words, you think that our society is set up in such a manner that people are not only denied these goals, but that their society depends upon their not being able to spend time like this?

Goodman: That's right. For instance, an enormous amount of the effort of people in our society is to create a synthetic demand. That's what the whole advertising business is about, isn't it? There is a natural use, a rational use, for advertising. It's to give news. If you look at newspapers in, let's say, 1800, you'll find that the ads were perfectly rational: "Shipment of smoked fish has arrived from Europe. On sale very reasonable at 14 Barrow Street."

The notion of *competitive* advertising has to do with the profit system, of course, and not with use altogether. But in advertising now, in semi-monopolistic advertising that's not even competitive, the main reason for it is artificially to stimulate demand. In other words, to trick people.

Ebert: This isn't the sort of demand, for example, you're talking about when you're talking of the desire people have to read or to gamble or play handball?

Goodman: No, no. It's *artificially* to stimulate demand; it isn't what the people would ordinarily want, but it distracts them into wanting something which they wouldn't even have *thought* of.

Ebert: And which wouldn't interfere with the society?

Goodman: Well, if they want these things and make a demand for them and are willing to pay money for them, to earn the money to buy the things, then of course the economic machine rolls faster. And people who are interested in the economic machine rolling faster are happy; but everybody else is that much *less* happy.

Of course, a good deal of it is done by threat. The whole suburban way of life is founded on the notion that if we don't have all these things, then in some way we are in outer darkness. We don't belong. Something is wrong with us. That is, the people don't look and say, "What would we really do if we did what we wanted to do?"

In other words, the standard of living is determined by two things. By emulation, that is, we have to be better than the other guy whether we want the thing or not; and by fear, that if we don't do that, we are going to end up on Skid Row.

Ebert: You were talking Thursday night about what de Tocqueville had to say about this element in our national character over a hundred years ago. You mention the transition in the news value of advertising. Do you think that, generally speaking, these organized activities are not what people would like to be doing, and the whole problem is getting worse from year to year?

Goodman: Yes, I think it's gotten to the point where it's pretty crazy. Adam Smith sets an absolute axiom—I don't think it's a true axiom, but it was a true axiom for him—that the only reason for economic activity is to provide goods and services.

Now it's obvious, it seems to me, that our economic activity is not being done for that reason. Only nominally is it to provide goods and services. The chief reason for economic activity is to keep the economic machine in operation. For instance, the great economic problem which faces Washington is the rate of unemployment. Now Adam Smith, I think, would have been utterly astounded at any such notion. He would have said, "But that's the whole point!" That is, we get rid of the real scarcities, and then—great! Then you don't work.

Of course that makes great social difficulties. I would rather look at it in this way. If, in fact, people absorbedly did what they had in them to do, then, far from fooling around, they would be extremely productive, their recreation would be valuable, and the whole distinction between working and not working would tend to vanish. But as we have it, we are caught in a terrific box. There are all kinds of feverish economic activity, seeking for jobs and salaries and status, which have nothing to do with the provision of real goods and services. But then precisely because of that, we're caught in an economic trap where more and more are unemployed because of automation, et cetera; therefore, you heighten the synthetic demand, you build, for instance, obsolescence into expensive machines like automobiles.

What I mean by building obsolescence is simply that the auto companies press to pass laws that they need not provide repair parts for more than five years. There's such a state law, in New Jersey I think, which the car companies have pushed. This means that after five years this expensive machine is supposed to be thrown away. Now to have an automobile, especially in a country district, is not only a great thing but probably indispensable. But it doesn't make any difference whether the car's fifteen years old or two years old. But the whole economy would crash if everybody believed that. Because the economy is geared to the health of General Motors. When Charles E. Wilson said, "What's good for General Motors is good for the country," unfortunately it was true. That's just what's wrong with the country.

Ebert: In describing this problem, particularly in *Growing Up Absurd,* you have pointed out that a good many people—high school dropouts, in some cases, or people who are unemployed under certain circumstances—are actually, as you put it, doing the right thing.

Goodman: I'm glad you brought that up. Take a Puerto Rican kid in New York. They aren't made for a scholarly life by their family background, their conditions. Their parents often came from a rural background in Puerto Rico. They have, on the other hand, a very tight community life. Their extended family relationship is extremely lovely. There's considerable richness to that life. And they love to play games, for instance handball. The Puerto Ricans have taken that up in New York and they play marvelously. In fact, the Irish, the Jews and the Puerto Ricans—it's a pleasure to see this game going on. It's our big city game. And these kids will try to drop out of school at thirteen if they can, often with forged documents so that they can get away with it and avoid the truant officer.

Are they making a bad choice? It is pointed out that their entire future is jeopardized; that is, if they do not get a high school diploma, they won't get jobs. Well, in the first place there's something hoaxy about the statistics. The unemployment among those who get high school diplomas is fifty per cent anyway, for four or five years after graduation. But suppose you get the high school diploma and you get the job. The increment of salary, say between those who have the diploma and those who don't, might after ten years be maybe five or six dollars a week. Supposing I make a rational choice, say at the age of twelve. I, now, am going to have to endure four years of torture in classrooms where I'm not doing anything that's of any value to me, however valuable it might be to some other kind of person. All of which time I could spend engaged in what really is interesting to me. Now wouldn't it be a rational choice to choose that rather than an increment in salary of five or six dollars, more than ten years from now? It seems to me rather dishonorable on the part of the President and the National Education Association and so forth to try to push these dropouts back into school, unless the school itself has more intrinsic value.

But now let's look at some middle-class kid. Let's say the child of a factory worker who has now edged into the middle class because the union has gotten him a better salary. He sees that his father and mother have struggled along working terribly hard and the great achievement is that they've been able to get the superior refrigerator instead of the old one they had. And it is for this there is all of the difficulty about paying the installment bill.

He might well feel that this is a very bad choice. ("I must make it because if I don't do that in terms of all the evaluation I see around me, we are just going to sink into the depths of degradation.") Nevertheless, it doesn't make his heart leap up as really the kind of thing that his life wants to be about. And when he has to make that choice, he must make it, it seems to me, with a real feeling of inner defeat.

From that point of view, I think that he would be wiser to drop out. I'm not saying that education is not a valuable thing, but what it ought to do is to give one more and more ways to be able to enjoy the world and grow as a person, and not teach how to spend money. It has been said that the best things in life are free. I'm afraid that's true. Much more than we're willing to allow. And if that's true, then our economy is founded on a hoax and it must be clear in some dumb way to the majority of the people that this is a hoax. And they can't get out of this thing and that's why it looks like a rat race.

Part of an interview with Goodman conducted by Roger Ebert, Editor of the *Daily Illini* at the University of Illinois (Urbana). The text here is from "Growing Up Absorbed," *Liberation* (April 1964).

"Power
Struggles"

Q. You have been called a utopian thinker on the ground that the things you propose cannot conceivably be achieved. How do you move in the direction of getting these things done?

A. If any of these things are to be accomplished they must be accomplished by pressure. The important thing is to try to make the unit of pressure the small local unit, the renewal of which is one of the things you're trying to accomplish. In trying to achieve decentralization in the city, for example, it is the settlement house, the school, the neighborhood that should be exercising the pressure, not the election district, the aim being that the neighborhood finally *becomes* the election district.

Q. If the desire for power corrupts, as well as power, and if the neighborhood settlement house had charge of its own budget, and the budget was public money, wouldn't your neighbors like to climb from their place in the hierarchy to the place which would inevitably be there, the tax collector's office and the disbursement office at the top?

A. No, no, I don't think so. I don't think so because I think the corruptibility of mankind is caused by frustration. People don't want power as such. What they want is activity. They want to

255

actualize potentialities, and insofar as they want power they want it in order to make decisions, in order to act. Now in a situation where more and more rights to make decisions are taken away from people, there gets to be more and more need to identify with big decision makers. But in a family for instance, where decision making remains, a pretty much all-right family let's say, isn't there pretty much of a continual town meeting going on?

Q. Not if mama controls the purse strings, as mama does pretty often.

A. Now wait a minute. Papa brings home the money and both mama and the kids have pressures whereby they get the money from him. But what are they? My kids have pretty good pressures. Some of their pressures largely consist in the fact that the activity their money is going for seems so worthwhile, that I want them to have it. And once that is established, in fact there *are* no unreasonable demands ever made. After a while if one of them would say to me I want five bucks, I wouldn't even ask what he wanted it for, because I know it would be used well. It always is. Because there hasn't been at the beginning a denial of his activity. And I don't think that's extraordinary. Do you?

Q. It seems to me there's a valid point that's been lost somewhere here. A great part of the time, perhaps due to the fact that frustration is inevitable, there are power struggles. Let's acknowledge this first, and then your idea of neighborhoods can be talked about in terms of more available power.

A. That's right.

Q. Somebody almost inevitably is going to be holding that power, some one person or small group.

A. I don't see why that follows. What was the idea of our federal system to begin with?

Q. What happened, though?

A. Well, yes, but, did it have to happen? You're saying it had to happen.

Q. Just a pure empirical argument: it does happen.

A. But that isn't altogether true. We tend to be very blind to those cases where it hasn't been true. Let's take the history of science. Up to the last thirty years, you'll find that science has been run in an international and completely decentralized way. Perfectly. There've been scientific academies, there've been universities that cooperated. They've advanced science by leaps and bounds; each little group has been in charge of its funds. And there hasn't been much of an attempt by anybody to dominate from above.

Q. I'm going to pick on this one, because I don't think you have a valid example, simply because there isn't much conflict of basic personal importance.

A. Oh, the devil that's so!

Q. Well, maybe there wasn't any need for this degree of organization before.

A. Scientific work has been extremely organized. I never said it wasn't organized. In every country there were academies of science, conventions, publications. The organization was immense, but there was no power struggle in the sense of some group struggling for centralized domination.

Q. There wasn't any need for a power struggle.

A. There never is a need for a power struggle. This is a neurosis.

Q. But today big organizations are giving out the money, and if you want any part in research in science you have to have money, and you have to get it from the people who control it.

A. That's right. In other words what's happened is that we are interfering with this great history of science with goals that are not the ideals of science. But centralization does not have to happen. It's a style exactly the way baroque was a style. In fact it is a baroque style, as Lewis Mumford points out. That's just what baroque planning is: in the middle is the big palace and all the rays come from the center.

Q. You think though that this is not necessary either in science or in the planning of the neighborhood, that we could choose to do otherwise.

A. Choose is too strong a word because choose gives the idea that you can get out of your skin. I think that we could edge in directions where it would become less necessary to do it this way. Let's put it that way. By creating other kinds of small institutions, we can take the venom out of the centralized institution. You have to fight against it with ideas of alternative activities. You can't fight against it with words, thought, a beatnik withdrawal. A beatnik withdrawal, however, is not a bad first step. To stop is often a very good step. Just to stop, in the beatnik way. You just won't do it. Then maybe you will think of something else to do.

Q. What kind of children would come out of the dormitory situation you propose?

A. What I was proposing was the family structure of the kibbutz, and the psychological theory behind it is Freudian. The trouble that leads to the Oedipus complex is the problem of the good and bad mother. The aim of the kibbutz is to make the mother only the good mother; that is, she teaches you nothing. She doesn't teach you table manners, you learn table manners from society. But when society gets too rough then you can run home crying and mama comforts you.

Q. I've heard some conflicting things about the effects that the kibbutz has had on children.

A. That's why I said to begin at age eleven. It seems beyond doubt that if a child is brought up, especially from the age of about six months to two years, without personal attention, he develops a cold personality which may eventually become a psychopathic personality. In Israel it was not implicit in the notion that the child should not get individual attention; they placed the child in the kibbutz too early because they needed the woman's work in the fields.

Q. I wonder when you talk about putting the children in a dormitory like that. I would not want to give my children up to some one else.

A. You're living in a dream world, dear. Wait till you have children. You'll find that your children get their standards from the street and not from you.

Q. Well, if they are still living at home and I have some influence on their lives, I might be able at least to modify the standards of the street. But if they are off somewhere else, I can't control them at all.

A. Yes, that's true. But even then if the standards you have at home are really more worthwhile and, what is more important, interesting, the child will get something from them even though he lives in the dormitory. But if we take the average situation, I think that almost any street situation is better than most family situations with regard to standards, culture, or love. Moreover, there is no such thing as absolute power over the child anyway.

Q. I'm not talking about absolute power. I just want to maintain an influence over my children by having them live at home.

A. And I'm saying that in urban slum conditions, by and large, I would rather make the influence a little less.

Q. But you said that you would not recommend anything that you would not do for your own children.

A. That's right.

Q. And I would not want to do it to my children. It would be all right if people agreed to it, but I want mine at home.

A. That's right. That's right. That's why I certainly would recommend any such policy on a voluntary basis.

Q. You mentioned something about the importance of interest. Why does it have this importance?

A. I'll tell you why. There are some things that have to be done against people's wills, but we do them at peril. For instance, if a child drifts out into the traffic, you get him by the neck and swat the tar out of him so that he learns his lesson. But every time that's done or a child is made to do something which isn't interesting to him, he is going to do it with less grace and talent; that is, less of himself initiated from inside is going to be involved in it. So insofar as we're interested in the perfection of everybody's life, we must try as much as we can to have a basis of spontaneous interest for anything that is done. The reason is that it will be done better, more accurately, with more grace, more intelligence, and more force.

Q. Would there be adult supervision in these dormitories?

A. If I were running them there would not be. There would be rules, for there is a necessity for structure. The kids would not be left completely to their own devices, for I would combine the dormitory system with a form of urban renewal which would attempt to give the kids the kinds of jobs which adolescents can do, such as renovation. The kids would not be neglected by adults, for if one comes over to a man working and watches, the man will talk to him. And they will be paid for working in the urban renewal program. Isn't this what happens in a primitive culture; Youth House and community work?

Q. You mentioned that with local planning there might be tremendous messes. What would happen? People might think that the planning was a terrible idea and public opinion might become so strong that the planning could not be carried through.

A. That's right. That's exactly what happened to progressive education when they began to try it. So that instead of giving it a real try, things stopped at the level of minor messes and then panic.

Q. Well what would you suggest doing about this?

A. I would suggest more courage.

Q. If power is given to the small group, who is going to lead its members?

A. The people who are wiser, compassionate.

Q. How are they going to establish themselves in this group?

A. Well, now look. Let's pretend for a moment that since I'm sitting here at the head of the table, I'm wiser. How have I established myself? It's not the physical plan of the room. There is no other answer, except that I care. I care enough to think about it; I care enough to write an article; I care enough to talk about it to other people who know something about it.

Q. Is there anything beside courage that might serve to overcome panic?

A. Well, perhaps motivational research might serve the same function at this level that psychotherapy does at the individual level; that is, you use sociological and psychological techniques not in order to put something into the person, but in order to get rid of those things which prevent him from being himself. In psychotherapy we call this unblocking. Thus we might use motivational research to get the people out of the idea that the planning can't be done. That would be quite sufficient. Then I would rather let nature take its course, so that the community is natural. I really deeply think so.

Q. Somewhere you have described yourself as an anarchist. What do you mean by that?

A. I'm for diminishing the exercise of coercive authority as much as possible. I don't think there's any anarchist thought at present which is interested in a total revolution of society or has any picture of a total society. The aim in general is to turn involuntary organizations into voluntary organizations, to turn as

much as possible the pre-organized into the spontaneously organized. To remove as far as possible the principle of fear as a strong
force in human relations so that other feelings will emerge, such as
anger, love, excitement, interest.

Q. I don't understand what you would do if, for instance, on a
small community level the majority of the members decide to do
this or that, and an individual or a few individuals are outvoted.

A. In principle in a good society things would not be put to a
vote. If there was disagreement nothing would be done. The matter
would not be tabled forever, because people would keep attempting
to understand the others' point of view, for the motives of all
would be trusted. But frequently things can be decided fairly easily.
Suppose you go out with a few friends and one says let's go to this
movie and another says let's go to a different movie. How is it
decided?

Q. You vote.

A. Oh, you do not. What happens is that somebody really
cares and really wants to go to a particular movie, and the others
don't really care that much and say O.K. Isn't that what would
happen in a society where people trust one another?

Q. But people don't always have the same set of principles.

A. That's right. And that's another reason for decentralism.
When you have a nice decentralized system, those who disagree
with the way one neighborhood is run can pack up and find
another one more to their liking.

Q. It's pretty obvious that a lot of people want, or think they
want, green space. The suburban way of getting green space has
produced some fairly undesirable side effects such as sprawl,
transportation problems, etc. How can we provide for this desire
for green space, given considerably greater density than presently
exists in the suburb?

A. Is it really the case that people want the green space? Isn't it
possible that when they say they want green space, they're trying to
say something but they're confused as to what it is they want; that
the green space is a sentimental rationalization for some real need?

Q. If people are merely rationalizing when they say that they
need space and green lawns, and they scream about slow bus
service and about slums, then all these things and the reaction to

them may be a result of the quality of life that we live in America.

A. Doesn't it seem obvious that a large part of the flight to the suburb is an effort to find a place where you have some say in your life?

Q. To get back to the criticism of your work as utopian, there are those who say that people spend a lot of time talking about impossible ideals, the utopias if you will, and that this keeps them from getting down to the things which actually might be accomplished.

A. I think that there is a false estimate of the general public involved here. The basis of this sort of criticism is the conception that the average man does not have profound ideals, that he doesn't have high hopes and castles in the air. In fact, the more simple people are, the more they tend to go in for future thinking. But because there is so much potential conflict in such ideas, the people who want to get elected soft-pedal them. It is a matter of how people really are, and therefore of what is *really* feasible.

Q. What is feasible though is partly dependent on the present organization of society.

A. I would suggest ameliorating the present organization. This can be done by people who withdraw from the larger society to carry on experimentation in new patterns, or it can be done by centralized planning for decentralization.

Q. But to get that central plan you'd have to have a fight in the center of power politics.

A. That's right, that's why I bother to write books. But this notion that the central plan would have to support further centralization is a myth which has been foisted by certain big industrialists on you. It is a germ which they put into your mind, a disease. There has been nothing like it in the history of mankind.

Q. What about the farm problem, the farm problem that is centrally managed from Washington? That wasn't foisted on anybody by industrialists. It was foisted on our country by simple laws of economic growth.

A. No, I don't believe that, I don't believe it. If you go back you'll see that there was every encouragement for not doing diversified farming, but for doing cash crop farming. This was altogether unnecessary. The farmer fell into a trap.

Q. We all recognize then the problems of the city are not only the problems of the city but also of the suburb.

A. I think suburbs ought to be wiped out. They are a bad idea. Get rid of them.

Q. What happens if the people who live in the suburbs are delegated decentralized power and choose to live in the suburbs?

A. Well, now look. If all the brass and the intellectual planners begin to set their minds against the suburban fringe, we have to assume that this will create a new cultural tone. It must be so.

Q. This will be education and not manipulation?

A. I think so.

Q. One of the troubles is just plain sheer numbers of people. When we first moved out of the city we weren't moving to the suburbs but rather to the country. But the country later became the suburbs.

A. What do you mean, sheer numbers of people? You can't mean actual population growth. I don't see crowds when I look out the window here. This crowding in the suburbs isn't because of an increase of population. It is caused by redistribution. And you can set up counter-forces in the suburb to go in the other direction. Tax policy, road policy, FHA policy. Or take Cape Cod National Park. It is going to say "no further" and it is also saying "we will buy up the land of people who move out."

Q. But then the city will expand and overtake the suburb.

A. Yes, but it is also possible to set up forces in the direction of keeping people from going to the suburb or the city, to keep them in the small town and the farm.

Q. Some day there just won't be room to stay on the farm.

A. That's a long time from now, and I don't believe it—I mean, I'm not convinced.

Q. How long is a long time?

A. That depends on what population figures you study. I frankly think this business of the population explosion is a somewhat bourgeois notion, and it is also something of a red herring which is thrown in the way of settling immediate problems. Why suddenly bring this neo-Malthusianism into the picture? They said the same thing exactly in the time of Malthus.

Part of an interview first published as "The Unity of Planning" in *The Carleton Miscellany* (Summer 1962).

Last
Public
Speech

I.

*T*he Department of Agriculture in one of its publications points out that you can feed a family of four on a sixth of an acre if you don't have animal products. If you have animal foods you might go up to three acres. That's a figure not too different from one Ralph Borsodi mentioned some forty years ago. This means good land, good seed, and so on. A sixth of an acre isn't much. The reason I use this introduction is to say that mankind for a long time has had that sixth of an acre and a good life in sufficiency. The notion that to live well requires modern conditions or something or other is false. For instance, if we can believe Lewis Mumford, in the high Middle Ages, 12th and 13th Century, the people lived very well and didn't work very hard. They had 180 religious holidays a year when they didn't do anything.

If we consider industrial sufficiency—in 1860 the United States clearly had an industrial sufficiency to allow everybody to live quite well. The proof of that is that they fought the biggest and most expensive war in all history at that time. Even though supporting soldiers, etc., the standard of living in the North went down not a bit. So there obviously was the productivity to make it pretty good for everybody. Marx had the notion that you could initiate Communism only when there was a technological base in the means of production to support Communism. He said this in 1848 and he seemed to feel that the specter of Communism was haunting Europe at that time. So Europe, in Marx's mind, had an excellent sufficiency to introduce Communism. That's a long time ago.

Now let's take another view; say decentralization, the ability to decentralize. Patrick Geddes, one of Mumford's teachers, around 1905 proclaimed the coming of electrification because this at last would allow us to decentralize. We would no longer need the steam-power prime-mover which had made big cities like Birmingham and Manchester. We could decentralize and, as Borsodi has recommended, use small power tools and small factories for industrial production. Now, the effect of electrification, of course, has been exactly the opposite; we are concentrating more and more. But this was not a technological consideration. Just about the same time the automobile was coming in and, about 1905, with Henry Ford, the automobile became cheap and ubiquitous. If you take electricity, power tools, automobile and the beginning at that time of distant communications (widespread telephone and telegraph, and since then radio and TV) you see that the technical means of decentralization have been with us quite a long time.

The actual demography, of course, has been just the opposite. I point out to you that the centralization of populations has gone on at a greater pace in the underdeveloped world than in the developed. That is, Asia, Africa and Latin America have centralized, urbanized, at a much more rapid pace in this century than Europe or the United States. It is quite clear then that the reason we live as badly as we do has nothing to do with technological considerations. The reasons are institutional, political, psychological and religious. Of those, I think the religious happen to be the most important.

One word about the psychological, being a psychologist. The use of a meeting like this is really not to teach people new technical gimmicks as to how they can make do on a small scale, though you all want to know that, but you all know how to find out by yourselves. The use of meetings like this is purely psychological, it seems to me. It is to bolster us up who feel powerless in large centralized institutions by showing that there are viable alternatives and by being able to prove that economically and statistically. That's the kind of thing Ralph Borsodi is superb at. I think one of his books, *Prosperity and Security,* is one of the masterpieces of the century, just as an economic analysis. I don't know what you think of the book, but it certainly influenced me profoundly. In other words, what has to be overcome is the psychology of powerlessness which everybody feels. You know, "you can't fight city hall," or "that's the system and what can you do about it?" And the young generation now is quite sure that there are many viable alternatives. Some of us, I include myself, have been talking up all kinds of alternatives. Mine are mostly made off the top of my head, but they are quite clever and why not those, because the aim is psychological. I mean, if they're not practical, you think of a more practical one; the important thing to do is to try, so if I think of one that you think is practical and then you find it is impractical, by then you'll have thought up a practical one. That's one of the uses of writers, by the way.

Political changes. I'm an anarchist; I don't buy political changes much because they all seem to devote themselves to a change of power, so a different group, an oppressed group, takes power. But then you find the oppressed group is no smarter than the group that oppressed them—how could they be?—because all they ever learned was what they learned from their oppressors. They might have certain better moral values but their sense of how to live within a technology is very rarely any better. And so you just repeat, say under socialism, what you had in capitalism, except that you have to try to catch up and surpass the capitalists, which gets even worse sometimes.

Now the religious issue; that is, given the fact that we could live differently, and sometimes you get an urge for people to live differently. Don Newey speaks of "What Price Miracle," in his new book. I think that's the right word. Miracle is the type of thing messiahs or prophets whose lips are touched by coals of fire by God produce. Well that ain't me. Consider especially the young people, who I think are religiously extremely naive although very deeply religious. You have to believe the religion—let's say a central part of it—you can't get to believe something just because it would be sensible and convenient to believe it.

Now the present world structure's belief, without question, is the scientific technology as at present used. That's what everybody believes. If you're sick that's what you do; you try to get the latest medical gadgets in the most centralized hospital possible. And that's what everybody does. That's what they believe. That has displaced for the last two hundred years, at least, the old Christian religion. And we want a different use of that scientific technology, but to get a different use will require a great change of thought, which I am not sure we can get. And, in fact, the people who speak of change of heart in recent times have always laid the emphasis quite the other way from the way that, say, I would want, or Mumford would want, or that Ralph Borsodi would want or Scott Nearing would want. It's in a different direction. For instance, when I was young the big book of social criticism of my adolescence and twenties was Huxley's *Brave New World*, which was then repeated in a kind of darker form—Huxley was kind of bright and funny about it—but in a darker form by Orwell in *1984*. The notion being that the new scientific technology and the centralized political organization would lead to a highly regimented, conformist, highly disciplined, mechanized, robot-like humanity. And people were going to be changed, having electrodes implanted in their brains, given drugs, watching Big Brother on TV. Well at least this prediction hasn't come out right.

One of the satisfactions of being a social critic like myself is to realize that if you can do it for real, the social criticism, everything you predict, won't come out. That is, you are like the prophet Jonah; he prophesied and because he prophesied it doesn't happen. That is a very important use of social criticism. Critics prevent the things from happening which they say are inevitable. To take a recent social critic of this kind who speaks of a change in human nature, Marshall McLuhan, we all live not in decentralized communities but in a global village. And because of the TV and the news media—and it's more centralized than you can possibly imagine and it's world wide—a lot of the present ecological thinking (like the Club of Rome) is founded on the same notion, that somehow there will be some commissars who will make rules so you won't dare step on the grass or eat anything because it's going to be against these worldwide ecological rules. If it's going to be that bad, I'd sooner take the risks of the present pollution. I don't think that's the way it needs to be done. But, in any case, the whole trend of the futurologists from my boyhood up to the present is toward more and more centralization; because what futurologists do, of course, is to take present trends and extrapolate them.

Now the good fortune that we have is that human beings are so ornery, capricious, etc., that present trends don't mean a thing. They tend to last fifteen years, ten years, five years sometimes. That is, the most remarkable trends such as the population growth are subject to sudden change. That doesn't mean that it's not useful to look at the trends and try out scare words; it is also the case that scare words work. Let me just give an anecdote about futurologists which is a good one: Ralph Nader, in his office in Washington, has got a typed card over his desk, an editorial from the *New York Herald* of 1895, hailing the coming of the automobile to New York City. It points out that with this wonderful new invention at last our city will be clean, meaning there won't be any horse shit on the streets, and it will be quiet because of these wonderful new machines which are going to run on rubber tires. Now that was a bum prediction, a real bummer. But Nader has it up there just for that reason, lest he get carried away by his own predictions of doom.

My own feeling is that the only thing which makes for this kind of religious change in people is facts. That is, calculations, reasons, etc., don't work. This isn't because people are stupid, but, because of the intimate way of life a person has, reason just isn't enough. What I mean by fact is when a thousand people, maybe more, died of the smog one day in London. They cut down the smog by enormous amounts, something like 90%, but only because a lot of people died. In New York City it would probably take ten thousand deaths. Then something would be done. When it became clear to women that the milk was being poisoned by the atomic testing and milk was their babies', then there got to be a worldwide screaming with the Women's Strike For Peace and so forth, and then they got the first test ban, the atmospheric test ban. Unfortunately, there has got to be something going on that gut level. My own guess is that we are not going to get rid of the atom bombs by SALT talks or anything like that. We'll get rid of them when accidentally a bomb falls on Akron, Ohio, and that'll be just too bad for the people in Akron, Ohio, but then there will be a world-wide movement, beginning here, to cut back on the atom bombs. I'm afraid that's how it is, and that isn't because people are stupid. I'm not saying people are stupid. It's just that if you want a big change which really changes your whole way of life and your sources of income and so forth, it has really got to hit you as a fact. Now the present system, unfortunately, is going to produce this kind of fact, just technologically.

I wrote an article once in which I outlined a week in which there were ten plagues in New York City and every boy ran away into the mountains and began to homestead. I'll just mention some of the plagues. There is a big power failure. Now we have had several power failures in New York City and we have had a brown-out this year already, so there could easily be a big power failure. When there is a big power failure, the subways don't run so all the cars have to go. There might be an atmospheric inversion just that day when all these cars are going, and the dangerous condition the atmosphere is always in will become deadly. So we'll have our ten thousand or fifty thousand people all dying of the smog. Now the same week (what terrible luck!) the new SST was finally sailing, and it was making its maiden voyage when it bumped right into the Empire State Building. Just the worst luck! Every city in the United States is bankrupt, the reason for that being that a city doesn't pay taxes. In New York City the bankruptcy operates as it does in other cities so we really can't renew the City's services. For instance, the sewage system we are running in New York City is about forty years out of date and as Mayor Lindsay pointed out in Washington recently, it would take fifty billion dollars to repair the city services of New York so that they would be adequate. Let's say this week the power failure takes place and the smog killings occur and the SST crashes and finally the water system begins to leak badly and breaks down and the garbage men are on strike again. It takes very few things like this, all of which are highly probable, and the combination is not terribly improbable, to be a total catastrophe. And then you can easily say, "Gee, I've had it."

Now under these conditions, and we needn't have ten plagues, we could just have too much annoyance from one plague or two or three at a time. Over the next twenty years in this country, there will be an increasing amount of disorder of the kind we've gotten used to. That is, there will be more and more liberation movements in which more and more people who have been quiet will suddenly come out of the walls and begin to shout out. For instance, I am beginning one myself called the gray liberation, because as you get older you realize that we are the oppressed group. In that kind of disorder, if only the radicals don't try to lead the disorder, and if only the reactionaries don't try to stamp it down with law and order, which would just aggravate everything and make it blow up—but if disorder can develop, then my faith as an anarchist is that very many things will fall apart to just the right size. Because people have got a lot of sense. And it is here that I put my hope for decentralization and for homesteading and for all that kind of thing; and I myself think that if we had 20% of the population homesteading and we decentralized 20-25% of our big industries, that would be fine; the whole thing would be quite livable. You don't want a 100% solution of anything; all you need to do is to relieve tension and then everybody looks better. Out of that disorder, if it is not radicalized and if there is no attempt at repression, we will find that the kind of attitude you people have will suddenly burgeon and there will be many million, perhaps 20 million, and 20 million is quite enough to make the thing livable. It gives alternatives, it gives another life style which works better and it takes the pressure off the cities. That's the kind of thing I put my hopes in to create a deep change in people.

II.

Question: Many educators are suggesting drastic reforms in American secondary education—what are your ideas?

Goodman: My own opinion is that we should abolish the high schools, period; except for a few really academic kids, 2 or 3% of the population who will do what they always do—go to little academies. But for the average bright kid it is a ridiculous institution. In 1900 only 6% went to high school and this was the time of Edison and Ford and Teddy Roosevelt and Edith Wharton—this wasn't the Dark Ages. Even with only 6% going to high school, the country seemed to get on quite nicely with high technology and all that stuff. It's just an idiotic institution. The lower school presents the advantage of getting the kids away from their mamas which I think is good. That's the chief reason of elementary schooling, to get the kids away from the home.

Question: What political advantage is there to decentralism?

Goodman: The advantage of the decentralist system and of anarchy in general is that power doesn't get concentrated. The reason that Thomas Jefferson, for instance, put such great faith in the small farm was a purely political reason. If you were a freehold farmer then nobody could force you how to vote, the way you had a forced vote in a rotten borough in England where the lord determined who the tenants voted for. Therefore there were members of Parliament from these rotten boroughs forever dictated by the landlord of those tenants. But if you are a freehold farmer, you can retire into your shell, you grow your own food, all you have to do is to stay out of debt. And if you stay out of debt, then nobody can compel you to do anything. In Jefferson's time they didn't even have the military draft. You are under no political compulsion whatsoever.

Question: But people are naturally greedy—without some political compulsion they'll do harm to each other and never reform.

Goodman: Let's assume, as you say, that people are greedy. Fine, people are just what they are; the beauty of the decentralist, anarchist position is that nobody can do much harm. As an anarchist, and all anarchists are decentralists, our view is not that human nature is good, but on the contrary, that human nature is probably lousy. It's improvable, but probably lousy. People are corrupt as hell, therefore don't give anybody any power, because that's where the trouble comes from, because the people who have power are not going to be any better than the other people. In fact we know by experience the more power people have the more corrupt they become. Let's make sure that everybody has an independent free-hold of their own, and if they've got that then there will be a limit to how bad things can get. And that's all you want out of politics. You don't want politics to give you a good society.

All you want is a tolerable background so the important parts of life can go on. We all know what the important parts are, the arts, the sciences, sex, justice, worship of God, love of nature. The political things are insignificant. But if they are bad, wow, can they cause damage! I don't want to change human nature. I couldn't care less. All I want to make sure is that there are enough goods to go around, and there will be enough goods to go around in this highly productive and intelligent race, on this highly productive planet, if you don't allow it to get concentrated.

This is the text of Goodman's last public speech, given to The New England Conference on Adequate Action for a Human Future on June 23, 1972, a month before he died. From *Humanizing Our Future,* ed. R. Bruce Allison, Hinsdale, Ill.: School of Living Press, 1972.